Spies

Spies

*The U.S. and Russian Espionage Game
from the Cold War to the 21st Century*

SEAN N. KALIC

Praeger Security International

PRAEGER™

An Imprint of ABC-CLIO, LLC
Santa Barbara, California • Denver, Colorado

Library of Congress Cataloging-in-Publication Data

Names: Kalic, Sean N., 1970- author.
Title: Spies : the U.S. and Russian espionage game from the Cold War to the
    21st century / Sean N. Kalic.
Description: Santa Barbara, CA : Praeger Security International, [2019] |
    Includes bibliographical references and index.
Identifiers: LCCN 2018049628 (print) | LCCN 2018056107 (ebook) | ISBN
    9781440840432 (eBook) | ISBN 9781440840425 (hbk. : alk. paper)
Subjects: LCSH: Espionage—United States. | Espionage—Soviet Union. |
    Espionage, American—Soviet Union—History. | Espionage, Soviet—United
    States—History. | United States—Foreign relations—Soviet Union. |
    Soviet Union—Foreign relations—United States. | Cold War. | World
    politics—1945–1989. | World politics—1989-
Classification: LCC UB271.U5 (ebook) | LCC UB271.U5 K35 2019 (print) |
    DDC 327.1247073—dc23
LC record available at https://lccn.loc.gov/2018049628

ISBN: 978-1-4408-4042-5 (print)
        978-1-4408-4043-2 (ebook)

23 22 21 20 19   1 2 3 4 5

This book is also available as an eBook.

Praeger
An Imprint of ABC-CLIO, LLC

ABC-CLIO, LLC
147 Castilian Drive
Santa Barbara, California 93117
www.abc-clio.com

This book is printed on acid-free paper ∞
Manufactured in the United States of America

To Tracie and Katheryn,
the loves of my life

Contents

A photo essay follows page 124.

Acknowledgments

The completion of this project brings with it the need to thank a host of people who contributed in very diverse and necessary ways to the final project. First and foremost, I need to thank James Willbanks, who actively encouraged me to pursue this project, despite the fact that I was assuming a new position in the Department of Military History at the U.S. Army's Command and General Staff College. I truly appreciate your leadership, wisdom, friendship, and mentoring, even though you left us to go to Texas. Within the same vein, I have had the great fortune to work under Thomas Hanson and Dave Cotter as they both assumed leadership roles in DMH. Your leadership has been inspiring and your support unwavering. Thank you for continuing to fight the good fight.

In addition to having the support of great bosses, I have the rare benefit of being part of a truly outstanding faculty. The professors in the DMH are first-rate colleagues who make work a genuinely fantastic place. I am truly honored to toil away with an inspiring group of professional historians. Beyond my colleagues at CGSC, I also must thank my many students over the years, who have graciously accepted a civilian academic into their unique world and culture. I am truly humbled to have the privilege to teach you military history, knowing that some of you will inevitably make history.

The process of writing a book also entails a long list of supporting efforts conducted by a whole host of professionals. Padraic (Pat) Carlin at ABC-CLIO, who stayed committed to the project, even when it fell behind schedule—thank you for staying the course; I truly appreciate it. To the staff at the Combined Arms Research Library, thank you for not getting frustrated with requests for interlibrary loans and having large piles of books checked out year after year. A hearty thanks is also necessary to the various public affairs professional at the CIA, FBI, and National Reconnaissance Office who assisted with photographs and other details. In addition to these agencies, I also had great assistance and service from Nathaniel Weisenberg from the Atomic Heritage Foundation and Alan Carr from the Los Alamos National Laboratory.

Writing a book can be an isolating and focused effort; however, thankfully, I had the fine people of Perry Yacht Club to ensure that I did not spend too much time with my head in books. To the crew of "Black Death," it has been a sheer joy to be in the Foredeck Union on the most feared Hobie 33 in the Midwest. Beyond spending quality time sailing, I also had the unwavering support of my parents, Sandy and Dennis Kalic, who always had time to assist when we needed them. I am always thankful for having such great parents who will selflessly make trips to Kansas City, just because we need them. Thanks, Mom and Dad.

Last and most importantly, I need to thank my family. My wife, Tracie, continues to be all I could ever ask for in a partner. Despite her own impressive and very worthwhile career, she still always finds time to read and offer comments on my work, as well as ensure that we have quality time together as a family. I truly am blessed to have such a great and wonderful wife. Tracie, you are still aces, baby! To my daughter, Katheryn, who has been a sheer joy and a great distraction from the rigors of writing, you are the best ski, sailing, and skateboarding buddy a father could wish for. I love being your father more than you will ever know. Finally, our family is not complete without Murphy and Olivia, two great dogs that have vastly different personalities, but yet fit very well into our lives.

Abbreviations

ATC	Amtorg Trading Company
CBC	Canadian Broadcast Corporation
CGSC	Command and General Staff College
CIA	Central Intelligence Agency
CIG	Central Intelligence Group
COMINTERN	Communist International
CPUSA	Communist Party of the United States
DCI	director of central intelligence
DMH	Department of Military History
DOD	Department of Defense
ELINT	electronic intelligence
FAECT	Federation of Architects, Engineers, Chemists, and Technicians
FAPSI	Federal Agency for Government Communications and Information
FBI	Federal Bureau of Investigation
FCD	First Chief Directorate
FSB	Federal Security Service
FSK	Federal Counterintelligence Service
GPU/OGPU/GUGB	Soviet Security and Intelligence Service
GRU	*Glavnoye Razvedyvatelnoye Upravlenie* (Chief Intelligence Directorate)
GUO	Main Guard Directorate
HUAC	House of Representatives' Un-American Activities Committee

HUMINT	human intelligence
ICBM	intercontinental ballistic missile
ISI	Inter-Services Intelligence
ITT	International Telephone and Telegraph Corporation
JCS	Joint Chiefs of Staff
JIC	Joint Intelligence Committee
KGB	*Komitet Gosudarstvennoy Bezopasnosti*
KH	Key Hole
MACV	Military Assistance Command Vietnam
MAD	mutual assured destruction
MB	Ministry of Security
MIRV	multiple independently targetable reentry vehicle
MIT	Massachusetts Institute of Technology
MRV	multiple reentry vehicle
NAACP	National Association for the Advancement of Colored People
NACA	National Advisory Committee on Aeronautics
NASA	National Aeronautics and Space Administration
NATO	North Atlantic Treaty Organization
NCO	noncommissioned officer
NEP	New Economic Policy
NIE	National Intelligence Estimate
NKGB	People's Commissariat for State Security
NKVD	People's Commissariat for Internal Affairs
NSA	National Security Agency
NSC	National Security Council
NSDAP	National Socialist German Workers Party
NSDD	National Security Decision Directive
ORE	Office of Reports and Estimates
OSO	Office of Special Operations
OSS	Office of Strategic Service
PCF	French Communist Party
RAF	Royal Air Force
RYAN	*raketno-yadernoye napadenie* (nuclear missile attack)
SAC	Strategic Air Command
SALT	Strategic Arms Limitation Talks
SDI	Strategic Defense Initiative
SG-A	Special Group–Augmented
SG-I	Special Group–Insurgencies
SIGINT	signal intelligence
SLBM	submarine-launched ballistic missiles
TCP	Technological Capabilities Panel

UP	Unidad Popular
USAF	United States Air Force
USAFE	United States Air Forces Europe
USIA	United States Information Agency
USMC	United States Marine Corps
VChK (Cheka)	All Russian Extraordinary Commission for Combatting Counter-Revolution and Sabotage

Introduction

In 2013 the television channel FX aired a new series titled *The Americans*. The premise of the series is that the KGB developed and infiltrated a network of "illegal" Soviet citizens into the United States.[1] The series focused on two main characters who appear to be part of a normal American family. They own a house in the suburbs of Washington, D.C., own their own travel agency, and suffer the standard family issues associated with American families during the 1980s. Yet, all is not as it appears, as the two "Americans" are actually highly trained and developed KGB "illegal" operatives who are intent on collecting intelligence and getting American citizens to provide the latest information on defense programs such as the strategic defense initiative, stealth aircraft, military operations in Latin America, and U.S. policy in Afghanistan. This popular television program, which is high drama, is not in fact just a great tale from Hollywood but rather is based on true events caused by the KGB and its development of KGB officers through its Directorate "S" program.

For the duration of the Cold War and even in the aftermath, spies and tales of espionage have captivated the imagination. The fact that the Western press occasionally found a "true" story and published its exploits only further fueled the fascination of the clandestine exploits of the spies on both sides of the Cold War. This public fascination with the "war in the shadows" did not wither as did the Cold War itself. In fact, as the archives of the former Soviet Union opened and the Central Intelligence Agency (CIA) declassified volumes of documents from its Cold War operations, the public finally got a look at the people, operations, and structure of some of the intelligence operations associated with the Cold War.

The objective of this book is to provide a chronological narrative of how the governments of the Soviet Union and United States strove to maintain a strategic advantage through the use of intelligence operations, using a wide variety of means. In the quest for more and better national intelligence, the two main agencies responsible for collecting intelligence, the CIA and the KGB, developed a "game" by which each used human, electronic, and other means to collect the necessary intelligence. As each nation strove to achieve an advantage in the international security environment, it was imperative to be aware of and prepared to counter the capabilities of each nation's primary nemesis.

Therefore, as the Cold War period unfolded between 1945 and 1991, the quest to maintain up-to-date intelligence mandated that the process by which the "game" was played had to encompass a wider variety of intelligence-gathering means. Moving beyond the use of human spies and the development of human intelligence (HUMINT) assets, a main objective of this work is to highlight the advanced technological means by which both the United States and the Soviet Union worked to ensure that they had a strong understanding of their enemy. Focusing on the period from 1945 to the start of the 21st century, during which each side used spies, airplanes, satellites, and other national technological means to collect intelligence, an understanding emerges of the process by which the United States and Soviet Union maintained robust and effective intelligence-gathering capabilities as a means to their strategic position in the dynamic international security environment of the Cold War.

Though the topic of espionage has long been a topic of interest for a wide variety of media and has produced a vast collection of literature focusing on spies, technology, and covert operations, this book is unable to cover the immense ground already discussed by authors on intelligence services, spy missions, and the technology of spies. Rather the intent is to provide an understanding of how the action and interaction between the two main intelligence services of the United States and Soviet Union worked to achieve their individual missions and national objectives through the duration of the Cold War. Moving beyond the standard understanding of human spies, this work strives to provide a broader understanding of spying, as well as the trials and tribulations faced by the intelligence services of the two main actors in the Cold War. Specifically, three main points differentiate this more general work from previous and contemporary works.

First, by exploring the espionage game from the perspective of the two major actors, a more detailed understanding of how and why the United States and the Soviet Union strove to collect intelligence on each other will evolve. Second, in the tense and dynamic international security environment of the Cold War, an understanding of the passion of the "need to know," which was fueled by ideological tenets as well as the demands to be ready and able to respond to a prompt attack, acted as a catalyst that drove both sides to seek more accurate and better means to collect intelligence. Last, while exploring the evolutionary nature of intelligence gathering, a more thorough appreciation for the advanced technological means will emerge within the context of the struggle between the United States and the Soviet Union, but at the same time, neither the CIA nor the KGB were ever to move completely away from heavy reliance on intelligence officers and agents.

These three points combined provide a detailed history that explains the quest for security and stability that both the United States and Soviet Union believed were essential for the duration of the Cold War. In fact, the need to be aware of the intentions and capabilities of other nations did not begin with the Cold War and therefore did not end with the Cold War. Therefore, this work will also provide a glimpse into how the CIA and KGB/FSB adapted to the end of the Cold War in an effort to maintain their fundamental mission in the post–Cold War security environment. To accomplish the objectives and goals established above, the work is composed of seven chapters that span the period from 1944 to the first decade of the 21st century.

ORGANIZATION OF THE WORK

"Chapter 1: Allies Become Enemies, 1944–1946" begins with a discussion of the Manhattan Project, which was the intensive scientific effort by the United States to develop an atomic bomb, and explores how the Soviet Union, though an ally, had thoroughly infiltrated the highly classified project in an effort to ensure that the Soviet Union did not end up in a significant position of weakness. Specific focus will be on how the Soviet Union cultivated and used Ted Hall and Klaus Fuchs as vital sources for gathering intelligence on the scientific and technical details of U.S. progress on the design and production of atomic bombs.[2]

In addition to the background story of the Soviet Union's infiltration of the Manhattan Project, the first chapter highlights the process by which the United States and the Soviet Union came to distrust one another as World War II ended and the Cold War began. The first battleground in the Cold War was a fight over the solidification of spheres of influence left in the wake of the collapse of the Nazis' empire and the destruction of World War II. As Joseph Stalin and the Soviet Union worked feverishly to control Central and Eastern Europe, the United States and its Western allies strove to ensure that the specter of communism did not seep into and establish a foothold in Western Europe.

Hence, a significant portion of this first chapter looks at how the Soviet Union skillfully worked to achieve control over Czechoslovakia and Hungary, by using intelligence and a strong network of spies and informants to maintain tight communist control. As a result of the inroads into Hungary and Czechoslovakia, the United States became deeply concerned about the political potential of domestic communist parties in France and Italy.[3] As the United States wrestled with the need to combat the encroachment of communism, this era produced the first significant use of Cold War covert operations and espionage designed to contain communism and that had authorization from President Harry S. Truman.

In addition to fortifying the political foundation in Western Europe, the Truman administration also focused on the military intentions of the Soviet Union in the immediate aftermath of World War II. Operation Grail was a short but intensive effort by the United States to gain intelligence on the military capabilities of the Red Army and to gain insights into their plans for East Germany and Central Europe. In addition to Operation Grail that focuses on the military capabilities and plans, the United States also maintained a program started in 1943 by U.S. Army Intelligence that decrypted and analyzed Soviet intelligence traffic from agents abroad and official KGB and GRU sources back to Moscow. Project Venona became a long-running intelligence program that gave the United States key insights into operations and intelligence-gathering targets that the Soviet Union used throughout the Cold War. Ultimately, the first chapter provides a robust foundation for understanding the essential objectives, methods, and operations by which the espionage game developed at the close of World War II and carried over into the Cold War.

Picking up where chapter 1 concludes, the second chapter, "Europe: A Contested Environment, 1946–1949," focuses on the Soviet Union's solidification of control in Hungary and Czechoslovakia, both of which were blows to the West.[4] The chapter will explore how the Soviet Union made extensive use of intelligence assets to shape and control the political and social environment as a means to bring two "democratic nations" under communist control. A parallel concern emerged from the United States and its Western allies over a perceived "bomber gap" and the military capabilities of the Soviet Union based on the intelligence gathered during Operation Grail. Though the United States and the newly minted CIA continued to focus on the political containment of communism in Western Europe, the United States also began to shift priorities to begin to gather better intelligence on the military and strategic capabilities of the Soviet Union. The U.S. knowledge of the military capabilities of the Soviet Union had atrophied in the aftermath of the conclusion of World War II.

Moving beyond the use of HUMINT assets, the United States Air Force developed advanced signal (SIGINT) and electronic (ELINT) intelligence-gathering methods to begin to assess the air defense capabilities of the Soviet Union and its satellite nations. These "ferret" missions provided the United States with critical military intelligence as it prepared to fight and win a nuclear war, if necessary. In addition to the use of aircraft for intelligence gathering for strategic and military purposes, the United States also focused on combating the propaganda of Moscow and its puppet regimes in Central and Eastern Europe. The Voice of America become a central, nonthreatening, but very dynamic force by which the United States and its

Western allies attempted to influence the popular perception of the West through the use of radio signals in communist-controlled Europe.

For its part, the Soviet Union worked to rebuild a robust KGB organization that focused not only on internal and domestic security but also on the collection of intelligence of its "main adversary."[5] In parallel with the Soviet Union's reinvestment in the development of the KGB, the American public became transfixed by the "infiltration" of the United States by communist spies. The case of Ethel and Julius Rosenberg, as well as the beginning of the House of Representatives' Un-American Activities Committee (HUAC), fueled an obsession with spies and infiltration only served to further the game being advanced and perpetuated by the Soviet Union and the United States.[6]

Chapters 1 and 2 demonstrate how, in the first five years of the Cold War, the world of espionage and intelligence gathering had quickly proliferated in the tense, dynamic nuclear security environment. Though the basic organizations were now in place, both nations continued to excel at the game of espionage as each attempted to gain greater and more insightful intelligence on the other.

Chapter 3, titled "Global Confrontation, 1950–1960," moves beyond the focus of Europe and the establishment of the organizational structures of the CIA as well as the KGB. The main focus of this chapter is to highlight how the United States and the Soviet Union actively pursued the use of direct action intelligence in an effort to assist, foment, or encourage revolutions, coups, and mass demonstrations in nations that were susceptible to social and political unrest.[7] The objective of both the Soviet Union and the United States was to try to sway nations into their respective spheres of influence, or at least make sure they did not affiliate with the Soviet Union or United States, respectively. The goal of the chapter is to build on the evolution of the espionage game in the first two decades after the end of World War II and in a period when the Cold War had become an established part of the international security environment. Of significance during this period is the fact that the intelligence services of the United States and the Soviet Union began to be emboldened in their use of espionage, not just as a means to collect intelligence but rather also as an active tool to combat the expansion of the other.

In the course of dynamic expansion of espionage operations in places like Berlin, Iran, and Guatemala, designed to sway nations into the one of the two major spheres of influence, the United States and the Soviet Union did not back away from the need to collect strategic military intelligence.[8] As the nuclear arsenals of the two main adversaries expanded—as did their respective military alliance structures—the pressing need for intelligence on the military capabilities, plans, and structures blossomed under the threat of nuclear war and military invasions. President Dwight D. Eisenhower's authorization of U-2 flights over the Soviet Union is an excellent example of how the United States was willing to take large risks in an effort to gain intelligence on the strategic nuclear capabilities of the Soviet Union.[9] Though not as overt, but every bit as bold, the Soviet Union attempted to rebuild its on deeply imbedded intelligence-gathering programs in the United States, by using legal and illegal agents to gain as much information as possible regarding the military intentions and technological capabilities of the United States and our North Atlantic Treaty Organization (NATO) allies.[10] Often these operations involved elaborate attempts to infiltrate the U.S. government and the U.S. military as a means to gain greater insights in the military capabilities of the United States and its allies and thus ensure that the Soviet Union and its satellites did not get caught off guard by a Western attack.

"Chapter 4: Crisis and Response, 1961–1968" uses the background of the Bay of Pigs invasion, the Cuban Missile Crisis, the Second Berlin Crisis, and Prague Spring as significant events that spurred the action-reaction paradigm of intelligence gathering. While the KGB and the CIA strove to maintain their robust HUMINT collection programs and worked ever harder to develop effective counterintelligence programs, the need to be aware of the enemy's strategic nuclear resources increased.

Though the espionage game had become rather routine, the era covered in this chapter highlights the rapid development of air and space-based intelligence capabilities used by both sides. Again, the objective of the chapter is to highlight the evolution of the espionage between the Soviet Union and the United States as they both reacted to the tense, dynamic security environment of the 1960s. Beyond the various operations centered around Cuba, this chapter also documents the development of the use of a whole host of reconnaissance satellites, this chapter captures how the intelligence agencies of the United States and the Soviet Union worked to ensure that they had the best and most up-to-date information on each other, in a very tense and demanding security environment.

In many ways, Chapters 3 and 4 provide an expansive composite of how the nature of the Cold War and technological advances, associated with the Cold War and the space race, dovetailed with the hotspots in Africa, Europe, Latin America, and the Middle East and drove the CIA and KGB to constantly assess and reassess their abilities to provide key and valuable intelligence to their respective governments.

Though this period, 1950–1968, is often viewed by the CIA as the "golden years" of its operational capabilities, the KGB worked hard to build its programs and met with decent success. So by the end of this eighteen-year period, the CIA had reached its apogee and would have to deal with a backlash against covert intelligence operations in the coming years, especially from within the U.S. Congress. From the KGB's perspective, this same eighteen-year period served as a foundation upon which the coming decade enabled them to believe that the "world was going their way."[11]

Therefore, in many ways, this period represents an inversion between the perceived capabilities of the CIA and the KGB.

Coming out of the turbulent and trying times of the middle and late 1960s, the fifth chapter, "Détente and Ostpolitik, 1968–1976." Recognizing the impact of détente on the overall strategic relationship between the United States and the Soviet Union, as well as their respective allies during this unique period of the Cold War, the focus on intelligence operations moves from Europe back to an intense focus on Latin America, Africa, and the Middle East. Specifically, this chapter strives to detail the evolution of the intelligence within the context of the United States' loss of global influence as a result of its experiences in Vietnam.

In a direct response to the declining influence of the United States, the CIA came under significant public scrutiny.[12] The public's general distrust of the U.S. government after Vietnam and the Watergate trials had a profound impact on the covert nature of the CIA. The CIA therefore faced a new period that saw its use of covert operations questioned by the public, as well as the U.S. president. Coinciding with the CIA's attempts to repair and improve its image and intelligence-gathering capabilities, the agency moved to embrace advanced technological means to gather strategic intelligence. Though these means improved the ability of the United States to gather more strategic intelligence, they came at a cost to the fledging HUMINT program.

From the perspective of the KGB and the Soviet Union, the waning of U.S. global influence and the public's scrutiny of the CIA and its use of operations represented an opportunity for the communists to regain a lead that had been lost at the close of World War II. Therefore, the KGB used this time period to focus on rebuilding and developing its network of "illegals" and other agents.[13] Having struggled to recapture its success of the pre–World War II years, the Soviet Union focused on two specific objectives to gather intelligence. The first, which in many ways had long been an objective, was to get agents and illegals to infiltrate government agencies. The second area of focus was on the need to gain technological and industrial intelligence on research and development (R&D) on advanced technology used and developed for military use.

By the late 1960s and early 1970s, the Soviet Union had begun to suffer economic stress and had begun to assess that their its industrial and technological capabilities were lagging behind the capabilities of the West.[14] As a result, the KGB intensified its operations with the intended purpose of procuring intelligence on advanced technologies and electronics being developed in the United States.

Therefore, within the greater context of détente and Ostpolitik, the CIA and KGB both had significant struggles as they adjusted to changes in the international security environment and the nature of collecting intelligence. Yet despite the massive political and technological forces, both agencies and nations had to maintain a steadfast commitment to continuing the game, as neither could afford to be caught off guard.

Continuing the chronological evolution of the espionage game, Chapter 6, "Carter, Reagan, and the Denouement of the Cold War, 1976–1988," elaborates on the espionage and intelligence operations of the CIA and KGB in Latin America and Africa, as the Soviet Union believed that, due to America's issues in Vietnam, the Third World was a vast opportunity from which the KGB and the Soviet Union could improve its global position. A major difference in this later period, compared to the period covered in Chapter 5, is the emerging recognition, first by the Carter administration and later by Reagan's administration, that the CIA could be used as a tool to advance the cause of human rights within the context of the Helsinki Accords, which could in turn be a viable strategic thread to exploit for the United States.[15]

As the world responded to the Helsinki Accords and began to look at the potential of using human rights as a touchstone against the Soviet Union, the emergence of anticommunist groups, such as the Solidarity labor movement in Poland, as well as the election of Pope John Paul II provided opportunities for the CIA to exploit. In addition to working behind the scenes to fund and support the inherent anticommunist message of these two examples, the CIA also saw the Soviet Union's struggles in Afghanistan as yet another azimuth to attack and weaken the United States' ideological nemesis.[16]

The KGB, having been aware of U.S. technological advances, now had to contend with stealth material and the possibility of the strategic defense initiative.[17] These two advanced military capabilities led to the Soviet Union becoming even more obsessed with the strategic nuclear triad of the United States. Taken in conjunction with U.S. President Ronald W. Reagan's strategic force modernization programs, the KGB and the leadership of the Soviet Union became particularly focused on the potential of the United States and its NATO allies to launch a surprise nuclear attack on the Soviet Union and the Warsaw pact.[18]

Operation RYAN, Operation ABLE ARCHER, and the case of John Walker, as well as U.S. aid to the Mujahideen in Afghanistan, provide the overall case studies in this chapter to reinforce the key themes of the chapter and the text. Unbeknown to both sides, by the close of the 1980s, both governments and both intelligence agencies needed to readjust fundamentally their operational outlooks, as the Warsaw Pact crumbled in 1991. The collapse of the Soviet Union would not be far behind.

The turbulent changes in the international security environment, especially with regard to the Warsaw pact and the collapse of the Soviet Union, offered hope for a new post–Cold War international security environment. At the heart of Chapter 7, "The New World Order and Beyond, 1989–2014," is the process by which the KGB and the CIA adjusted to the changes in the world. Though there was an optimistic fervor that emerged with the end of the Cold War that the espionage game had withered in the wake of the collapse of the Soviet Union, 50 years of intrigue and tension did not evaporate easily.

The reality was that the post-Soviet security was, in many ways, more dangerous than the previous period, which had become relatively stabilized, compared to other periods of international history. Though the KGB became the FSB and instituted some basic reforms to reflect the political and social changes of the former Soviet Union, threats still remained.[19] From the perspective of the CIA, its officers also had to readjust its primary purpose and objectives that had come to focus on the Soviet Union and its other satellites.[20]

The intelligence services' mutual recognition that the Cold War tension and threat of nuclear war had dissipated allowed both the FSB and the CIA to look at the new international security environment with an eye toward "other threats." For the FSB, threats from within the newly created commonwealth of independent states presented distractions from the former "main adversary."

Concerns over Chechnya and the infiltration of radical Islamists allowed the FSB to focus on internal matters while at the same time keeping some tabs on the United States in its self-professed role as the winner of the Cold War.[21] Ultimately, we expand the scope of the seventh chapter in an effort to capture the struggle the FSB faced as it fundamentally adjusted to a new international security environment, a new government, new social structures, and new internal threats. Against the backdrop of these major changes, the FSB also had to deal with the "defection" of longtime KGB officers such as Oleg Kalugin. In short, the FSB scrambled to adjust and find its way in the first decade of the post–Cold War world.[22] Yet by the first decade of the 21st century, the FSB seemed to be employing some of its traditional means by using "illegals" and sleeper cells to infiltrate and gather intelligence.

Likewise, the United States and the CIA had to make adjustments as their primary enemy of the Cold War evaporated. In the initial years following the Cold War, the CIA and the United States wrestled with future threats and the stability of the post–Soviet Union security environment. As the FSB adjusted to the radical changes in the Soviet Union and around the world, the CIA also refocused its attentions on other potential threats to the United States. Adjusting to the damage done by Aldrich Ames and his identification of CIA agents in the Soviet Union, the CIA refocused its attention to the Middle East and the growing concern about radical Islamists and Al Qaeda.

Though the fundamental nature of the international security environment had changed, the United States and the Soviet Union/Russia, as well as their intelligence agencies, still maintained their suspicions of one another. The game, which had emerged 50 years earlier, still maintained itself, though with some distractions.

The final capstone chapter in this work provides a fitting conclusion in the sense that the main theme of the chapter is the recognition that Russia, since the beginning of the 21st century, reemerged as a significant regional power, if not an international force. This rebirth came at a time when the United States and its Western allies had expanded NATO to include several key members of the former Warsaw Pact. With this newfound tension of NATO creeping into the Russian sphere of influence, the FSB and the CIA returned to their old habits of maintaining a robust espionage game between our two nations.

Looking at Russia's use of "sleeper cells" within the United States, discovered by FBI counterintelligence efforts, provides a fitting conclusion to the project. The discovery of Russian intelligence agents within the United States conveys a sense that the Cold War game of espionage between the United States and Russia did not end with the demise of the Cold War. In fact from the perspective of 2018, the release of this information parallels a phrase from the music group Talking Heads: "same as it ever was, same as it ever was."[23]

BACKGROUND AND STRUCTURE OF THE CIA

Prior to attempting an understanding of the evolution and history of the espionage game, it is critical to offer a short history and basic organizational structure of these two very complex and inherently secretive national intelligence agencies. The Central Intelligence Agency evolved from the Office of Strategic Service (OSS), which was headed by William Donovan during World War II. On orders from President Harry S. Truman, the OSS disbanded on October 1, 1945.[24] However, in the immediate period after World War II, the need for a covert organization was vigorously debated as the new security environment took shape.[25] On January 22, 1946, Truman signed a presidential directive that "established a National Intelligence Authority that was comprised of Secretary of State, Secretary of War, Secretary of the Navy, and the President's personal representative Admiral William D. Leahy."[26] The purview of these executive-level advisors to the president oversaw the work of the Central Intelligence Group (CIG).

The CIG, numbering roughly eighty people, was an amalgamation of military, Federal Bureau of Investigation, and State Department intelligence personnel who coordinated and analyzed intelligence for the president.[27] The CIG had divisions such as the Office of Reports and Estimates (ORE) that produced "daily intelligence summaries" for the president that focused on "foreign, economic, and scientific" issues that were pertinent to the United States and the development of foreign policy.[28] Beyond the analytical side of the new and evolving intelligence bureaucracy in the United States, the CIG also inherited covert operations from the old OSS. The new division that retained international covert operations that focused on espionage and counter-espionage was the Office of Special Operations (OSO).[29] As the Cold War security environment developed, the CIG expanded in personnel. By June 1946, only six months after its official creation, the CIG had a workforce of roughly 1,800 personnel.[30] Though the new intelligence bureaucracy was expanding and providing critical information to President Truman, it was not a well-synchronized or streamlined operational organization.

The process of making the intelligence bureaucracy more effective and efficient came with Truman's signing of the National Security Act of 1947. Put simply, this act created the Central Intelligence Agency (CIA) and also outlined the creation of the director of central intelligence (DCI) to preside over the new agency.[31] The DCI would be appointed by the president and confirmed by the Senate and serve as a cabinet-level position to coordinate and oversee the collection, analysis, and dissemination of strategic intelligence to the president of the United States. The DCI also served as the bureaucratic head of the CIA, which was the new organization that replaced the CIG and its various components.

The structure of the CIA was relatively simple at first. By 1950 the organization had a director (DCI) and a deputy director. The DCI also served as head of the Board of Estimates and the Intelligence Advisory Committee.[32] In addition to these two positions, the CIA had an executive director and a deputy executive director who managed and controlled the management staff, budget staff, and personnel staff.[33] Together these positions formed the core administrative elements of the CIA. The next level of bureaucracy contained sections outlined as "Operations and Policy Staff," "Legal Staff," "Advisory Council," "Medical Staff," "Inspection and Security Staff," "Administrative Staff," and "Special Support Staff."[34] The final level of the CIA was composed of the divisions that actually collected and analyzed intelligence and ran covert operations. The duties and functions of these units were housed in the "Office of Reports and Estimates," "Office of Collection and Dissemination," "Office of Scientific Intelligence," "Office of Policy Coordination," "Office of Operations," and "Office of Special Operations."[35]

This basic structure evolved and adapted through the duration of the Cold War. The biggest adjustment was the development of specialized and focused offices that allowed the CIA to better allocate its resources and direct its intelligence and counterintelligence operations to best suit the strategic objectives of the Cold War. As the game of espionage evolved during the Cold War, the CIA also made sure to adapt and adjust its operational abilities to ensure that it remained capable of providing critical and necessary intelligence to the president of the United States.[36]

BACKGROUND AND STRUCTURE OF THE KGB

The history of the intelligence service of the Soviet Union (KGB) is much more complex than the evolution of the CIA.[37] The first step in the evolution of what would become the KGB started in the immediate aftermath of the Bolshevik Revolution, with the establishment of the All Russian Extraordinary Commission for Combatting Counter-Revolution and Sabotage (VChK, commonly known as Cheka). In contrast to the calls for greater democracy, freedom, and fairness for the people of Russia, the Bolsheviks quickly established the Cheka, which was an organization designed to arrest, torture, and imprison enemies of the regime. Led by Felix Dzerzhinsky, the Cheka became a comprehensive security service used by the Bolsheviks to maintain order and discipline to the tenets of the Revolution. Though originally established as a means to check the efforts of the White Russians and other counter-revolutionaries, the need to control and suppress contradictory ideas and other interpretations beyond those advocated by the Bolsheviks only further solidified the extraordinary police powers of this intelligence service that focused both on internal and external enemies of the state. The Bolsheviks outlined the duties of the Cheka as follows:

1. To investigate and nullify acts of counter-revolution and sabotage throughout Russia, irrespective of origin.
2. To bring before the Revolutionary Tribunal all counter-revolutionaries and saboteurs and to work measures to combat them.
3. The Commission is to conduct the preliminary investigation only, sufficient to suppress (the counter-revolutionary act). The Commission is to be divided into sections: (1) the information section, (2) the organization section (in charge of organizing the struggle with counter-revolution throughout Russia) with branches, and (3) the fighting section.

   The Commission shall be set up tomorrow. Then the fighting section of the All-Russian Commission shall start its activities. The Commission shall keep an eye on the press, saboteurs, right Socialist Revolutionaries, and strikers. Measures to be taken are confiscation, imprisonment, confiscation of cards, and publication of the names of the enemies of the people.[38]

With Vladimir Lenin's approval, on December 20, 1917, Felix Dzerzhinsky began building the basic structure of the internal security service of the Soviet State. Between the Bolshevik Revolution and the end of the Soviet State in 1991, the intelligence services evolved in various forms and gained greater power.

The evolution of Soviet security and intelligence services can be understood by understanding the duties and foundation of the Cheka, as it evolved from 1917 until 1922 as the Bolsheviks' organ to maintain strict control of the Revolution and any counterideas that threatened the stability of the new regime. The Cheka's primary focus was on internal enemies, but it also had to be aware of outside threats. With the conclusion of the Russian Civil War and the Bolsheviks' solidification of power, the Cheka transitioned into the People's Commissariat for Internal Affairs (NKVD). Within the NKVD, there was also the division of the Soviet Security and Intelligence Service (GPU).[39] The security and intelligence services continued to expand with a focus on state security from internal as well as external forces. Between 1923 and 1943, the internal security and intelligence services (GPU) of the Soviet Union morphed into the OGPU, which was a minor name change facilitated by some organizational changes that sought to further refine the security and intelligence capabilities of the Soviet State.

As it tried to recover from the German invasion in 1941, the Soviet Union again adjusted its intelligence and security structure by renaming the OGPU the GUGB, which was the Russian acronym for Soviet Security and Intelligence Service.[40] During World War II the GUGB persisted within the structure of the NKVD until it was renamed the People's Commissariat for State Security (NKGB). The focus and mission of the new bureaucracy was still internal and external intelligence and security operations for the benefit of the Soviet State.

With the conclusion of World War II and the quick onset of the new Cold War, the leaders of the Soviet Union tinkered with the structure and function of their security services while also stressing the need for greater emphasis on collecting and analyzing foreign intelligence. Though this had been a function of Soviet intelligence services since 1920, the tense security environment of the Cold War placed a greater emphasis on the need to keep track of Western military, political, and economic advancements. The Soviet State Security, known as the KGB, emerged in 1954 with a robust and focused organizational structure that maintained the traditional blend of internal and external focus. However, the security environment dictated that external intelligence gathering was necessary and of equal, if not greater, importance that internal security.[41]

The structure of the KGB in many ways parallels the structure of the CIA, with a major difference: at the top of the organizational chart resides the Communist Party and governmental oversight.[42] Under the chairman of the KGB are traditional administrative functions of "Personnel, Finance & Planning, Mobilization, and Administrative & Supply."[43] The operational levels of the KGB fall under the Chief Directorates.

The Chief Directorates are composed of five separate sections. The section that handles foreign intelligence is the First Chief Directorate. The Second Chief Directorate handles internal security and counterintelligence. The third Chief Directorate focuses on military counterintelligence.

The only non-numbered Chief Directorate is Border Troops. And the final Chief Directorate is the eighth, which is responsible for communications and cryptology.[44] Further down the organizational chart are the Directorates, Department, and Services that provide administrative reports to the Chief Directorate.

The Directorates responsibilities are categorized as follows: Protection of the Constitution, Operational Technical, Communications and Interception, Economic Counterintelligence and Industrial Security, Surveillance, Security of Government Installations, and Military Construction.[45] Parallel to these Directorates are the Departments and Services of the KGB classified thus: KGB Protection Service, Investigation Department, KGB Higher School, Archives, Government Communication Service, Interception and Inspection of Correspondence, and Eavesdropping.[46] As one can see, the KGB still maintains a balance between internal and external intelligence and security measures, which makes the KGB a much different and more complex organization compared to its Western counterparts such as the CIA.

To understand this complexity, the First Chief Directorate (FCD) is used as an example, as this organization has a robust and large complement of specialty functions that the KGB used during the Cold War, especially as the FCD was the primary actor in foreign intelligence operations. The Directorates and Services within the FCD are broken down into letter-designated Directorates, which distinguish them from the number-designated Chief Directorates. Within the FCD these functions are assigned as follows: Directorate R Operations and Planning; Directorate K Counter-Intelligence, Directorate S Illegals; Directorate T Science and Technology, and Directorate RT Operations within and from the Territory of the Soviet Union; Directorate OT Operational Technical Support; and Directorate I Computer Service.[47] In addition to these Directorates, there are three hosts of Service departments: Service A Disinformation Covert Action; Service R Radio Communication; and Service A Code Section.[48] Further refinement for regional operations fall under fourteen departments that divide the world into regions.[49] The subdivisions and organization of the FCD serve only as the most useful examples of the vast, multilevel bureaucratic structure of the KGB. It must also be noted that the structure of the KGB does not include the parallel organization of the Soviet military, which had its own intelligence structure known as the GRU.

A CAVEAT

The topic of espionage has generated a significant number of nonfiction books, studies, and manuscripts, not to mention the vastness of the spy novel genre. However, it must be acknowledged that although the overall objective of this work is to highlight the evolution of the espionage game between the CIA and the KGB for the duration of the Cold War and the onset of the 21st century, there are limits to what is covered and referenced in this work. Whole works have been written on specific spies, such as Aldrich Ames, or specific programs, such as Venona or Corona, or even specific technologies such as the U-2 or poison-dispensing umbrellas designed to kill rogue agents or spies. The intent of the work, therefore, is not to provide a comprehensive history of every spy, every operation, or every piece of technology. Rather, the methodology has been used to highlight events, technologies, and operations that demonstrate shifts in the evolution of the espionage game, as well as to reinforce the fact that the nature of espionage has remained focused on using people as a primary means of intelligence gathering since before the start of the Cold War. By selectively picking specific events, spies, and technologies, a general trend is more easily discerned for those with a budding interest in espionage during the Cold War.

CHAPTER 1

Allies Become Enemies, 1944–1946

It is a well-known fact that the Soviet Union used spies to gather intelligence and collect research and development data on the Manhattan Project. The intelligence gained through the use of espionage assisted the Soviet Union in the development of its own atomic bomb in 1949, years ahead of the best estimates made by the United States' technical experts.[1] Though names like Klaus Fuchs, Ted Hall, and Julius and Ethel Rosenberg emerged from the early Cold War period as stunning examples of the Soviet Union's ability to penetrate even the most secret U.S. government programs, these four agents were just the proverbial "tip of the iceberg."

The period between the end of World War I and the end of World War II represents a "golden age" for the Soviet Union's use of spies in the United States. Though the penetration of the Manhattan Project has received a significant amount of attention, the decades prior to the start of World War II and our alliance with the Soviet Union are really toward the end of the story. In the period between 1920 and the beginning of 1939, the Soviet Union developed an active espionage program that sought to collect significant amounts of intelligence on the development of advanced technologies such as "aircraft engines, radar, military electronics, synthetic rubber, and photographic film."[2]

In addition to these technologies, the Soviet government had established a pattern of industrial espionage that had started in the 1920s when they assisted in the establishment of the Amtorg Trading Company (ATC), which become the Soviet Union's "purchasing agent" in the United States.[3] Though it was an official business that served as a conduit between U.S. corporations and companies in the Soviet Union, as the Soviet Union focused on modernizing its economy, ATC became a haven for industrial spying, which led to the Federal Bureau of Investigation's (FBI) investigation of the activities and objectives of the ATC.[4]

In tandem with the activities of the ATC, the Communist Party of the United States (CPUSA) also served as a venue by which the Soviet Union kept abreast of activities in the United States. The communists used the civil rights movement and worked with the National Association for the Advancement of Colored People (NAACP) as a means to advance the social agenda of communism. These actions spurred more and more investigations by federal authorities.

Even though by the start of World War II, it was relatively well known in certain U.S. government circles that the Soviet Union had a robust espionage program against the United States, the war posed a bit of a conundrum, as the Soviet Union was an ally of the United States and Great Britain. By the end of the war, the United States had established a counterespionage program that collected and analyzed diplomatic cables sent from Soviet diplomatic officers back to Moscow. This highly secret program, known as Venona, produced significant intelligence on the depth of the Soviet Union's espionage program within the United States.[5]

At the same time that the United States was intercepting and deciphering the Soviet Union's diplomatic traffic, the situation at the close of World War II produced a situation that caused the United States and its allies deep concern about the spread of communism in recently liberated Western Europe. In the immediate aftermath of the war, the political situation in Italy and France was such that the local communist parties were on the verge of achieving success. Having just defeated fascists and watched as the Soviet Union slowly tightened its control over Eastern and Central Europe, President Truman became focused on not allowing France and Italy to turn communist.

In the turbulent and fluid political environment of the very early Cold War, President Truman saw France and Italy as prime opportunities for the use of covert action to help shape the political environment.[6] This first era of espionage, covered in this chapter, captures three distinct forces in the period from 1940 to 1946. The first is the Soviet Union's infiltration of the Manhattan Project and the subsequent reaction by the United States to control and limit the loss of secret intelligence. Second, the United States developed and evolved its Venona program as a way to keep abreast of and counter Soviet intelligence operations. The third and last focus of this chapter is the United States' use of active covert forces to assist in shaping the political environment of postwar Europe in a way that was beneficial to the United States and its allies.

Overall, this chapter demonstrates that the espionage game between the United States and Soviet Union was well underway as World War II raged on and eventually transitioned to the early Cold War period. In fact, many of the objectives and missions outlined and developed in this first period of focus provided the foundation for the continuation and evolution of the espionage game that came to represent the Cold War.

BACKGROUND PRIOR TO THE MANHATTAN PROJECT

In the aftermath of the Bolshevik Revolution and the subsequent Russian Civil War, V. I. Lenin had the difficult task of rebuilding and industrializing the economy of the newly founded proletariat state.[7] A key element of this process was the advancement of the New Economic Policy (NEP), which served as a quick infusion of capitalism and industry into the Soviet Union's economy as a means to jumpstart the development of the industrial sector.[8] A main tenet of this economic policy was the need to develop official ties with international businesses that were interested in collaborating with the Soviet Union. Being a booming industrial economy, the United States became a lucrative target to collect industrial intelligence as a way for the Soviet Union to enhance and develop its fledgling economy. Though the United States had not officially recognized the Soviet Union in the aftermath of the Bolshevik revolution, this did not stop Lenin and, after 1924, Stalin in courting American businesses and industry as conduits for economic development.[9]

The establishment of the ATC served as an ex officio diplomatic entity by which the Soviet Union developed and fostered business relationships with U.S. companies.[10] The main goal, beyond establishing a trade relationship with the United States, was the Soviet Union's need to build its industrial base on the latest technology. Lacking advancements, and facing stiff resistance from official U.S. governmental channels, the ATC, under direction from Moscow, become an espionage vehicle; the Soviet Union used the mission of ATC as a screen to cover its espionage as it sought access to advanced technologies. Stalin's first five-year plan drove the quest for industrialization, which, in turn, necessitated the need for industrial espionage as the Soviet Union lacked the technology possessed by the United States and other capitalist powers.

In 1928 the chairman of the ATC, Saul Bron, stated:

Beyond doubt in the future we . . . shall be able to extend our industrial relations with the United States, from whose high technical level we shall gain advantages.[11]

This statement seems to imply an atmosphere of friendship and respect that is not typically associated with the relationship between communist and capitalist countries. But the Soviet Union's need to gain access in an attempt to modernize its economy drove the awkward relationship even though it was against the tenets of Karl Marx. Even though the U.S. State Department remained steadfastly committed to nonrecognition of the Soviet Union, the business community in the United States welcomed the opportunity to develop new markets. By 1931, the Soviet Union was America's "largest foreign purchaser of industrial machinery" as well as the "seventh largest customer of the goods produced in the United

States."[12] The concern over espionage remained small and focused, and it was largely overcome by the profits associated with the development of new markets within the rapidly expanding Soviet economy.

As odd as the U.S. government's lack of concern may seem against the backdrop of what we now know from the perspective of the 21st century, historian Katherine A. S. Sibley best characterizes this economic relationship. Sibley states in her book *Red Spies in America:*

At the time, the US government's overall security agenda and its concerns about the threat of the Soviet Union in particular were limited, and most Russian visitors continued to be welcome to make purchases and visit American plants. The threatening atmosphere in Europe by the end of the decade [1930s] increased concerns about domestic subversion of both the Communist and Nazi variety, but an understanding of Soviet espionage nevertheless remained indistinct.[13]

By the time of Stalin's second Five-Year Plan (1932–36), this close relationship continued to develop, which allowed E. H. Hunter of the U.S.-based Industrial Defense Association to proclaim:

Practically all the large industries like the Harvester Company, Ford Motor, General Electric, A&P Stores, etcetera are teaching technical men from Russia all the secrets of their great organizations. This is being done openly and above-board and those people come here under the quota privileges.[14]

Even though the Russian and American industrial relationship blossomed from the perspective of E. H. Hunter and industrialists, increasing concern over communist activity emerged in Congress.

In 1930 Speaker of the House Hamilton Fish Jr. (D–NY) stated:

The government . . . has practically no power to deal with the activities or the propaganda of any of the communists in the United States, and the communists, knowing that, have increased their activities within the last 6–7 years . . . [and] become a menace in the great industrial centers of the United States.[15]

Fish's concerns led him to establish the Special Committee to Investigate Communist Activity. This committee heard testimony on ATC members and their connection to Soviet military intelligence (Glavnoye Razvedy-vatelnoye Upravlenie, GRU). Of specific concern was the GRU's focus on gaining industrial intelligence on aircraft, aircraft engines, artillery, and naval ships, specifically battleships.[16] The ATC's interest in these items worried not only Fish and his committee but also the Office of Naval Intelligence. Fish and his committee recommended that "alien communists should be deported and that the Justice Department's power be strengthened to more closely scrutinize all communists."[17] Public opinion in the United States ran counter to recommendations of the

committee, and the committee was accused of grandstanding and foster-
ing anticommunist hysteria.[18]

Within the context of the espionage game, it can easily be seen from these
very early events in the 1920s and 1930s that the Soviet Union actively
used ATC as a vehicle to infiltrate the United States. Once in, the agents
used the cover of ATC as a means to collect, analyze, and disseminate critical industrial and military intelligence back to the Soviet Union. Using
quasi-government organizations as a means to develop and promote espionage within the United States, as well as later around the globe, became a
hallmark of the Soviet spy masters in Moscow. What is even more interesting to note is that although security and concerns over enemy infiltration
increased under the pressures of World War II, in the late 1920s and early
1930s, these hyperaware security concerns were generally dismissed as
politically or economically driven hysteria. Not until the onset of World
War II did the United States become keenly interested in increasing its vigilance regarding security and the need to protect secrets from espionage.

THE MANHATTAN PROJECT AND SOVIET ESPIONAGE

In the 1930s German scientists Otto Hahn and Fritz Strassman, aided by
chemist Lise Meitner, had been working on the theory of atomic fission.
In 1938, Hahn and Strassman finally succeeded in splitting the nucleus of
a uranium 235 atom.[19] This research was cutting-edge in the late 1930s; it
was greatly celebrated throughout the international scientific community
and was openly debated and discussed by scientists around the globe.

The significance of this discovery was that by splitting the nucleus of
the uranium 235 atom, a great amount of energy was released as the atom
transformed into atoms of krypton and barium. This prompt and powerful release of energy captured the attention of scientist as a potential
means to create a new category of weapon, if the process could be repeated
and sustained in such a way as to create a chain reaction.

Leo Szilard, who had been working at the University of Berlin prior
to leaving Germany due to the rise to power and Hitler and his National
Socialist German Workers Party (NSDAP), had been working on the theoretical concept of sustaining the chain reaction in atomic fission. Concerned
over the thought of Hitler and his NSDAP having a weapon of such great
potential, Szilard enlisted his friend Albert Einstein to write a letter to U.S.
President Franklin Delano Roosevelt. Einstein and Szilard stressed to FDR
that the United States needed to begin a crash program to research the use
of nuclear fission for potential use as a bomb. Einstein and Szilard wanted
to make sure that the Germans were not the first to have such a weapon.
FDR approved.

Between 1939, when FDR supported the continued research, and 1942,
when the Manhattan Project was officially started, research into nuclear

fission was maintained and conducted throughout the United States. On September 17, 1942, the United States officially funded and devoted significant resources to the development of an atomic bomb. The ultrasecret program, known as the Manhattan Project, named after the Army Corps of Engineers district office in New York City, came under the direction of Colonel (soon to be Brigadier General) Leslie Groves.

Groves had the difficult task of not only building the infrastructure necessary to support and advance the research and engineering necessary to work toward the development of an atomic bomb but also of hiring a vast army of approximately 500,000 people to complete the task.[20] To assist him in developing the several teams of scientists and engineers across the country, Groves hired J. Robert Oppenheimer, a scientist working at the Radiation Laboratory (Rad Lab) on the campus of the University of California Berkley.

Though Groves insisted that the Manhattan Project receive the utmost security and stressed that the various teams focus only on their part of the "project," his appointment of Oppenheimer raised some suspicion with the FBI and military intelligence, as Oppenheimer's family had been connected to the CPUSA.[21] Though suspicion continued to follow Oppenheimer well into the 1950s, when he eventually lost his security clearance under the investigation of the U.S. House of Representatives' Committee on Un-American Activities (HUAC), there are no definitive documents that point to Oppenheimer as an agent for the Soviet Union.[22]

Even as suspicion had been raised, and many in the United States knew that the Soviet Union had an active and intensive espionage campaign dating back to the late 1920s and the development of ATC, Groves and Oppenheimer pushed ahead with their work to complete an atomic bomb. The work done by Hahn, Strassman, Szilard, and many others on the use of atomic fission as a bomb had been well known in the international scientific community, until the Manhattan Project closed the open international discourse on the project. Of course, the Soviet Union, using its connections developed through ATC, worked to maintain awareness and gather intelligence on the science and engineering of the gun-type bomb. Of greater interest to the Soviet Union was the second type of design being explored by the Manhattan Project, which was the use of the more readily available plutonium to build an implosion-type atomic bomb. The Soviet Union had great interest in this device and did not have to work very hard to recruit and develop agents willing to provide them with the necessary technical intelligence.

Capitalizing on loopholes in the security vetting of the Manhattan Project, whereby British scientists who were already vetted as British nationals did not have to undergo a second round of security vetting when the United States requested their assistance on the Manhattan Project, the Soviet Union was able to use Klaus E. J. Fuchs to gather significant amounts of intelligence on the Manhattan Project, as well as the science and engineering hurdles toward weaponizing the plutonium-based bomb.

In addition to the use of British agents to infiltrate the Manhattan Project, the Soviet Union used its network of agents affiliated with ATC, as well as the CPUSA to gather intelligence. The two most significant examples are Theodore Hall and David Greenglass. Examining Fuchs, Hall, and Greenglass leads to a greater appreciation of the extent of the Soviet Union's knowledge of the Manhattan Project.

KLAUS FUCHS

Emil Julius Klaus Fuchs was a significant source of intelligence for the Soviet Union and provided critical information that would save the Soviet atomic project years of research and development in the design of a plutonium bomb.[23]

Fuchs, German by birth, was born in Rüsselsheim in 1911. Coming of age in the turbulent times of the Weimar republic, Fuchs excelled in math and physics.[24] Though he identified with the political agenda of the Social Democratic Party in Germany, he rejected the tenets of the party in 1931 and gravitated toward the political agenda of the Communist Party in Germany.[25] By 1933, the year Adolf Hitler and the NSDAP came to power, Fuchs officially joined the Communist Party of Germany.[26]

Sensing the NSDAP's quest to purge Germany of communists, Fuchs, now training as a physicist, left Germany to go to France and ultimately ended up in the United Kingdom, at the Bristol University.[27] He completed his doctorate of philosophy (PhD) in physics in 1937, and in 1939 he had landed a job in the United Kingdom as a research physicist at the University of Edinburgh.[28]

With war in Europe erupting, Fuchs, as a German national, was investigated by the British government as being a potential "Nazi agent" and was sent to an internment camp in Canada in 1940.[29] By 1941, the British government cleared Fuchs as a security risk and allowed him to return to his position at the University of Edinburgh, even though he had maintained his overt allegiance to communism. Banned from working on ultra-secret projects, such as Britain's development of radar under the direction of Marcus Oliphant, Fuchs worked with Rudolf Peirels on atomic physics, which was deemed a less "important project."[30] To put the security issues behind him and advance his career as a scientist, Fuchs signed the "Official Secrets Act" of the British government and became a British citizen in 1942.[31] His naturalization as a British citizen proved exceptionally valuable as his double life as a communist spy evolved over the next three years.

In 1943 the Manhattan Project was stuck with the slow production of uranium 235, and its scientists, physicists, and engineers sought a secondary design for an atomic bomb. Using research by Glenn Seaborg on the potential of plutonium, Groves and Oppenheimer asked the British for help in the development of a plutonium-based bomb. Though Groves argued for the vetting of the British scientists, the British held that they had already thoroughly checked and vetted their own scientists who were British citizens. Groves acquiesced. Fuchs was a British citizen and therefore did not have to undergo a security check before being allowed to work on the Manhattan Project.

Though the British had vetted Fuchs, he had been providing the KGB and GRU intelligence on his research in England since late 1941.[32] Working with Simon Davidovich Kremer, a member of the Soviet military attaché's staff in London, Fuchs provided the Soviet Union with atomic intelligence prior to traveling to the United States to work with the Americans on the Manhattan Project.[33]

In December 1943, Fuchs traveled to New York City to assist with the Manhattan Project. In February 1944 he met with Harry Gold.[34] Gold was a Russian Jew who was born in Bern, Switzerland, in 1910 to parents who had fled Kiev in 1907.[35] His family immigrated to the United States in 1914. In the early 1930s, Gold worked and saved his money as to way to pay for his college education as a chemist at the University of Pennsylvania.[36]

Gold joined the Federation of Architects, Engineers, Chemists, and Technicians (FAECT) and was cultivated by NKVD agents as a potential source of intelligence. Gold embraced the communist cause and accepted financial assistance from the Soviet Union as a means to complete his studies, which he did at Xavier University in Cincinnati, Ohio.[37]

Having secured work as an analytical chemist, Gold actively passed intelligence to his Soviet contacts.[38] By 1943, his handlers identified him as the best source to meet with Klaus Fuchs and work as a courier to gain access to atomic intelligence on the Manhattan Project. In February 1944, Fuchs and Gold met for the first time. Soviet intelligence reported to Moscow:

On 5th February a meeting took place between "Gus" [Harry Gold] and "Rest" [Klaus Fuchs]. Beforehand [Gold] was given a detailed briefing by us. [Fuchs] greeted him pleasantly but was rather cautious at first; during the discussion [Gold] satisfied himself that [Fuchs] was aware of whom he was working with. [Fuchs] arrived in September as a member of the British mission on "Enormous" [the atomic bomb project]. According to him work on the atomic bomb in the United States is being carried out under the direct control of the United States Army represented by General [Brehan] Somervell and [Secretary of War] Stimson: at the head of the British is a Labour Member of Parliament, Ben Smith. The operation amounts to working out the process for the separation of isotopes of uranium.[39]

After this first meeting, Fuchs was firmly committed to providing Gold with intelligence on his work. In a short time, Fuchs and the British team transferred to Los Alamos, New Mexico, to work on weapon design and other critical issues associated with building the plutonium-based atomic bomb.

The science, research, and design of the "gadget" that would come to be called "fat man" was more advanced than the gun-type bomb using uranium. To make Fat Man a viable weapon, Fuchs and the team at Los Alamos, which included Hans Bethe, Enrico Fermi, Niels Bohr, and Robert Oppenheimer, had to solve the problem of how to create a sustained chain reaction within the sphere of approximately fourteen pounds of plutonium.[40] The main issue was how to compress the softball-size sphere of plutonium with approximately five thousand pounds of high-explosive materials to the size of a tennis ball, which was thought to be enough force to generate the pressure necessary to create the sustain chain reaction in the Plutonium atoms.

While this sounds like a relatively straightforward research and engineering problem, the team needed to ensure that the pressure generated from the high-explosive materials created the same pressure distributed equally around the core of the bomb. This impressively difficult task required the use of lenses and other devices to ensure that the detonation of the high-explosive materials would be constant, consistent, and focused equally to create the proper force for the sustained chain reaction.

Fuchs was part of the team that worked on the details and engineering of these issues. By 1944, he was supplying Gold with regular technical intelligence on the research being done at Los Alamos. Gold, in turn, passed the intelligence on to Soviet officials, who sent the reports back to Moscow. Often this process took less than two weeks.[41]

With the test of the Trinity bomb, which was the plutonium core bomb worked on by Fuchs, in the summer of 1945, the research, science, and engineering provided the United States with a second bomb design. As U.S. President Harry Truman traveled to a meeting with Joseph Stalin and Winston Churchill at Potsdam to discuss political issues relating to the situation in Europe, as well as plans to conclude the war in the Pacific, he received a coded message of the successful test. In the course of his meeting with Stalin, Truman let him know of a secret project that the United States had been working on. Truman mentioned in his memoirs that Stalin had no real reaction to the announcement.[42]

Stalin already knew about the test at Trinity and was well aware of the progress of the Manhattan Project.[43] The Soviet Union's uses of Fuchs and Gold ensured that they had the latest intelligence on the progress of the atomic bomb. The intelligence passed on to the Soviet Union by Fuchs provided the Soviet Union's own atomic bomb research program with valuable information as to the successes and failures of U.S. and British research efforts. This critical information from Fuchs, regarding what worked and what did not, allowed the Soviets' atomic bomb program to avoid the dead ends and false starts encountered by the United States and the British. Therefore, Fuchs, via his intelligence, directly assisted the Soviet Union in building a bomb years before the projected date identified by the U.S. intelligence community in the immediate Cold War period.[44]

At the end of World War II, Klaus Fuchs returned to Great Britain and worked on the British atomic bomb project. Based on his research and work with the United States on the Manhattan Project, Fuchs was a highly placed and central scientist in Britain's effort to build its own atomic device. However, U.S. Army Intelligence, working with the FBI, broke into the Soviet Union's cable traffic from the United States back to Moscow. Having succeeded in forming a signals intelligence program called Venona (which will be detailed later in this chapter), U.S. authorities turned their information over to the British, who confronted Fuchs. Fuchs confessed.[45]

By the time of his arrest in 1950, Fuchs had been providing the Soviet Union with intelligence on not just the U.S. Atomic bomb project but also on Britain's research on the hydrogen bomb for approximately seven years. In fact, Soviet sources confirmed that they believed the "most valuable information provided by Fuchs" came when he returned to Britain and maintained his connections to Soviet intelligence-gathering sources.[46]

Though historians identify Fuchs as the most detrimental Soviet intelligence source, due to the atomic secrets he passed to Moscow, the well-developed communist espionage network in the United States had a host of other spies working in the Manhattan Project. Theodore Hall, the youngest scientist to work at Los Alamos, also supplied the Soviet Union with critical intelligence. In addition to Hall, an army enlisted man by the name of David Greenglass would also play a critical role in spying for the Soviet Union, as his sister was Ethel Rosenberg and his brother-in-law was Julius Rosenberg. The cases of Hall and Greenglass demonstrate the ease with which the Soviet Union easily penetrated the Manhattan Project and gathered significant intelligence.

THEODORE HALL

Theodore Alvin Hall, like Klaus Fuchs, worked on the plutonium bomb at Los Alamos and also spied for the Soviet Union. Hall, at the age of twenty, was the youngest scientist to work on the Manhattan Project. Hall was, by all accounts, a "child prodigy" during his studies at Harvard University.[47] Being naturally gifted in mathematics and physics, Hall easily excelled at his studies.

While at Harvard, Hall befriended Saville Savoy Sax, who was a member of the Young Communist League. Through his friendship, Sax introduced and exposed Hall to the tenets of communist ideology. Hall began to attend meetings and eventually joined the Young Communist League.[48] Throughout his time at Harvard, the quiet, reflective Hall, under the tutelage of Sax, began to "idealize Russia as a simple worker-peasant state."[49]

Using the utopian vision outlined by Marx along with the powerful pro-paganda churned out under the tenure of the Stalin, the Soviet Union and its international affiliates easily sold their state as a progressive nation that focused on the ideal worker's life. The totalitarian nature of the Soviet regime under both Lenin and Stalin ensured that the state controlled a deliberate and positive international and peaceful image, although in fact they were purging large elements of their society who did not adhere to the new vision for the Soviet Union.[50] Hall was convinced by the propa-ganda of the benefits and goodness of the Soviet system.

By November 1944, Hall had secured a job at Los Alamos, working on the implosion of the Plutonium pit. Being sympathetic to the Soviet cause, his friend Sax convinced him that he should provide information on his work.[51] In fact, Sax served as Hall's first courier; Hall supplied him with the first piece of intelligence in which Hall outlined the names of heads of research departments and other critical projects being conducted at Los Alamos.[52] Though the initial report supplied by Hall had limited utility, and the information was rudimentary, it proved that Hall would spy for the Soviet Union and that he could be trusted as an intelligence source.

Historian Michael D. Gordin, author of *Red Cloud at Dawn*, makes the point that Theodore Hall "may have been the first intelligence source by which the Soviet Union learned of the implosion method," rather than Fuchs.[53] Though Soviet intelligence greatly welcomed two sources that they could use to "cross-check one another,"[54] it is important to note here that a major operational tenet of the KGB was to ensure that competing agents and couriers were not known to one another as a way to maintain cover and ensure that if captured, they had very limited knowledge of the extensive intelligence-gathering network. This way, even with a disruption caused by an arrest, the espionage network could continue to function. Therefore, Fuchs and Hall, though they might have known each other through their work at Los Alamos, did not mutually know that they were both providing the Soviet Union with U.S. intelligence on the atomic bomb program.

Hall's coworkers at Los Alamos, including the "father of the neutron bomb" Sam Cohen, had no idea that Hall passed secrets to the Soviet Union.[55] In an interview well after Hall had been identified as a spy for the Soviet Union, Cohen recollected that Hall was "the most disheveled and eccentric GI in the camp."[56] During his tenure at Los Alamos, Hall provided the Soviet Union with critical information on the process to build an implosion bomb with plutonium. Of equal importance was Hall's iden-tification of the locations and people doing the work.[57] Though location and the identification of people may seem relatively simple and lacking necessary specificity, especially in the context of the vast size of the work force at Los Alamos, the intelligence provided by Hall allowed the Soviet Union a greater understanding of the program and potential sources that they could further exploit for additional intelligence.

Throughout Hall's time at Los Alamos, neither the U.S. military nor the FBI suspected him of being involved in espionage for the Soviet Union. Hall, with his sympathies toward communism, believed that "no nation should have a monopoly on atomic power."[58] Therefore, his decision and commitment to pass information to the Soviet Union seemed to be driven by ideological reasons, as was the case with Fuchs. Though Hall had a past that involved communist sympathies and known affiliation with the Young Communist League, the United States did not concern itself with the possibility of Ted Hall being a spy.

In 1948, Hall attended the University of Chicago to complete his PhD. While in Chicago, Hall joined the Communist Party.[59] His past caught up with him in 1951, when the FBI became interested in his work and contacts while at Los Alamos. Based on information obtained from the Venona deciphers, the FBI had information and cause to suspect Hall as being a spy, but not enough evidence to convict him.[60] Hall's past was not fully exposed until the 1990s, when the Venona deciphers were fully declassified, and historians and research pieced together the puzzle. Hall issued a written statement in response. Hall stated "that he might have been a spy for Russia, and that as a young man, he had felt it dangerous for the United States alone to have the nuclear weapon."[61]

There were early indicators that both Hall and Fuchs had communist sympathies prior to their classified work on the Manhattan Project. Despite these political proclivities, both men were able to work for the United States and the Soviet Union simultaneously without arousing significant suspicion. Without the Venona program, it is possible that neither one of these spies would have been identified. Furthermore, Hall, like Fuchs, provided the Soviet Union with intelligence that fed directly into its own atomic weapons research. The end result was that the Soviet Union could check and double-check its research and progress based on the intelligence of Fuchs and Hall. These streams of intelligence, combined with additional information from other U.S. agents like David Greenglass, accelerated the Soviet atomic bomb program.

DAVID GREENGLASS

The story of David Greenglass has commonalities with Fuchs and Hall. Like these two other spies at Los Alamos, Greenglass was also a committed communist prior to his work at Los Alamos. Though there are similarities with Fuchs and Hall, the case of David Greenglass, who was the brother of Ethel Rosenberg and brother-in-law to Julius Rosenberg, placed him at the center of one of the most famous and controversial cases of espionage during the Cold War. Known more for his identification of Julius and Ethel Rosenberg as spies for the Soviet Union, he served as a primary source for the U.S. government's case against the Rosenbergs. Greenglass was nevertheless also a spy that provided the Soviet Union critical atomic intelligence through his work at Los Alamos.

Having had a semester of college at Brooklyn Polytechnic Institute before dropping out of school to work as a machinist, David Greenglass had already been exposed to the tenets of communism and the organization of the Young Communist League.[62] His sister Ethel, who married Julius Rosenberg, introduced her younger brother to communism. Working as a machinist, Greenglass maintained his interest in communism and worked diligently as a union organizer. He married his childhood sweetheart, Ruth Prinz, in November 1942. Ruth was also a dedicated communist.[63] Shortly after their marriage, the U.S. Army drafted Greenglass in early 1943. Greenglass maintained his commitment to the tenets of communism while the U.S. Army assigned him to work on the Manhattan Project, even though he was not aware of the nature of his work while at Oak Ridge, Tennessee.[64]

Greenglass's letters to his wife, who remained in New York, reflect his commitment to communism. Filled with positive sentiments, such as "the future is socialism" and "we are in love and have our Marxist outlook" the letters emphasize the fact that Greenglass firmly believed that the future was certainly going to be a socialist one. In one of his last letters to Ruth prior to his transfer to Los Alamos, Greenglass wrote:

I have been reading a lot of books on the Soviet Union. Dear, I can see how farsighted and intelligent those leaders are. They are really geniuses. Everyone of them. . . . I have come to a stronger and more resolute faith in and belief in the principles of Socialism and Communism. I believe that every time the Soviet Government used force they did so with pain in their hearts and the belief that what they were doing was to produce good for the greatest number. . . . More power to the Soviet Union and a fruitful abundant life for their people.[65]

Considering his strident commitment to the communist cause, it is amazing that Greenglass got orders to report to Los Alamos in August of 1944. His assignment at Los Alamos was to work on "implosion detonators" for the plutonium bomb.[66] Committed to his work and his loving wife, Ruth, who was still living in New York, Greenglass regularly sent letters back to his wife let her know that he was working on an important project. In turn, Ruth Greenglass provided small details and insights into David's work to his sister, Ethel Rosenberg. Ethel, in turn, talked with her husband, Julius Rosenberg, about the work of her younger brother.[67] Julius Rosenberg was already working as a spy for the Soviet Union and was very interested in the possibility of recruiting his brother-in-law to provide atomic intelligence to the Soviet Union.[68]

Working through his KGB handlers, Julius Rosenberg penned a report of the potential use of his bother-in-law and sister-in-law as spies for the Soviet Union.[69] With approval from the KGB to develop David Greenglass as a spy within the Manhattan Project, Julius and Ethel Rosenberg worked through Ruth Greenglass to confirm that David Greenglass was indeed interested and willing to work as a spy. In November 1944, David wrote a letter to Ruth in which he stated that he would be "most certainly will be glad to be part of the community project that Julius and his friends have in mind."[70] By January 1945, David Greenglass had provided his contact, Julius Rosenberg, with his first set of intelligence on the progress of the atomic bomb.[71]

The information David Greenglass supplied the Soviet Union pertained to the lenses needed to focus the explosion of high explosives in an effort to compress the pit of plutonium to create the sustained chain reaction necessary to achieve critical mass in the plutonium bomb.[72] Again, as with the intelligence being forwarded from both Fuchs and Hall, the intelligence from Greenglass was greatly welcomed by the Soviet Union, as it focused and directed their work for the development of their own plutonium bomb in 1949.

The revelation of Greenglass as a spy for the Soviet Union did not come to light until 1949, when the FBI talked to Greenglass about people whom he had worked with while stationed at Los Alamos. The investigation by the FBI was not focused on Greenglass, because they were looking into the espionage conducted by Fuchs. Greenglass told the FBI that "he had heard of Fuchs, but knew nothing more."[73] Even though the U.S. government had the Venona cables that provided links to Greenglass and the Rosenbergs and their spying for the Soviet Union, it was not until 1950 that David Greenglass told his story to the FBI, after Julius Rosenberg tried to talk David and Ruth Greenglass into a plan to move to Mexico with $5,000, which the KGB had supplied.[74] At this point Greenglass and his wife became fundamental players in the Rosenberg espionage case, which will be covered in later chapters.

The fact that Fuchs, Hall, and Greenglass had been dedicated communists who supplied critical information to the Soviet Union on the U.S. effort to produce an atomic bomb could potentially have been lost to the march of history, as it appears that the United States had little knowledge of these spies. However, the development of a counterintelligence program, later to be known as Venona, provided the United States with critical counterintelligence and deciphering capability that finally allowed the United States to become aware of the depth the Soviet Union's penetration of not just the Manhattan Project but a whole host of U.S. government agencies.

VENONA

Though it had long been suspected by the U.S. government that the Soviet Union had made significant inroads into infiltrating the U.S. government, industry, and society with communist spies, there was a general lack of proof that confirmed the suspicion of domestic and international communists. The Venona project provided the U.S. government with the smoking gun it need to prove that the Soviet Union did indeed have a robust and resilient intelligence-gathering network within the United States. Furthermore, once the initial deciphered messages began to emerge in the initial years of the Cold War, the U.S. government became astounded at the depth and breadth of the Soviet Union's capability to collect a plethora of military, governmental, and industrial intelligence from Americans.[75]

Once the overall Venona project had finally been declassified on July 11, 1995, the U.S. public as well as the international community finally saw the extent of Soviet espionage within the United States during the 1920s through at least the 1950s. The extensive volume of declassified material—approximately 2,900 messages—proved that the Soviet Union's use of Americans was not only focused on a few well-placed, diehard committed communists but rather that the CPUSA served as a conduit to entice a large number of American citizens to spy on behalf of the Soviet Union.[76] The use of the CPUSA as well as other connected organizations such as ATC and the Young Communist League provided an expansive network of spies that reported back to Soviet embassies on a vast array of governmental, industrial, and military programs within the United States.

In many ways the previous pages of this chapter have exposed and highlighted the Soviet Union's successful use of spies to gather industrial, military, and atomic secrets from the United States. The Venona project was an effort to pin down and eventually try to suppress the success of the Soviet Union's prewar and wartime intelligence-gathering networks.

The Venona project emerged slowly in the context of World War II. First, one must understand that the Soviet Union had NKVD stations, or *rezidenturas*, embedded within the Soviet diplomatic missions within the United States. The three primary rezidenturas were housed within the Soviet Union's embassies in New York City, Washington, D.C., and San Francisco.[77] A fourth rezidentura was run as an "illegal," by which NKVD and later KGB personally entered the United States with fake credentials and attempted to live and work as immigrants or even as eventual American citizens, but with an overall objective of developing agents and building spy networks within the United States and its government.[78] These diplomatic stations served as the points by which Soviet intelligence officers forwarded messages back to Moscow. However, in the turbulent years of 1941–1943, the U.S. government was much more concerned with the infiltration of Germany and Nazi spies than it was with spies from the Soviet Union. This focus of priority changed in 1943.

While attempting to "search the airwaves for clandestine Nazi radio transmitters" in the United States, the Federal Communications Commission stumbled on illegal radio transmissions coming from consulates of the Soviet Union in New York and San Francisco.[79] Having confiscated the illegal radio transmitters, the U.S. government had forced the Soviet Union to revert to using commercial telegraph agencies to transmit messages back to Moscow.[80] Having thought that they had suppressed the flow of intelligence to the Soviet Union, the U.S. government remained somewhat concerned about the actions of its wartime ally.

Specifically, the U.S. government was concerned that if conditions got bad enough in the Soviet Union's fight with Germany, Stalin might try to duplicate V. I. Lenin's separate peace with Germany, as he had done in 1917. The United States wanted to ensure that the allies in World War II retained a unified commitment to the tenets of Germany's unconditional surrender. U.S. Army Colonel Carter Clark, working for the U.S. Army's Special Branch, which was a component of the U.S. War Department's Intelligence Division, had been assigned to try to discern the intentions of the political leadership of the Soviet Union vis-à-vis negotiations with Nazi Germany.[81] To begin to ascertain his objective, Clark worked to collect, decipher, and translate Soviet diplomatic cable traffic from New York, Washington, D.C., and San Francisco. Clark's efforts proved futile as the Soviet Union used an elaborate system of onetime-use codebooks, which proved very difficult, if not impossible, to break.[82]

The two-part code system required that once a specific message had been coded by Soviet officers in the United States and then sent to the Soviet Union, officers in the Soviet Union deciphered the coded message using a onetime code from a book of codes. The idea behind the system was that the code for the specific message was used only once, and then the code page was torn from the book and destroyed. Once all the pages of the codebook had been used, the Soviet intelligence officers started with a new book and new codes. As one can imagine, Clark's attempt to decipher the diplomatic messages of the Soviet Union's rezidenturas proved slow and daunting, despite a tremendous amount of effort thrown at the system by the U.S. Army and the U.S. government.

The code-breaking effort took place in Arlington Hall, a former girls' school in Virginia that the U.S. Army had taken over during the war.[83] Despite the fact that this was primarily a military-based operation, only 10 percent of the personnel assigned to the project were military officers. The remaining 90 percent were young men and women who had special aptitude for math or foreign languages; very few had any experience at code breaking.[84] Despite the importance of the project, the civilian personnel hired by the U.S. government for Venona retained a relatively low rank, such as GS-2—or GS-3 if they had attended some college.[85] This civilian rank was the equivalent in pay to an enlisted private in the U.S. Army.[86]

Though the process was difficult and slow, by 1945 the United States' code-breaking efforts at Arlington Hall began to collaborate with their British allies and had identified and compiled a list of over two hundred thousand cables that needed attention. By this time, the FBI was also brought into the project, even though it remained a very tightly guarded and highly classified program, even to the extent that President Harry S. Truman was not aware of the program.[87]

By the end of World War II, the Venona program at Arlington Hall had made some progress due to wartime conditions in the Soviet Union. In 1943, when the Soviet Union and its Red Army was engaged in savage fighting with Germany, the Soviet Union faced a production shortage of its onetime-use codebooks. Therefore, resourceful Soviet diplomatic officers saved pages and even entire books, with the idea to conserve limited resources. This frugal action by the Soviet Union's diplomatic and intelligence corps provided the United States with a lucky break.

The Soviet Union's reuse of codebooks allowed the code breakers at Arlington Hall to begin to at least identify the code names of U.S.-based intelligence agents passing information to the Soviet handlers. Throughout the process Soviet agents inside the U.S. government, most notably Lauchlin Currie, Elizabeth Bentely, and William W. Weisband, steadily informed their Soviet handlers about the origin and progress of the code-breaking effort.

By 1948, the United States, with assistance from the British, were able to decode and begin to translate and analyze a very small portion of the mountain of diplomatic traffic. Even though the original intent of the Venona program had failed to provide any intelligence as to the objectives of the leadership of the Soviet Union, it did provide some key insights into the espionage network developed and used by the Soviet Union in the interwar and wartime periods.

Though the Venona project failed in its original mission, in the immediate postwar years, it provided intelligence that led the U.S. government to identify Klaus Fuchs, Ted Hall, and David Greenglass as spies who had worked with Soviet intelligence officers to pass atomic information to the Soviet Union. Despite the limited success of initial program, the U.S. government maintained and continued to work through the backlog of unbroken coded messages. In fact, the Venona program remained operational and was folded under the National Security Agency (NSA) until its termination in 1985. At the time of termination, the program had decoded three thousand messages—an impressive number, but only approximately 1.5 percent of the over two hundred thousand messages intercepted and collected by the United States and its British allies. The U.S. public, as well as the rest of the world, became aware of the program in 1995, when the NSA declassified the Venona messages under pressure from the U.S. Senate.

The significance of the Venona program within the context of the espionage exploits of Fuchs, Hall, and Greenglass was that the program provided evidence that the Soviet Union did indeed have a vast array of people spying for them within the United States, especially within the Manhattan Project. The Venona program provided critical evidence and allowed the United States to begin work toward reducing the infiltration of Soviet spies operating within the U.S. government. Venona, though limited in its ability and exactness, did provide the necessary evidence that the U.S. government had been slow to recognize the extent and seriousness of the Soviet Union's use of American citizens and other foreign nationals as intelligence-gathering sources.

In the period from 1946 to 1960, the information from Venona combined with the work by done by the FBI, CIA, and NSA provided a springboard for an anticommunist crusade to sweep through the United States. Borrowing heavily from the tactics used by Hamilton Fish and the HUAC during the first Red Scare decades earlier, Wisconsin Congressman Joseph McCarthy (R) revived the Red Scare, largely based on information devised and decoded through the Venona program. Though the "Second Red Scare" generated suspicion and paranoia about Soviet spies within the United States, the overall outcome, with specific focus on the U.S. government, was that Venona allowed the FBI to reduce and suppress many of the Soviet spies who had worked in the years between the 1920s and the end of World War II. Furthermore, it demonstrates how the United States began to develop a system by which it could identify and build cases against the spies in the United States working for the Soviet Union. The espionage game therefore began in the period prior to the start of World War II and would maintain itself for the duration of the Cold War. By the time the first Venona telegrams had been decoded and analyzed, the U.S. government had begun to take the business of espionage very seriously.

CONCLUSION

The Bolshevik Revolution and the subsequent Russian Civil War created significant political, social, and economic upheaval in the Soviet Union, but these changes also had an international influence throughout the world. As V. I. Lenin and, after 1923, Joseph Stalin worked to build the political, social, and economic infrastructure of the new Soviet State, they realized that the new country had significant deficiencies, especially in the industrial sector. Seeing the United States as a major industrial leader, yet also as a major political rival, the leaders of the Soviet Union saw industrial espionage as a means to gain the technology needed to recast the worker's paradise as a new model for the rest of the world to emulate. The major problem was that World War I, the Bolshevik Revolution, and the Russian Civil War left the Russian State in shambles. International espionage provided a means by which the Soviet Union could rebuild itself and attempt to rival the traditional Western industrial powers.

The ATC was a critical vehicle for the Soviet Union to acquire industrial and technological information from corporations in the United States. This semiofficial trade organization provided a conduit through which Soviet intelligence operatives developed relationships that suited their need for information and access to technology and industrial secrets. Prior to the official recognition of the Soviet Union by U.S. President Franklin D. Roosevelt in 1933, ATC served as the quasi-diplomatic, industrial, and technology conduit by which the Soviet Union could acquire the hardware, machinery, and information needed to rebuild its industrial capacity. Furthermore, ATC capitalized on the rise of the CPUSA and used U.S. nationals with sympathies to communism and the Soviet Union as agents to provide military and technological intelligence they were barred from acquiring.

The twin pillars of ATC and CPUSA provided the Soviet Union with not only a bureaucratic infrastructure to acquire and transport technology and information back to the Soviet Union from the United States but also a budding intelligence network that used U.S. citizens as agents in this initial round of espionage. The experience and insights gained from this interwar period proved valuable to the Soviet Union once FDR recognized it as an official state, which allowed the communist nation to establish rezidenturas in the United States. These diplomatic establishments allowed the Soviet Union to expand its intelligence-gathering capabilities in the United States. With the onset of World War II, pledged as an ally to the United States and Great Britain in the fight against Hitler's Germany, the Soviet Union used the opportunity to infiltrate the U.S. government's most classified program, the Manhattan Project.

In many ways the Soviet Union's infiltration of the program to develop an atomic bomb and the use of Klaus Fuchs, Ted Hall, and David Greenglass to gain knowledge of the organization of the Manhattan Project, as well as key technological progress, mimicked its use of spies through ATC. However, the main objective of gaining intelligence on U.S. progress on the atomic bomb was not just about establishing parity in industry and technology but also about maintaining parity in military and political power.

The espionage efforts of Fuchs, Hall, and Greenglass provided Soviet scientist with key pieces of research, engineering, and technology that allowed the Soviet Union to develop its own atomic bomb much quicker than the intelligence experts in the Truman administration predicted. It is interesting to note that during World War II, the United States seemed to be more interested in finding German spies than making sure the Soviet Union had not infiltrated the Manhattan Project, which was a very highly classified project. In fact, were it not for the efforts by the Federal Communications Commission's attempt to locate illegal German radio transmissions, the U.S. government may not have stumbled onto the Soviet Union's use of illegal radio transmitters to project information from the

United States to the Soviet Union. This lucky break proved highly beneficial to the U.S. government, as it made the Soviet rezidenturas use commercial telegraphs lines, which could be intercepted.

These events combined with concerns within FDR's administration about Stalin's potential to negotiate a separate peace with Germany. Based on these political concerns within the context of the allied effort to fight the Axis powers to an unconditional surrender, the U.S. Army worked on collecting, deciphering, and analyzing Soviet cable traffic in an attempt to gain greater insights into the political intentions of Stalin and other key political leaders in the Soviet Union. Stymied by difficult codes, this original project proved futile in its original mission.

However, the program did begin to provide insights into the highly developed Soviet espionage network as well as reveal that the Soviet Union had effectively penetrated the Manhattan Project. The problem was that these revelations came after the end of World War II. The Venona program become a key fixture of the early Cold War program by the United States to identify, track, and arrest Soviet spies in the United States.

This initial period of espionage set the stage for the remainder of the Cold War, whereby both the Soviet Union and the United States strove to develop the means to collect intelligence on their primary adversary. The espionage "game" established in this first period identified the parameters and would become an ever-evolving process by which the two sides worked to collect intelligence on one another. Beyond just using people as spies, both sides worked throughout the Cold War to ensure that they had the necessary intelligence so that they would not be caught off guard or even fall behind in the tense atmosphere of the nuclear security environment.

Though the ideological tenets of the United States and the Soviet Union were always at odds, World War II offered an opportunity for the United States and the Soviet Union to be allies in the fight against Nazism. However, this common enemy did not slow the espionage efforts. As a result of the information gathered from Venona, the United States realized the extent of Soviet espionage; and in the tense years of the early Cold War, this only further fueled American suspicion of communists. With the end of World War II, the allies had little in common, and their suspicion of one another only escalated in politically turbulent Europe in the years 1945–1948. With the release of the first decoded Venona intercepts, the allies of World War II became Cold War enemies.

CHAPTER 2

Europe: A Contested Environment, 1946–1949

In the aftermath of World War II, the former allies increasingly became suspicious and aware that the wartime alliance had waned in the new political vacuum across Europe, especially Central and Eastern Europe. As the Soviet Union attempted to consolidate a communist security sphere across Eastern Europe, the Truman administration focused on stabilizing Western Europe in a way that would promote democracy and capitalism.[1] Truman's main objective was to ensure that communism would not gain a foothold in Western Europe, despite the dilapidated economic and political environment.

Building on the foundation established in the first chapter, whereby the Soviet Union and the United States engaged in an espionage game over the Manhattan Project and atomic secrets, in this early period of the Cold War, the nemeses of the Cold War strove to understand the threat posed by each other.

Therefore, the attempt to understand the new security environment focused on two major fronts from the perspective of the United States. The first was the need to understand and become more aware of the military threat posed by the Soviet Union. The second concern for the West, and Truman and his administration, was the need to ensure that the specter of communism did not encroach into Western Europe.

From the perspective of the Soviet Union, their intelligence service had enough intelligence on the U.S. Manhattan Project to develop and test its own atomic bomb in 1949.[2] However, they still needed to be aware of the advancements made by the United States in the development and deployment of atomic and shortly nuclear weapons. The main objective from the perspective of the Soviet Union was to build its large, effective spy network within the United States. This proved to be much more difficult, as the development of the U.S. Venona program led to the erosion of the previous network and many of its agents were either compromised or exposed.[3] Therefore, the Soviet Union had to work extremely hard at rebuilding its withered espionage network.[4]

While focusing on the efforts to rebuild its espionage network in the United States, the Soviet Union also strove to ensure that Poland, Czechoslovakia, and Hungary become cemented within the new Soviet security zone. This tension in the immediate postwar years was reflected in a speech given by Stalin at the Bolshoi Theater in Moscow in February 1946. Stalin argued that despite the alliance between the West and the Soviet Union during World War II, "democratic capitalism and communism could not live together peacefully."[5] A major part of Stalin's effort to advance the eventual end-state, as advocated by Karl Marx, was to ensure that the countries of Central and Eastern Europe remained well within the influence of the Soviet Union, which meant that they became communist states. This obsession with security by Stalin and his belief in the international incompatibility of the East and West further drove the international tension in the opening years of the Cold War.

By 1947, just a short two years after the end of World War II, the Soviet Union had worked to gain control of Central and Eastern Europe. However, Truman and Western Europeans (specifically the British, French, Germans, and Italians) were deeply concerned about the tense and economically turbulent period following the end of World War II. Clark M. Clifford, White House counsel, wrote a policy paper for Truman, in which he stated:

The expansion of Communism was "the gravest problem facing the United States," as the Soviet Leadership appeared to be on a course for aggrandizement designed to lead to eventual world domination.[6]

Clifford's assessment of the strategic objective of the Soviet Union was not the first instance of a member of Truman's administration making this assessment. In February 1946, George F. Kennan, a diplomat and foreign service officer wrote a seven-thousand word telegram in which he outlined the political objectives and methods used by the Soviet Union and its government to obtain it objectives and control its people.[7] A year later, Kennan, now director of the policy planning staff in the U.S. State Department, penned an article in *Foreign Policy* entitled "Sources of Soviet Conduct."[8] The insights highlighted and outlined by Clifford and Kennan reflected the dynamic and turbulent political security environment of the new Cold War and concern on the part of Truman and many in his administration about the expansion of communism.

As these internal debates evolved within the administration, the populace of the United States began to learn about the Soviet Union's infiltration of the Manhattan Project. Together these forces drove Truman and the U.S. government to focus on building efforts to combat the spread of communism within the context of the Cold War. Although the traditional elements of national power such as political, military, and diplomatic forces would be used, Truman also focused on the use of active and passive covert activities to make sure that the West stood firm against any further communist encroachment. For the United States Espionage served a central part in this critical focus on the United States. Additionally, Truman had to make sure that the West clearly understood the military capabilities of the Soviet Union. By 1947 espionage had become a complicated and multifaceted effort conducted across a variety of newly established U.S. agencies.

POSTWAR ISSUES: FRANCE

The security environment in Western Europe in the aftermath of World War II was a major concern for Harry S. Truman and the United States. In the wake of the destruction of the war, Truman and his administration worried about the rebuilding process and the potential for domestic communist politicians to make significant headway in the tumultuous social, economic, and political conditions. As the United States worked to assess the postwar security environment, France had to rebuild itself and adapt to the emerging Cold War.

The top security concern for the French was the need to ensure that they did not again get invaded from the east. Second, the French had to ensure that the balance of power in Europe accounted for a powerful Soviet Union and the as-yet undetermined role of Germany.[9] Last, as they were devastated from the war years, they had to ally with powers that would ultimately assist in retaining balance in Europe. The ultimate concern that faced French politicians was the fear of "economic marginalization and political irrelevance."[10]

To assuage these fears and concerns, the French focused on Germany as a catalyst to recast their position in post war Europe. Specifically, French politicians and military leaders believed that France, as a victorious power, could leverage this opportunity to position the nation as a leader in postwar Europe. However, before this action could happen the French had to account for their economic inferiority.[11] Germany, and more specifically, western Germany, lay at the center of the French plan to rebuild Europe. Even prior to the end of World War II, Charles de Gaulle emphasized to the allies that Germany dominated France's thinking about postwar recovery.[12]

France's immediate post war scheme aimed to cultivate a relationship with Germany's industry and use it as an engine of change for rebuilding a new post war Europe. To ensure that empowering Germany did not result in yet a fourth military invasion from their historically bellicose neighbor, French politicians and strategists argued that Germany would be "shackled by administrative controls" that would render their ability to "threaten the political equilibrium" in Europe void.[13]

An additional concern that emerged in the onset of the Cold War was France's worry that a new German government could ultimately come to be dominated by communists, and therefore France would be faced with a threat on its eastern frontier.[14] As far as the security environment was concerned the French faced dual concerns in the embodiment of a resurgent and rebuilt Germany, as well as a military strong Soviet Union that was quickly gaining control of Central and Eastern Europe.[15] To assist in hedging against these potential security concerns, the French opted for stronger ties with the United Kingdom and, to a lesser degree, the United States, as a way to work toward a strong Atlantic alliance that could assist with stabilizing and rebuilding Europe.

Despite these general objectives, French Prime Minister Felix Gouin faced powerful opposition to the envisioned role of France in postwar Europe.[16] Internal to French domestic politics, communists and Christian Democrats expected France to take a strong anti-German policy by extracting the Ruhr and Rhineland in an effort to suppress German militarism.[17] Though this position had strong support for these internal political parties, their objective did not synchronize with the emerging vision of Europe as seen from the perspective of the United States and Great Britain.[18] In many ways the Treaty of Dunkirk, signed by Britain and France on March 4, 1947, represents a solution to appeasing the pressing concerns of communist ministers in the French government. Identifying Germany as a principal threat, compared to the Soviet Union, allowed the French government to downplay the weak position of Western European military forces compared to the forces of the Soviet Union. Also, the treaty provided the French government with the ability to pacify the communist ministers as it treated Germany harshly.[19]

In addition to working on strategic issues, France had to overcome significant social and economic issues that were perceived by the United States as potential breeding grounds for the communist party. George Bidault, who had been a critical member of de Gaulle's cabinet and continued to serve France into the Fourth Republic, spoke to the General Assembly of the United Nations at its opening in New York. In his speech, Bidault outlined the political tension in Europe, and France specifically, as between forces of communism and anticommunism.[20] In many ways this parallels the famous speech by Winston Churchill about the "iron curtain" that had descended on Europe.[21] Furthermore, the Truman administration had been growing increasingly concerned with the rise of communism in Europe and with the potential strength of communist parties in France and Italy in particular.[22] This was not just a Western European and American concern; a month before Churchill's "iron curtain" speech in Fulton,

Missouri, Joseph Stalin, in a speech at the Bolshoi theater in February 1946, declared that "democratic capitalism and Communism could not live together peacefully and that Communism would eventually overcome the west."[23] Therefore, in the critical period of 1946–1947, tensions that came to represent the Cold War were already in place. Furthermore, U.S. President Harry S. Truman had to work to ensure that communist parties in France and Italy did not come to power, as this could be a foothold for Soviet-backed communism to spread into Western Europe. Truman and his administration worked to make sure that the domestic communist party in France was quieted within the tense, dynamic period of the immediate postwar era.

Reeling from the impact of Venona on its illegal operations in the United States, the Soviet Union's security services attempted to capitalize on the dynamic nature of the security environment in the immediate aftermath of World War II. Using its relationship within the French Resistance from World War II, the Soviet Union empowered the French Communist Party (PCF) as a means to influence the postwar political situation in France.[24] After being invited to be part of the Provisional French government by Charles de Gaulle in August 1944, the PCF, in just over a year, had succeeded in gaining 26 percent of the popular vote to secure its position as the largest political party in France with roughly 800,000 members.[25] This was a stunning success for the forces of communism and an opportunity for the Soviet Union to exploit.

Having used the success of the PCF, the Soviet Union developed an intelligence network within the party that provided roughly 1,100 reports back to Moscow on a wide variety of topics.[26] Though declassified documents later highlighted that KGB headquarters in Moscow chastised the Paris Centre for the lack of good intelligence within this first batch of information, the PCF and the KGB worked to gather better and more specific intelligence that could assist the Soviet Union in gaining an ally in Western Europe.[27]

In the next few years, the PCF and the KGB worked to build a better intelligence network that could provide more insightful and useful intelligence to the Soviet Union. Specifically, the Soviet Union was very interested in placing and cultivating agents in the scientific and intelligence organizations in France, as it had done in the United States in the 1930s.[28] A major victory for the communists was the appointment of Frederic Joliot-Curie as France's director of scientific research. Joliot-Curie was a devoted communist, and intelligence operatives assured the Soviet Union that the "French Scientist will always be at your disposal without asking for any information in return."[29] Having secured access to the latest research and development being conducted by France's top scientists, the KGB moved to focus on cultivating agents within the Foreign Ministry.

Concern over the building anticommunist rhetoric in the United States and Great Britain drove the KGB's quest to obtain access to diplomatic information being exchanged among the Western allies. Therefore, the primary focus of the KGB's operations within France's Foreign Ministry was gaining access to ciphers used in French diplomatic cable traffic. The most successful agent the KGB cultivated was only known by the code name ZHUR, and this agent provided the KGB with decades of intelligence covering a wide variety of diplomatic intelligence useful to the Soviet Union.[30]

Despite the seemingly stunning success the KGB and the PCF had in the initial years after the end of World War II, by May 1947 the PCF suffered a large-scale dismissal of its ministers from the French government. This single action assisted in significantly slowing down the intelligence operations that the KGB had cultivated since the establishment of the Provisional French Government in August 1944. Though thwarted in its quest for more intelligence, the Soviet Union continued to work on building networks of agents in Western Europe to ensure it was not caught off guard by the policies and actions of the Western allies.

U.S. CONCERNS AND COVERT ACTION

Against the backdrop of Europe in the period of 1945–1948, U.S. President Harry S. Truman and his national security team became significantly concerned about the encroachment of communism across Europe. With the Soviet Union holding Eastern and Central Europe and working to ensure that they became strong pillars in an emerging communist bloc, Truman's key foreign policy advisors, George C. Marshall (Secretary of State), Dean Acheson (Undersecretary of State), George F. Kennan (Head of Policy Planning Staff), Robert Patterson (Secretary of War), and James Forrestal (Secretary of the Navy and later the first Secretary of Defense) became convinced that the United States needed to start a covert program to assist in hedging or containing the spread of communism in Europe.

By 1947, a short two years after the end of World War II, Truman and the United States faced a series of security crises as the post–World War II security environment solidified. On March 12, 1947, Truman spoke to the people of the United States concerning the encroachment of communism across Europe. With specific reference to communist insurgencies in Greece and Turkey, Truman stated:

The very existence of the Greek state is today threatened by the terrorist activities of several thousand armed men, led by communists, who defy the Government's authority at a number of points.

Greece's neighbor, Turkey also deserves our attention. . . . Since the war Turkey has sought additional financial assistance from Great Britain and the United States for the purpose of effecting that modernization necessary for the maintenance of its national integrity. That integrity is essential to the preservation of order in the Middle East.[31]

Furthermore, Truman proclaimed that "it must be the policy of the United States to support free peoples who are resisting attempted subjugation by armed minorities or by outside pressures."[32] In an effort to start building a containment policy against communism, Truman asked Congress to authorize $400,000,000 for assistance to Greece and Turkey for the period March 1947 to June 30, 1948. In addition to providing fiscal support, Truman authorized the government to send civilian and military personnel, at the request of Greece and Turkey, to assist them with their momentous tasks of reconstruction.

In addition to the tenets of what became known as the Truman doctrine, Secretary of State George Marshall gave a commencement address at Harvard University roughly two weeks after Truman's address to the people and government of the United States. In his speech, Marshall outlined the harsh economic conditions that hampered the recovery of Europe in the post–World War II security environment. He championed the idea that the United States needed to do "whatever it is able to do to assist in the return of normal economic health."[33] The ultimate objective of the European Economic Recovery Act, or Marshall Plan, as it would come to be known, was the "revival of a working economy in the world so as to permit the emergence of political and social conditions in which free institutions can exist."[34]

The underlying belief within the Truman administration was that European countries left with underdeveloped economies and high unemployment became increasingly susceptible to domestic communist parties and, more importantly, the attention of Soviet communism. Together the Truman Doctrine and the Marshall Plan strove to provide the economic and political assistance necessary to hedge against the spread of communism throughout Europe. With these measures, the United States agreed with Georges Bidault's assessment that with substantial foreign and economic aid, France could weather its economic and political crisis and emerge as a stronger nation that was less susceptible to domestic communists as well as Soviet communists.

Fearing that France's population was still susceptible to communism, the Truman administration decided to authorize the newly created Central Intelligence Agency (CIA) as the primary government agency with responsibilities to conduct covert operations.[35] Essentially, the Truman administration was building a multifaceted foreign policy strategy that encompassed overt (white), semi-covert (gray), and covert (black) means to contain communism. The Truman doctrine and Marshall covered the "white" means of containment, and meanwhile the Truman administration worked to define the use and direction of the "gray" and "black" means.

Concern over increased communist activity, both overt and covert, in Europe led the National Security Council (NSC)—yet another newly created entity that emerged from the National Security Act of 1947—to focus on developing two "streams of US countermeasures" to keep communism at bay in Europe.[36] The first stream would be the use of "overt foreign information activities," while the second stream would focus on the generation of covert propaganda and psychological warfare.[37] On December 17, 1947, the National Security Council approved NSC 4/A, which was a secret annex to another NSC document, NSC 1/4.[38]

Within NSC 4/A, the NSC provided the director of central intelligence (DCI), the head of the CIA, with $20 million to "initiate and conduct covert psychological operations designed to counteract the Soviet and Soviet inspired activities which constituted a threat to the world peace and security."[39] The specific operations authorized in NSC 4/A included "propaganda, sabotage, demolitions, subversion of adversary states, and assistance to indigenous and anticommunist underground movements."[40] Therefore, by the end of 1947, the Truman administration established the foundations of a robust espionage system that worked to counter the political influence of the communist party in France, as well as other European countries, specifically Italy.

ITALY: A HEDGE AGAINST COMMUNISM

In addition to the Western allies' concerns about the domestic situation in France, Italy also presented a significant threat based on its own unique domestic political situation. As the post-World War II security environment tried to stabilize in Europe, Truman and his administration increasingly focused on ensuring that the political, economic, and social conditions in Italy were properly supported as a means to hedge against any further communist encroachment.[41]

By 1947 the backdrop in Europe had shifted since the promising days of the spring of 1945. Against what was perceived by Truman and his administration as a real threat posed by communists, supported from Moscow, the United States watched as the Red Army worked to control and occupy large swaths of Europe. Not only did the Soviet Union use its large military force to occupy the nations of Central and Eastern Europe, but the Soviet state also used its intelligence services to assist in shaping the political and social environments in a way that ensured that communist parties would easily win any elections. Seeing Czechoslovakia and Hungary both succumb to these communist forces greatly worried Truman and his staff.[42]

Seeing how the communists used labor unions and other means to gain support of the once "democratic" nations of Czechoslovakia and Hungary greatly concerned Truman and his diplomatic and national security staff as they saw the local communist parties in Italy begin to seize control of labor unions. Against the political and economic turmoil in Europe in 1947 and 1948, the Truman administration perceived most domestic situations within the larger context of the international struggle between the United States and the Soviet Union. In many ways the concerns about the increase in communist activities, as well as communist strength, greatly concerned noncommunist Italian politicians as well.

On January 5, 1948, Italian Prime Minister Alcide De Gasperi landed in Washington, D.C., in what was to become a first step in cementing Italy within the orbit of the United States and its Western allies. However, De Gasperi had to navigate through a complex political situation that defined Italy's foreign policy. Starting with the signing of the peace treaty in 1947, Italian politicians aimed to reestablish Italy's presence in Europe, as well as its "traditional sphere of influence in the Mediterranean."[43] Considering that the Mediterranean was itself going through fundamental changes with Tito's assumption of power in Yugoslavia and the Greek Civil War, it was against this context that pro-Western Italian politicians (mainly Christian Democrats), government officials, and even private citizens warned of the growing power of the internal Italian Communist Party, as well as the expansionistic tendencies of the Soviet Communist Party.[44] Truman heeded the warnings as they fit within his growing concerns, which led to his announcement of the Truman Doctrine in March 1947.

In addition to making the public pledge to assist nations in fighting communist subversion, Truman also signed the National Security Act of 1947. This significant piece of legislation not only created the independent United States Air Force (USAF), but it also created the CIA. In addition to these two new national security instruments, the National Security Act of 1947 also established the NSC to advise the president on relevant matters in the emerging Cold War.

In relation to the use of espionage in the political climate of Italy in the period of 1947–1963, the development of the CIA and the NSC proved to be two very important tools that the Truman administration leveraged in its fight against the expansionistic communist threat. Specifically, the political situation in Italy emerged as a central concern for both the CIA and the NSC. From its perspective of having to conduct the first review of the "world situation," the CIA stated that "the Italian economic situation is desperate and the political situation is unstable."[45] Building on the U.S. intelligence service's assessment of the domestic situation in Italy, the CIA reasoned that if the political and economic situation worsened, the Communist Party could capitalize on the opportunity and take over the country.[46] Truman could not allow this potentiality to arise. To act on the assessment of the CIA, the NSC presented President Truman with National Security Council Memorandum 1/1. This first document outlined the interests of the United States in an anticommunist Italy and assigned duties to the CIA that allowed the intelligence agency the power to take action to actively combat communism in Italy. NSC 1/1 stated:

The United States has security interests of primary importance in Italy and the measures to implement our current policies to safeguard those interests should be strengthened without delay: The United States should:

(a) Give full support to the present Italian government and to equally satisfactory governments by means and measures such as the following:
    1. Shipment of wheat and other essential commodities.
    2. Additional dollar credits.
    3. Further assistance to the Italian Armed Forces in the form of technical advice to increase their capacity to deal with threats to Italian internal security and territorial integrity.
(b) Extend economic aid to Italy by means of favorable US foreign trade policies.
(c) Press for the relaxation of unduly onerous terms in the Italian Peace treaty, and meanwhile interpret these terms liberally.
(d) Continue to support acceptance of Italy as a member of the UN.
(e) Actively combat Communist propaganda in Italy by an effective US information program and by all others practicable means.[47]

Against the growing concern from the CIA and the NSC, the Truman administration approved NSC 1/1 as a means to empower the United States with a tool to use against the increasing predictions that the communists in Italy were in a position to capitalize on the political and economic conditions.[48] In addition to these concerns, it was a known fact that Stalin and the KGB "worked hard to build intelligence networks of legal and illegal operatives throughout the west."[49] Though the FBI had done a good job of cracking the Soviet Union's intelligence ring using Venona, the efforts in Europe faced a much more significant task due to the political conditions and the historical popularity of leftist organizations.

The CIA outlined its assessment of the political situation in Italy in "The Current Situation in Italy." Specifically, the CIA stated:

The stability of the existing government depends primarily on its ability to obtain adequate economic support from the United States. Given interim aid sufficient to avert acute distress during the winter, it should be able to maintain its position until the general election in April. The communists and Nenni Socialists will continue their vigorous effort to intensify existing difficulties and dissatisfaction with the purpose of thoroughly discrediting the existing Government. . . . Assuming that the present Government survives the winter, the outcome of the April elections will depend not only on the results of interim aid, but also on the process for the success of the European Economic Recovery Program. Favorable developments in this regard would operate to the decided advantage of the Government. Adverse developments and the consequent disillusionment would enhance the possibility of a Communist electoral victory.[50]

While noting that the European Economic Recovery plan (i.e. the Marshall plan) served a significant role in the stabilization of Europe, the CIA also outlined what they believed were the objectives of the Soviet Union vis-à-vis France and Italy. In a report later in December 1947, the CIA reported:

The Communists, under Soviet direction, have launched a concerted campaign of disorder, strikes, and sabotage. . . . The primary Soviet objective is to defeat the European recovery program by bringing about a sufficient degree of economic deterioration: (a) so greatly to increase the cost of the recovery program to the U.S. that the U.S. Congress and the public will reject it; and (b) to cause the collapse of French and Italian centrists governments. To obtain this objective, the USSR is risking the political popularity of the Communist parties in France and Italy and will depend thereafter, on a hard core of militants possibly operating underground.[51]

Within the Truman administration, the consensus had reached a level whereby the common understanding of the situation in Italy, as well as other European countries, was that "Moscow had established in Europe the largest and probably most skilled collection of covert operatives the World had ever seen."[52] NSC 1/1 therefore served as a significant hedge to stem the expansion of this perceived political threat.

In addition to the approval and recommendation of actions taken by the CIA in Italy, in March 1948 the Truman administration issued NSC 1/2 as a means to further refine and develop intelligence operations in Italy. Specifically, NSC 1/2 approved the development and action of a covert propaganda program intended to "off-set similar Communist efforts."[53] In essence, the Truman administration was building a comprehensive program that had black, gray, and white means to offset and wither any communist advantage. Not only did NSC 1/2 provide the CIA with black means to develop propaganda, but the document also enlisted the U.S. State Department and recommended the development of the United States Information Agency (USIA) as an additional agency to combat the communists. Beyond using propaganda, NSC 1/2 further recommended that the United States also needed to be ready to use military force to "stop Italy from falling under the domination of the Soviet Union."[54]

As the Truman administration wrestled with the new Cold War security environment, the NSC continued to build on NSC 1/1 and NSC 1/2. In NSC 1/3 the concern had migrated from military intervention to the scenario that the Communist Party in Italy could gain a strong showing in the elections in a legal manner.[55] On this point, the Truman administration had to consider a very cautious path, as the major tenet of the Truman Doctrine upheld the virtue of democracy and democratic elections. However, in 1947 and 1948, Truman faced the possibility that the communists in Italy could potentially gain ground in a legal way. This situation led the Truman administration to develop two methods to mitigate this scenario. The first process involved overt means whereby the United States used the European Economic Recovery Act and the newly designated USIA as way to build a pro–Christian Democrat narrative among the Italian people with radio, newspapers, and print propaganda. The second method used by Truman and his administration involved covert means, specifically covert propaganda and psychological operations, which would be conducted by the CIA. On December 17, 1947, Truman signed NSC 4/A, which was a top-secret annex to NSC 1/4. In NSC 4/A the National Security Council provided the DCI with $20 million in funds for the CIA to conduct psychological operations as means to "counteract" the Soviet Union and its communist activities.[56] The operations outlined in NSC 4/A for which the funds could be used included propaganda, sabotage, demolitions, subversion of adversary states, and assistance to indigenous and anticommunist underground movements.[57]

With the authorization of NSC 4/A, the Truman administration had defined and outlined the roles and missions of the CIA within the context of Cold War security. In the increasingly tense race to stabilize Europe, the use of covert means became a vital tool for the United States to combat the perceived forces of communism.

Having empowered the newly created CIA with covert powers to assist in containing the spread of communism, the Truman administration wanted to ensure that it did not become public knowledge that the United States worked covertly with allies to sway democratic elections in a manner that was beneficial to the United States and its growing coalition of global allies. In June 1948, Truman signed NSC 10/2, which "required the CIA to conduct all covert programs in a manner that would provide the U.S. government the ability to have plausible deniability" of such action.[58] Furthermore, NSC 10/2 also stipulated that that the CIA was an instrument of foreign policy and was not the "initiator" of action designed to advance U.S. national interests.[59] Though he had provided the CIA with a wide berth of new abilities, Truman ensured that the power to develop and approve covert operations remained firmly within the purview of the U.S. president and his National Security Council.

The last major piece for building the covert means necessary to support the increasingly important goal of containing communism was NSC 20, signed by Truman in August 1948. NSC 20 authorized:

Behind the lines paramilitary operations, including assistance to resistance groups and sabotage missions inside the iron curtain and in the Baltic using émigrés recruited in the West. The overall objective was to reduce the power and influence of the USSR to the limits that which no longer constituted a threat to peace.[60]

Furthermore, NSC 20 provided the means for the CIA to develop, supply, and train "stay-behind organizations" throughout Western Europe and provide them with weapons and ammunition in hidden caches, in the likely event that these groups needed to initiate guerilla operations against communist governments.

By the end of 1948, the Truman administration had successfully established the foundations for the use of covert operations designed to combat the expansion of the Soviet Union and communism throughout Europe and, later, Asia. The NSC documents provided a capability for the United States as it sought to influence and stabilize the dynamic and complex post–World War II security environment. In addition to these actions, through which the Truman administration sought to build a hedge against communism in France and Italy, the administration also worked to define, resource, and apply a national security strategy for the United States that would contain the Soviet Union and allow its system to wither from within.

Taken together, the actions by Truman in the second half of the 1940s provided a comprehensive strategy of ends, ways, and means through which the United States would use overt and covert means to shape the international security environment to meet U.S. foreign policy objectives. While building a robust capability to combat the expansion of communism in Western Europe, Truman also was deeply concerned about the lack of intelligence on the Soviet Union's military and, more importantly, its capability to produce an atomic bomb. He turned to the USAF as a service that could generate the necessary intelligence.

THE NEED FOR ATOMIC AND MILITARY INTELLIGENCE: 1945–1949

Even though the Soviet Union had been an ally of the United States in World War II, by the end of the war in Europe, the former allies had already actively begun to consider one another threats to the uneasy peace in Europe, as well as around the globe. In the tense security environment period between 1945 and 1949, the Truman administration recognized a significant deficiency in its intelligence on the Soviet Union, specifically on the atomic bomb program of the Soviet Union. In October 1945, Britain's Joint Intelligence Committee (JIC) identified the need to have intelligence on the Soviet Union's efforts to produce atomic weapons as critical and of the utmost importance in the new strategic environment.[61] The Americans concurred with Britain's assessment. As a result the two allies with a "special relationship" worked to build a robust capability designed to keep track of the Soviet Union's quest to produce atomic weapons.

In addition to apprehension over imprecise knowledge about the current status of atomic bomb research and development in the Soviet Union, the Truman administration also faced two other significant strategic concerns. The first was a lack of photographic intelligence over the Soviet Union. As the Cold War evolved, and the United States starting building war plans for a strategic bombing campaign against the Soviet Union, the USAF's Strategic Air Command (SAC) had to acknowledge that it lacked the necessary target photographs and targeting data to build a comprehensive war plan. The second concern, which also related to the first, focused on the capabilities and placement of the Red Army's air defense systems. As they considered and planned a strategic air campaign against the Soviet Union, the USAF became obsessive about knowing and mapping the capabilities of the Soviet Union's air defense network.

These three concerns drove the Truman administration to empower the USAF to work to improve these significant deficiencies, though the traditional means of espionage had to be adjusted to new aerial technological capabilities. Espionage in the early Cold War evolved into a new and very sophisticated game whereby advanced aerial capabilities provided the necessary intelligence to satisfy the increasing demand for strategic, atomic, and military intelligence.

The recognition of the lack of atomic intelligence emerged not only with discussion with the British but also with the Truman administration's concerns about the status of Soviet air power. This drove Truman to establish the Air Policy Commission as a means to understanding the current balance of air power between the United States and the Soviet Union. An additional concern of the members of the Air Policy Commission was the timeline by which the Soviet Union would acquire an atomic bomb.

Concern over the status of U.S. airpower vis-à-vis the Soviet Union prompted Truman to appoint a committee to investigate the strategic military balance in 1947. Truman's Presidential Air Policy Commission, headed by the U.S. government's advisor to the U.S. mission to the United Nations, Thomas K. Finletter, focused on the need of the United States to improve its airpower and aeronautical technologies. In October 1947, Navy Rear Admiral D. V. Gallery stressed in a letter to Air Policy Commission member John A. McCone that he believed that "Russian capabilities are below those of the United States."[62] One month later, however, USAF Major General and Acting Deputy Chief of Staff for Operations E. E. Partridge, USAF Brigadier General and Air Force Liaison Officer to the Air Policy Commission B. L. Boatner, and Executive Director of the Air Policy Commission S. Paul Johnson raised concerns about the technological balance between the United States and the Soviet Union in the development of air power and missiles. These men argued that "Russia's developments in air power and missiles are probably further advanced than the United States."[63] The difference between the two positions demonstrated the lack of hard intelligence possessed by the United States in the immediate years after World War II as well as the increasing concerns about the need to modernize the USAF.

Reinforcing the view that there was inadequate intelligence on the Soviet Union, legal advisor to the President's Air Policy Commission E. C. Sweeney told Navy officials in a meeting with the Navy's Bureau of Aeronautics in September 1947 that "we have little specific knowledge of Russian developments."[64] The United States needed to keep informed of the expanding military capabilities of the Soviet Union, especially after the Soviet Union's detonation of its first atomic bomb on August 29, 1949. For the next several years, the United States worked at using various endo-atmospheric methods to collect vital strategic intelligence.[65]

Beyond the need for more intelligence, the Air Policy Commission gauged the Soviet Union's capability to develop, construct, and deploy missiles and atomic weapons as compared to that of the United States. In their preliminary report, the committee members assumed the Soviet Union would have atomic capability by 1953.[66] The members of the committee reasoned that if the Soviet Union started a program in 1943, it would likely achieve the desired results within 10 years.[67] In order to counteract any concern over the Soviet Union's scientific capabilities, the Commission's members noted that a 10-year program was "three times as long as it took the United States to complete the same job."[68] The Commission believed that its 10-year estimate was realistic.[69]

Despite the Commission's estimate, former Chairman of the War Production Board, Donald M. Nelson, testified before an executive session of the Air Policy Commission on October 23, 1947, that "the Russians will have the bomb in two to three years."[70] As Air Policy Commission internally debated when the USSR was expected to get guided missiles, the uncertainty of intelligence produced significant differences in the advice given to Truman by military and civilian experts. In August 1949, the Soviet Union tested its first atomic bomb. This action reinforced the need for the United States to gather intelligence on the Soviet Union's rapidly expanding military capability.

The loss of America's atomic monopoly made many Americans, including Truman, Curtis E. LeMay, and the head of the State Department's Policy Planning Staff, Paul H. Nitze, concerned about rearming.[71] Nitze and the members of the State Department's Policy Planning Staff recommended that the United States rebuild its conventional forces.[72] However, prior to the development of what would become NSC-68, the Truman administration undertook a massive aerial reconnaissance program in an attempt to get a more accurate understanding of the military capabilities of the Soviet Union.

The driving force that exposed this significant weakness was the initial planning and development of Operation Pincher, which was the first joint war plan developed in March 1946.[73] Prior to the development of the

Pincher war plan, the Army Air Force made three basic assumptions about future warfare in the atomic age:

The atomic bomb does not at this time warrant a material change in our present conception of the employment, size, and organization and composition of the post-war Air Force.

The Atomic bomb has not altered our basic concept of the strategic air offensive but has given us an additional weapon.

Forces using non-nuclear bombs will required for use against targets which cannot be effectively or economically attached with the atomic bomb.[74]

Despite the reaffirmation of the principles of strategic bombardment used during World War II, the Air Force began planning air offensives for the new security environment; however, unlike World War II, the United States did not have very good intelligence on which to build comprehensive war plans. In fact, starting in February 1946, the Strategic Air Command (SAC) suffered significantly from demobilization, which left it with only fifty-three reconnaissance aircraft.[75] This diminished capability was a serious problem as the nation's air service worked to conceptualize the future of warfare.

Ceding that the Soviet Union had a ground force that well exceeded the number of U.S. and allied ground forces in Europe, the planners in the United States believed that strategic air forces would be the blunting force to turn the tide in a conceived war with the Soviet Union. Though a primary part of the plan called for blunting Soviet military capabilities in Central and Eastern Europe, a parallel annex to the plan called for the outright destruction of the Soviet Union's capability to continue a war. This focus on the Soviet Union's capacity to sustain the war effort meant that the strategic bombers of the United States had to target the government, industry, and communication systems of the enemy. However, as war plan Pincher evolved into the planning stages, the Joint Chiefs of Staff (JCS) recognized significant problems with executing the plan due to the lack of intelligence needed to build the required target sets.[76]

Specifically regarding the lack of intelligence, the Joint Chiefs of Staff commented:

The scarcity of reliable and detailed intelligence on the USSR precludes the determination at this time of specific target systems for air attacks. Any strategic bombing program established at this time would be provisional even for the purposes of current planning; it is certain to be altered radically when additional information become available. The current lack of intelligence on the USSR is due not only to the rigid security maintained by that country, but also to the fact that such information as is available has not yet been properly assembled. It will be possible to improve this appreciation by incorporating in it new intelligence as the information now available to the various intelligence agencies is correlated.[77]

In short, the Air Force had rebuilt its reconnaissance and intelligence gathering capability due to the demands of the new and evolving security environment.

Having just completed the bombing campaigns in both the European and Pacific theaters of World War II, the Air Force knew that it needed information on "Soviet transportation networks, electric power grids, key plant locations, and raw material supply."[78] In addition to these demands, the aircrews charged with executing the operation outlined in Pincher needed "detailed maps, charts, weather information, and supplemental data" to build complete target packages for the crews to fly their missions.[79] Dr. James T. Lowe, who worked for Air Intelligence, observed that the Air Force needed intelligence on over "70,000 bombing objectives."[80] Gathering the necessary intelligence on 70,000 objectives would be a significant feat considering the marginal intelligence-gathering capability of the Air Force.

To begin this daunting process, SAC's 311th Reconnaissance Wing, which controlled the Army Air Forces reconnaissance assets and was also already working on increasing the global coverage of aerial maps by flying photomapping missions, also provided this intelligence to improve the maps and intelligence needed to conduct future strategic air operations. Though these missions had a routine, scientific nature, they also served to produce critical intelligence needed for future military operations against the Soviet Union. A component of these missions, along with operations conducted by the U.S. Navy was the effort to map the magnetic fields around the globe. The importance of mapping magnetic fields was not only that it yielded scientific data, but it was also used to produce military maps that provided the correct magnetic variation needed for precise navigation of warships and military aircraft.

Even though the 311th strove to perform its missions—and did so—the unit lacked the ability to penetrate and photograph inside the borders of the Soviet Union. This represented a significant obstacle that would eventually be overcome with aircraft such as the U-2 and SR-71 and also by satellites. Prior to the advent of these advanced technologies, the Air Force sought to correct intelligence imbalances by synergizing their mapping and photographic intelligence missions by retrofitting aircraft for these new missions. Also, the Air Force worked to produce a new variation of intelligence aircraft that could intercept, record, and pinpoint electronic signals. This new type of "ferreting" mission was a critical capability because the Soviet Union had significantly improved its air defense capability. In order for a strategic air operation to be executed, the Strategic Air Command had to know the whereabouts and capabilities of these robust systems.

The USAF recognized the need to have more electronic intelligence in August 1946, when Yugoslavia shot down an American C-47 using antiaircraft guns that the U.S. air intelligence officers thought, but could not confirm, were radar guided. In response to the lack of information, the United States Air Forces Europe (USAFE) began a hurried program that allowed aircrews to place receiver and direction-finding equipment onboard B-17 aircraft.[81] These aircraft, which had no visible modification, would then fly around the site at which the C-47 was downed in order to discern what type of equipment Yugoslavia had used to down the C-47. After several flights, USAFE detected and pinpointed radar fire control signals from a restored German Wurzburg radar that the Yugoslavs had rebuilt and put back into service.[82]

The confirmation of the presence of fire control radars confirmed to the USAFE that the Soviet Union could also be expected to have similar, if not better, systems for an effective antiaircraft defense. By flying more "ferret" missions, USAFE obtained critical electronic intelligence that allowed the United States to begin to build a comprehensive understanding of the defense capabilities of the Soviet Union. The initial ferret flights in 1946 and 1947 by the 7499th Squadron confirmed that the Soviet Union did indeed have early warning radars that operated in the 70 MHz range, but they did not detect the presence of fire control radars.[83]

With the use of the new method of gathering critical intelligence on early warning and antiaircraft radars systems, the USAF had confirmed the need for electronic intelligence (ELNIT) as a critical capability to understand the threat environment of Eastern Europe and the Soviet Union. As the JCS worked on building war plans, the knowledge gained from these initial ferret flights provided a much-improved understanding of the threat environment the Air Force would face in the event of having to conduct a strategic bombing campaign on designated targets in Eastern Europe and the Soviet Union. The tense events of 1947 and 1948 in Europe reinforced the USAF's belief that intelligence and reconnaissance missions had to be maintained in order to improve the chances of success for the various war plans that relied on strategic bombardment as the means to defeat the enemy.

Though these missions had long been part of air operations, they tended to be looked down upon by bomber generals, who saw allocation of intelligence and reconnaissance aircraft as the loss of bombing platforms that were needed to conduct bombing operations. In 1947 and 1948, the new, independent USAF slowly came to acknowledge the need for electronic and photographic aircraft as necessary components to air operations, especially since the dearth of intelligence was so significant. As the Air Force wrestled with internal questions as to how best to employ photographic, radarscope, and electronic intelligence-gathering means, USAF Major General George C. McDonald, Director of Intelligence at the United States Air Forces Headquarters, outlined the priority for areas in need of photoreconnaissance. In addition to his list, McDonald also noted the amount of information the USAF had on the potential targets as of January 1948. McDonald's list, with comments, was as follows:

a. Industrial area of the Urals (no cover at present)
b. Industrial area of Kuznetsk basin (no cover at present)
c. Industrial area of Dnepr and Don Basins (1941–43 coverage)
d. Central Industrial Region (1941-1945 coverage)
e. Stalingrad-Kuybushev Industrial area (1941–1943 coverage)
f. Leningrad Industrial area (1941-43 coverage)
g. Industrial area of Fergana Valley in Uzbek and Kirgis (no cover at present)
h. Petroleum Areas of Caucasus and Caspian (1941—1945 coverage)
i. Khabarovsk-Vladivostok Area (no cover at present)
j. Uncovered strips of the Trans-Siberian Railway
k. Industrial areas of Karaganda (no cover at present)
l. Industrial area of Alma Ata, Kazakhstan (no cover at present)
m. Industrial areas of Western White Russia (1941–45 cover)
n. Northern Regions, including Archangelsk, Kola Peninsula, and Pechora Valley (spotty 1941–43 cover)
o. Industrial area of Magadan in eastern Siberia (no cover at present).[84]

A quick glance over McDonald's list and his notes confirms that of the fifteen major industrial centers of the Soviet Union, the United States lacked coverage on eight of them. SAC worked hard to correct this significant deficiency by launching a wide variety of operations that worked to fill in the needed intelligence. In addition to trying to expand the coverage of photographic and radar mapping, SAC and the USAF also conducted air operations designed to collect weather data and navigational data in an effort to provide its aircrews with the necessary comprehensive intelligence to conduct bombing operations against the Soviet Union.

Taken together, in the period of 1946–1948, the United States Air Force ushered in a new era of espionage, which was driven by the lack of hard military and strategic intelligence on the Soviet Union. While trying to build war plans in the first phase of the new Cold War, the USAF had to devise new airborne methods to collect the necessary intelligence to build a comprehensive strategic bombing campaign. Though these intelligence-gathering operations may at first like seem traditional Air Force operations needed to devise, plan, and conduct offensive strategic bombing campaigns, the intelligence gathered in these operations provided Truman and his administration with critical information as they planned the possibility of a third world war. Simply, the information provided by the USAF was necessary as the United States had few insights into the capabilities of the Soviet Union. Therefore, Truman and his administration wrestled with developing a comprehensive national security policy designed to combat the encroachment of communism across the globe. Though the Air Force stumbled into this new era, it became a leading force in the collection of a wide variety of intelligence, which the CIA would eventually assist in collecting.

Whereas during World War II, intelligence gathering hinged on human intelligence and other traditional means of intelligence gathering, the closed nature of the Soviet Union significantly stifled these traditional means of the United States and its allies on gathering intelligence on its new enemy. At the start of the Cold War, the Truman administration was already well aware of the Soviet Union's penetration of the Manhattan Project, as discussed in Chapter 1; however, the major concern that emerged from these events was the stress over how far along the Soviet Union was in developing its own capabilities for an atomic weapon. Again, due to the lack of intelligence, the United States and Great Britain simply guessed. Recognizing that the possession of the atomic bomb by the United States fundamentally altered the international security environment, and that the Soviet Union already had technical and engineering details gathered from sources inside the Manhattan Project, the United States naturally assumed it was only a matter of time before the Soviet Union acquired its own atomic capability. This assumption emerged from the idea that the Soviet Union reasoned only the "elimination of the American monopoly could remove the threat" to the stability of the new international security environment.[85]

The Soviet Union tested its first atomic bomb on August 29, 1949. However, it was not until September 23 that President Truman announced to the world that the United States had "evidence that within recent weeks an atomic explosion occurred in the U.S.S.R."[86] The evidence that the United States had collected came from WB-29 (weather reconnaissance) that flew a mission on September 3, 1949, between Alaska and Japan.[87] Having collected atmospheric samples on this routine flight, the laboratory that analyzed the sample detected "higher than normal radioactive content." This was nothing new, as this indication had been identified 111 previous times, due to naturally occurring radiation in the atmosphere. Yet the Air Force flew two additional flights on September 5 and again on September 7 to collect more samples.[88] Analysis of the samples confirmed that it was not naturally occurring radiation, but rather traces of radiation had "been injected into the atmosphere by a non-natural occurrence."[89] The United States shared this important intelligence with its British allies on September 10, 1949, and asked that the Royal Air Force to also fly missions to collect atmospheric samples as a means to confirm that data obtained by the United States. By September 14, 1949, the Royal Air Force had collected and analyzed data that again indicated that there was an abnormal amount of non-naturally occurring radiation found in the atmosphere.[90] Together the British and Americans confirmed, based on their "weather intelligence" that the Soviet Union had indeed detonated its first atomic bomb. The surprise that this event occurred well before any of the intelligence professionals had predicted confirmed to both the United States and the British that aerial intelligence gathering was a critical means needed to keep a close on the Soviet Union. Since the end of the World War II, intelligence gathering and espionage had changed significantly.

CONCLUSION

The period 1945–1949 was a dynamic and important evolution in the espionage game between the United States and the Soviet Union. As the peacetime alliance between the United States and Soviet Union transitioned into the new Cold War period, there were two major concerns that troubled Truman and his administration. The first was how to contain the encroachment of the Soviet Union and communism into the Western Europe. Realizing that the unstable economic and political conditions in Europe, and especially in France and Italy, presented an opportunity for communism to take hold in these two Western European nations, the Truman administration established the organizations and institutions that could conduct espionage against communism. Though the United States had yet to officially fixate on containment as a national security strategy, the tenets of the policy evolved and coalesced in this era.

One of the major tenets of the era was to assist Western Europe in rebuilding after World War II. The European Economic Recovery Act was a major force designed to firmly fix Western nations in the Western alliance. Furthermore, it ensured that questionable political and economic conditions in France and Italy did not allow the communists to seize power; the Truman administration created and empowered the Central Intelligence Agency to conduct covert operations that were designed to influence the elections in France and Italy. Providing overt support to friendly governments allowed to the United States to continue along a more traditional foreign policy path, while using covert means to influence the elections in France and Italy created a new means for the United States to combat the forces of communism through espionage. The CIA became a primary means to this justifiable end.

The second consideration that Truman and his administration wrestled with was the lack of military and strategic intelligence on the Soviet Union. Having to rely on German officers and enlist soldiers only provided a small glimpse behind the iron curtain. The West needed the ability to see more. Airpower became the answer. Using long-range aviation to identify the Soviet Union's air defense capabilities, as well as identify the Red Army's military size and structure, the Truman administration gained a greater understanding of the Soviet Union military and techno-logical capabilities in the immediate period after World War II. Even though the use of strategic reconnaissance and intelligence gathering pro-vided some much needed strategic and military intelligence, the Truman administration still had to guess about the Soviet Union's ability to build and detonate an atomic bomb. Routine weather reconnaissance flights in the late summer of 1949 gathered samples of the atmosphere that led to the conclusion, with British confirmation, that the Soviet Union had indeed detonated its first atomic bomb in August of 1949.

The USAF's development of aerial reconnaissance and intelligence gathering in this era provided a small, yet important, expansion in the intelligence-gathering capabilities of the Cold War. As a result of these actions, the United States would continue, for the duration of the Cold War, to build on the foundation established in the first four years of the Cold War.

CHAPTER 3

Global Confrontation, 1950–1960

Moving beyond Europe and focusing on the global context of the Cold War, this chapter examines events in Latin America, Africa, and Asia as the United States and Soviet Union actively began to pursue the use of direct-action intelligence operations to incite revolutions, coups, and mass demonstrations across the globe. The goal is to demonstrate that the espionage game evolved beyond the simple collection of intelligence to the use of clandestine forces to shape and influence regional hotspots. A parallel discussion in this chapter focuses on domestic operations in both the United States and the Soviet Union to demonstrate that both nations ran a whole host of espionage missions in order to assess the strength of the other. Specific operations covered in this chapter are the start of Operations Silver and Gold, the Berlin Tunnel, the use of U-2 flights over the Soviet Union, and Operation Rhine.

Having established the foundations for the use of covert action in the period between 1945 and 1950, the United States used the period between 1950 and 1960 as a very active period to check the expansion of communism beyond the confines of Europe. The Cold War became global and spread to the four corners of the earth, with a special emphasis on Latin America, Asia, and even the Middle East.

Using the foundation established under the administration of Harry S. Truman, Dwight D. Eisenhower used covert action as a means to advance the objectives of the new national security policy of the United States, which focused on containing the global expansion of communism. Signed in September of 1950, NSC-68 provided Truman and, later, the Eisenhower administration with the stated political objective of using all elements of national power to contain the inherent expansionistic tendencies of communism as sponsored by the Soviet Union. Though the administration of Eisenhower has come to be associated with the strategic policies of new look and massive retaliation, both of which focused heavily on nuclear weapons, Eisenhower also became an advocate for the use of covert operations "where diplomacy alone was insufficient, and the risk of using overt military force was too great."[1]

In addition to expanding the capabilities and operational reach of espionage in this period of tense global adventurism, Eisenhower would also continue to refine the technological capability of intelligence gathering that the United States had begun under Truman. Specifically, Eisenhower would usher in the use of outer space as a means to collect intelligence on the Soviet Union.

From the perspective of the Soviet Union, the period between 1950 and 1960 represents a decade of hard work in which they had to rebuild their once-impressive network of spies within the United States. Having had their impressive system of illegal agents and technical experts exposed as the result of Venona, the KGB and the Soviet Union had to ensure that they did not lose access to vital intelligence. However, as the Cold War heated up and U.S. society faced a new wave of the Second Red Scare, the KGB and the Soviet Union could no longer rely on using the Communist Party of the United States of America (CPUSA) as a fertile ground to convince ideologically committed Americans to spy for the Soviet Union. Using a wide variety of means, mostly extra-legal, the KGB set about to convince U.S. citizens that they needed to spy for the Soviet Union as a means to ensure stability and prosperity in the world. However, this process became increasingly difficult in the strongly anticommunist era under Eisenhower.

Of significant importance to the KGB and the Soviet Union was the need to maintain awareness and knowledge of the scientific and technological advancements being made in military hardware. For both the Soviet Union and the United States, the transition of the Cold War into a tense nuclear stalemate meant that "lack of intelligence could lead to dangerous assumptions."[2]

In the nuclear era of the now global Cold War, both the United States and the Soviet Union became obsessed with making sure that they had the latest intelligence on the capabilities and intentions of their respective adversaries to ensure that they would not be surprised by a nuclear bolt from the blue.

For both the Soviet Union and the United States, the need to know more about each other drove both sides to expand their espionage capabilities. However, the two nations fostered the development of their capabilities in very different ways. The Soviet Union sought to rebuild its network of dedicated spies that had been built and cultivated in the 1920s and 1930s as a means to ensure access to information on the latest technologies being explored by the U.S. military. From the perceptive of the KGB's success within the Manhattan Project, this prospect was logical and made great sense. The period from 1950 to 1960 therefore represented an intense period when the Soviet Union aggressively stepped up its spying capability, not only in the United States but also around the globe. Though the Soviet Union came to have some notable success with building and developing networks of illegal spies entering and living in the United States, these expensive and cumbersome operations provided little real actionable intelligence to justify their continuation.

While the Soviet Union seemed to focus on the more traditional craft of developing human intelligence gathering networks, the United States took a different approach. Though Eisenhower and the CIA during his tenure still used and relied heavily on HUMINT sources, there was also a significant investment in the develop of technological intelligence assets that could provide even more information from behind the iron curtain. While expanding and cultivating its global intelligence network of humans, the CIA in conjunction with the Department of Defense, worked on developing aerial reconnaissance such as the U-2 that could provide photographic evidence of the military and strategic nuclear capabilities of the United States. In addition to the development of aerial intelligence gathering platforms, the Eisenhower administration also started the development of using space-based satellites to gather intelligence on the Soviet Union. The period of global confrontation, therefore, possessed the traditional human assets of earlier eras, yet it also witnessed the technological expansion of the espionage game to include the use of highly sophisticated aerial and space-based platforms to gather intelligence. Hence this period, which witnessed the Cold War confrontation taking on a global perspective, also saw the espionage game move into a new era of high technology as a means to gather the necessary intelligence.

THE SECURITY ENVIRONMENT

Building on the foundation established under the Truman administration, President Dwight D. Eisenhower continued to use espionage as a way to help shape the Cold War security environment. With Truman's approval of NSC-68 and containment becoming the strategy for the United States, Eisenhower and his administration maintained the tenets of containment and developed policies that would further entrench espionage as one effort within the overall national security strategy of the United States. In the waning days of the Truman administration, the CIA prepared an estimate on the global security environment as it prepared to hand over the White House to Eisenhower and his staff. In the document dated November 21, 1952, the board concluded:

For the time being the worldwide Communist expansion has apparently been checked. There are indications that the USSR has recognized this situation and has been shifting to less openly aggressive tactics. Since Korea the Soviet bloc has undertaken no new military adventures and it has not increased its aid to Communist insurrectionary movements during the last year. These changes are due in great part to the fact that the principal Western countries have grown politically, economically, and militarily stronger.[3]

Though the briefing to Eisenhower started with a positive assessment of the current operations and status of efforts by the United States and its allies to contain communism, the board members provided additional guidance about the immediate future. They stated:

We believe that the outlook is for a continuation of Soviet Efforts to undermine and destroy the non-Communist world by cold war [sic] tactics. The Communists will resort to armed aggression and to armed revolt by indigenous Communist parties when they believe these courses of action are the best means to achieve Communist objectives. If the growth of free world strength and unity continues, however, the Communists will probably place greater emphasis upon "unified front" tactics and upon propaganda and diplomatic moves designed to split the Western allies and to promote dissension within non-Soviet countries.[4]

Beyond highlighting the prospective of open war with the communists in the immediate future, by 1954, the members of the board also summarized the situation of key Western European allies based on the actions and operations started and perpetuated during Truman's tenure.

First and foremost, the members of the board commented on the situations in France and Italy, respectively. Regarding France, the members believed that "French economic and political instability appears likely to continue for some years to come, and as a result, France will most certainly be unable to meet its current NATO commitments while simultaneously maintaining a major effort in Indochina. However, France almost certainly will remain firmly aligned with the Atlantic Community."[5]

Regarding Italy, which had been an even greater concern for Truman and his national security staff during their tenure in the White House, the members of the board commented that "the present conditions, led by Christian Democrats, will probably win the 1953 elections by a narrow margin, but it appears unlikely that Italy will develop during this period sufficient economic or political strength to be anything more than a weak ally."[6] Despite the United States having spent considerable resources, both overtly and covertly, the political situation in Italy still remained problematic as the Truman administration transitioned to Eisenhower.

From the Soviet Union's perspective, the analysis of Truman's national security team was on the mark and the success they had had during World War II within infiltrating agents into the United States and turning U.S. citizens into spies within the Manhattan Project seemed like distant memories. As the Second Red Scare evolved in the first decade of the Cold War, and Senator Joseph McCarthy (R–WI) began his crusade against communist infiltration into the government of the United States, the Illegals directorate of the KGB had to figure ways to rebuild its program of agents in the United States.

By 1954, the KGB created a plan that focused on rebuilding its intelligence apparatus within the United States. The program aimed to develop a network of "130 'documented agents' whose sole responsibility was to obtain birth certificates, passports, and other documents to support the illegals legends."[7] However, the changing nature of the social, economic, and political environments in both the Soviet Union after Stalin's death in 1953 and in the United States after the end of World War II made the KGB's efforts excessively difficult.

The transition between Truman and Eisenhower caught the KGB at a low point, however, and interestingly enough, due to lack of intelligence, the United States was deeply obsessed with "spy mania" and therefore was unaware of the diminishing capabilities of the Soviet Union's ability to rebuild its program within the United States.[8] From the perspective of the United States, we had to maintain vigilance against the encroachment of communism. However, it must be noted that the success of the Soviet Union to recruit spies in the late 1920s and throughout the 1930s rested largely on an intellectual appeal of communism as the globe faced significant economic hardships. However, as World War II ended and the intellectual appeal of communism faded against the reality of Soviet Union's existence and wartime behavior, the intellectual appeal of communism faded as a catalyst to recruit new and younger agents, especially in the United States. Though the KGB continued to try to recapture its stunning success of the 1920s 1930s, and 1940s, they failed to obtain the same results, though they would not be deterred from spying on their "main adversary."

For Eisenhower, the onset of the Cold War and the security situations in Western Europe, Asia, and Latin America necessitated that he maintain and expand the programs and structure of spying developed under Truman for the duration of his tenure. Using covert means to collect intelligence and stabilize political situations across the globe became hallmarks of the Eisenhower years, though they, too, suffered limited success.

NSC 162/2, "The Basic National Security Policy," presented to the National Security Council on October 30, 1953, established the parameters within which Eisenhower and his administration maintained the espionage programs developed and defined during the initial years of the Cold War. Continuing to identify "Soviet hostility to the non-communist world, and particularly to the United States" as a major issue, the administration outlined its projections about the future of the security environment.[9] Focusing on the recent impact of Joseph Stalin's death, the NSC commented:

The author of the Soviet regime does not appear to have been impaired by the events since Stalin's death, or to be likely to be appreciably weakened during the next few years. The transfer of power may cause some uncertainty in Soviet and satellite tactics for some time, but will probably not impair the basic economic and military strength of the Soviet bloc. The Soviet rulers can be expected to continue to base their policy on the conviction of irreconcilable hostility between the bloc and the non-communist world.[10]

The NSC concluded this passage by highlighting that "the basic Soviet objectives continue to be consolidation and expansion of their own sphere of power and the eventual domination of the non-communist world."[11] After outlining the issues presented by the Soviet Union's transition of power and their general security outlook for the next several years, the members of the NSC focused on how the United States could defend itself from the Soviet threat.[12]

Specific action recommended to Eisenhower from the NSC was the need to "maintain a robust intelligence system."[13] Building on the covert programs developed and transitioned from the Truman administration, the NSC's report stated that Eisenhower needed to have a strong intelligence system that "collected and analyzed indications of hostile intentions that would give maximum prior warning of possible aggression or subversion in any part of the world."[14]

Furthermore, the NSC recommended that the intelligence system of the United States be capable of "accurately evaluating the capabilities of foreign countries, friendly and neutrals as well as enemy, to undertake military, political, economic, and subversive course of action affecting U.S. security."[15] Under the subtitle "Reductions of the Soviet Threat," the NSC recommended to Eisenhower that for the United States to "continue to exercise its control and influence in the free world," it had to retain and expand its covert and overt means.[16] In essence this meant continuing and expanding the programs of "white, gray, and black" means that developed in the years of the Cold War under the Truman administration. Specifically, the NSC recommended four courses of action:

Take overt and covert measures to discredit Soviet prestige and ideology as effective instruments of Soviet power, and to reduce the strength of the communist parties and other Soviet elements.

Take all feasible diplomatic, political, economic, and covert measures to counter any threat of a party or individuals directly or indirectly responsive to Soviet control to achieve dominant power in the free world.

Undertake selective, positive actions to eliminate Soviet-Communist control over any areas of the free world.

Accordingly, the United States should take feasible political, economic, propaganda, and covert measures designed to create and exploit troublesome problems for the USSR, impair Soviet relations with Communist China, complicate control in the satellites, and retard the growth of the military and economic potential of the Soviet bloc.[17]

With the establishment of peacetime objectives vis-à-vis the Soviet Union, Eisenhower used the courses of actions outlined in NSC 162/2 as a means to use covert actions as "a tool for achieving US policy goals where diplomacy alone was insufficient, but the risks and costs of overt military intervention was too great."[18] These loose criteria were not the only motivating force that propelled Eisenhower and his administration to increase the use of covert actions and espionage.

Eisenhower was a fiscal conservative and saw covert action and espionage as a "cost-effective tool" to thwart the expansion of communist ideology as well as the influence of the Soviet Union.[19] Furthermore, the use of white, gray, and black means provided a fiscally responsible way to combat the Soviet Union in a way that stayed consistent with the national security policy of containment. Moving beyond NSC 162/2, the Eisenhower administration replaced NSC 10/2, devised under Harry S. Truman, with NSC 5412.

NSC 5412 outlined the Central Intelligence Agency's responsibility for conducting covert operations around the globe.[20] The primary objective of NSC 5412 was to transfer more responsibility to the director of central intelligence (DCI) in the planning and conducting of covert operations. Specifically, the new document charged the CIA with:

Undertaking covert operations to counter similar Soviet operations (active measures); discredit Soviet ideology; support anti-communist guerillas or paramilitary operations; develop underground resistance organizations; counter threat to Communist attempts to achieve dominant power in a free world country; and undermine or reduce international Communist control of any area of the world.[21]

Though these tasks mimic the ones outlined in NSC 10/2, they reaffirm the importance of the CIA as the primary executive level agency in charge of conducting covert operations. Of significant note is that overall objective of these missions is to hedge against the expansion of communism around the globe, not necessarily to "roll back" communism. With the reasserted emphasis on the use of covert operations to contain communism, Eisenhower wanted to ensure that the United States maintained a "clean" international image.

THE SOVIET UNION AND ITS MAIN ADVERSARY

Having recognized the onset of the Cold War and the reality that the United States was indeed its "main adversary," the Soviet Union, in the aftermath of the release and exposure of the Venona intercepts, had a tough road ahead. The primary objective was to reestablish a network of spies within the United States as a way to gain military, political, and economic intelligence as a means to assess the Cold War competition.[22] However, the nature of the environment from which the Soviet Union had to rebuild its espionage network within the United States had changed substantially since the end of World War II.

First, the release of Venona demonstrated to the U.S. population that the Soviet Union had been very successful in cultivating agents within the United States, including within the highly classified Manhattan Project. Furthermore, with the exposure and trial of the Rosenbergs, Ted Hall, and Klaus Fuchs, the fervor in the United States over spies fueled the growing suspicion that the Soviet Union had fully infiltrated all levels and elements of American society. The onset of the Second Red Scare, perpetuated by Sen. Joseph R. McCarthy (R–WI), further challenged the Soviet Union and the KGB in its attempts to build and gather additional strategic intelligence.

The effects of these environmental changes challenged the KGB, as in its previous and more successful era of recruitment, Soviet's intelligence service tended to rely on using the CPUSA as a means to identify and cultivate potential spies for the communist cause. Essentially, the Soviet Union and its intelligence services used a complex variety of spies to gather information within the United States. By the end of 1950s, it was well known that beyond the standard use of recruited agents, such as the Rosenbergs, Fuchs, and Hall, who had ideological sympathies to communism, the Soviet Union also used a series of "illegal" operatives who had infiltrated the United States using fake identities and lived and worked among the normal population of the United States.[23] The third contingent of spies were those people who had official diplomatic papers but also worked at gathering intelligence beyond the scope of their normal jobs, which at times happened to be overt cover for their real purpose, espionage.[24] Simply put, the Soviet Union's intelligence network withered in the late 1940s and early 1950s.

As Eisenhower and his administration strove to readjust the balance of the international security environment, which also included the strategic nuclear balance, the KGB recognized the pressing need to reassert its efforts against the United States, as it now identified it as the "main adversary" in the new global struggle.

Feeling the pressure to succeed, the KGB's "illegals" Directorate S focused on building a new network of agents within the United States. In 1954, the "illegals directorate" established a plan for "130 documentation agents, whose sole purpose was to obtain birth certificates, passports, and other documents" to build the identities of a new generation of deep-cover KGB agents in the United States.[25] Their plan called for the stationing of KGB officers who specialized in illegal documentation in "twenty-two of their Diplomatic residencies in the Western world, Third world, China, and Soviet Bloc countries."[26] Beyond having to produce and generate the personnel experienced in forging documents, the KGB had other issues they had to overcome to achieve their goal.

Cultivating Soviet citizens "who had been brought up in the Stalinist Soviet system" was difficult as these people had a very hard time adapting and blending into the West, which ultimately meant that the KGB had to spend more time training and assimilating agents into the ways of the West.[27] The second major issue was that the net effect of the McCarty era was that the pool of ideological U.S. citizens effectively dried up. This meant that the Communist Party of the United States became an ineffective source from which to draw and train agents. The neutralization of the CPUSA was the direct effect of a synergy of Cold War forces. First and foremost, Venona tipped off the federal law enforcement officials as to the depth of Soviet's espionage penetration in the 1930s and 1940s. Hence, by the 1950s, the FBI had become vigilant in making sure that it focused on identifying and rooting out communist spies, whether legal or illegal.

Furthermore, the Soviet Union could no longer count on persuading U.S. citizens who had previously been sympathetic or even overtly open to the Communist Party as potential recruits because of the scrutiny from the FBI, McCarthy, and the Second Red Scare, suppressed the once appealing ideology of the Communist Party. Though these internal domestic forces in the United States helped to stifle the KGB's efforts, they also faced internal issues.

The primary obstacle within the KGB, and more specifically the "illegals directorate" was Aleksandr Korotkov, who was the director of the illegals directorate for the first era of the Cold War, and he had also put together the plan to use William Fisher, aka Rudolf Abel, as an illegal in the United States earlier in the 1940s.[28] Despite Abel's earlier success, Korotkov, having never lived in the West, had a very difficult time adapting to and understanding the changing environmental conditions facing Soviet agents in the late 1940s and early 1950s.[29] Hence, the KGB's bureaucracy believed they needed to change the way it recruited, trained, inserted, and managed illegal agents, as the Soviet Intelligence Service had its own internal issues that needed to change before it was able to rebuild its once-prominent espionage network.

THE CASE OF WILLIAM FISHER, AKA RUDOLF ABEL

In 1962 the United States exchanged captured Soviet spy Rudolf Abel for American U-2 pilot Francis Gary Powers. Powers had been detained in the Soviet Union since May 1961 when his aircraft was shot down while conducting an overflight mission over the Soviet Union. Though the U-2 will be discussed later in this chapter, the focus of this section is on the deep-cover illegal spy whom the Soviet Union used to try to gather intelligence on its "main adversary." The communist spy offered to recover Powers was none other than Rudolf Abel.

The spy who came to be known as Rudolf Abel started life as William (Vilyam) Genrikhovich Fisher in 1903, born to Russian parents who had deep sympathies for the Bolsheviks' cause in Russia prior to the October 1917 Revolution.[30] Fisher and his parents lived in England until 1921, when his parents, who both were Russian immigrants, decided to move their family back to Russia in the midst of the Russian Civil War. Fisher, who was 19 years old in 1921, worked as a translator for the third Communist International (COMINTERN), which was the central organization that advocated the worldwide advancement of communism, as outlined by Marx and Lenin. Beyond working as a translator, Fisher later joined the Red Army and worked in foreign intelligence in Norway, Turkey, Britain, and France.[31] Based on his extensive experience in intelligence matters, between 1936 and 1938, he directed an NKVD school that taught young officers to use radios to transmit intelligence gathered through illegal means. Though Fisher was removed from his post in 1938 during the height of Stalin's purges, he survived and joined the Red Army during the Soviet Union's bitter fight against Nazi Germany, where he worked on intelligence-gathering and sabotage operations.[32]

In the aftermath of the Soviet Union Great Patriotic War, Fisher again joined the intelligence service of the Soviet Union as the new Cold War began. The head of the recently reorganized "illegals department" within the Committee of Information was Aleksandr Korotkov. Korotkov saw an opportunity to use Fisher as an important foundation upon which the Soviet Union could rebuild and expand its illegal espionage network throughout the globe and especially within the United States, which was quickly becoming the primary threat.[33] According to Pavel Sudoplatov, Korotkov's original plan called for using Fisher as the manager of agent networks in Norway and France as the Soviet Union attempted to build a Western European network of spies who could supply intelligence on military installations.[34]

Based on his extensive experience with radio transmission, Sudoplatov recommended to Korotkov that Fisher could be better employed as a technical manager focusing on running illegal radio networks that provided the Soviet Union with critical intelligence.[35] In 1947 the apparatchiks within the Soviet intelligence system had decided how best to employ the talents of Fisher, who had been training to become an illegal with communist intelligence services. Fisher assumed his first identity as artist Emil Goldfus when he entered the United States in 1948.[36] At this juncture there are conflicting accounts as to his mission.

In Sudoplatov's memoirs, he explains that Fisher's mission was to focus on the West Coast of the United States, specifically on the military facilities around Long Beach, California, and provide intelligence on military hardware being shipped by the United States in support of the Chinese Nationalists.[37] Furthermore, Fisher built a network of other illegals who emanated from Latin America. These agents were Soviet spies with extensive guerilla experience from World War II and posed as businessmen from Latin America, and their objective was to provide additional intelligence on the shipment of U.S. military hardware but also "implement sabotage operations" within the port facilities.[38] By the start of the Korean War in June of 1950, Fisher had built an elaborate intelligence network that also had the plans and capability to launch sabotage operations within the United States, yet by 1952 his mission had changed, and he assumed his more infamous identity as Rudolf Abel.[39]

In other accounts, in the period between 1947 and 1952, Fisher "acted as case officer" for agents working for the Soviet Union who were inside the United States, such as Morris Cohen, Lona Cohen, Theodore Hall, and Helen Sobell.[40] Though there is a major discrepancy among sources as to the exact nature of Fisher's work in the early period, there is consensus that he was a highly competent Soviet illegal who had made great gains at building networks of agents within the United States that produced intelligence for the Soviet Union.

By 1952 Fisher had become a "naturalized" U.S. citizen under the alias of Rudolf Abel and relocated via Canada to the Eastern half of the United States, mainly settling in New York. Under his new alias, Fisher posed as an artist and painter while he once again built networks within the United States to gather intelligence for the Soviet Union.[41] Furthermore, using his expert knowledge of illegal radio transmitters, Fisher established centers for agents to transmit their material in New York, Virginia, around the Great Lakes, and again on the West Coast.[42] All seemed to be going well for the next five years until the FBI arrested Abel on June 21, 1957.

The background of how the FBI came to arrest Abel is clouded. However, there seems to be consensus that the shoddy work of his subordinate, Reino Hayhanen, who was an "incompetent alcoholic, a liar, and a convicted drunk driver," led to the unraveling of Abel's operations.[43] The Soviet Union recalled Hayhanen in May 1956 to make sure that he did not expose the work being done by Abel. However, on his return to Moscow, Hayhanen defected in Paris. The KGB ordered Abel to leave New York and offered him a new identity as Robert Callow.[44] However, he disobeyed the order, and before he could transition to his new identity, he was arrested in New York.

Under interrogation Abel admitted to being a spy for the Soviet Union spy, but refused to give a name, until he finally asserted that his name was Rudolf Ivanovich Abel. Though he had never been assigned this name, Fisher used the name of an old dead friend as a way to signal his superior in Moscow that William Fisher had been caught.[45] In a very public trial, Abel was tried and sentenced to 30 years in prison, until the United States used him in an exchange in February 1962 for U-2 pilot Francis Gary Power, who had been detained in the Soviet Union for approximately fourteen months. Fisher was hailed as a hero upon his return to the Soviet Union.[46]

Fisher's story details the success the Soviet Union had in inserting illegal operatives into the United States and building networks of agents to transmit needed information back to the Soviet Union. The need to keep apprised of the military capabilities of the United States and the West in the late 1940s and into the 1950s was of the utmost importance for the Soviet Union, especially as the strategic nuclear balance tipped in favor of the United States. Though the Soviet Union had much success with inserting Fisher and having him develop clandestine intelligence networks on the west and east coasts of the United States, they still seemed to fall short of the insightful technological intelligence that the Soviet Union had succeeded in collecting in the 1930s and prior to the end of World War II. For years to come, the KGB looked to rebuild and succeed with other illegal networks within the United States, always alluding to Fisher as the model of a successful illegal Soviet spy, yet without fully acknowledging that the program failed to gather the necessary intelligence craved by the Soviet Union's government.[47]

THE BERLIN TUNNEL

On April 22, 1956, in the Soviet sector of Berlin, East German and Soviet soldiers began digging near the boundary between the U.S. and Soviet sectors. Within an hour after they started their process, the work party discovered telecommunications lines that had been tapped into and that the lines ran into a trapdoor.[48] Beneath the trapdoor, which the Soviet soldiers easily breached, was an elaborate subterranean tunnel that had been purposely built to collect intelligence on Soviet and Warsaw Pact military and political actions. The story behind the Berlin tunnel reveals that while the Soviet Union focused on rebuilding its human intelligence-gathering networks within the United States and around the globe, the United States worked at more sophisticated ways to gather intelligence as a means to understand the intentions and actions of the Soviet Union and its satellite partners.

The history of the Berlin tunnel, or Operation Gold, as it became known, actually started with a British intelligence operation in Vienna, Austria, in the period 1948–1952. Much like Berlin during the Cold War, Vienna was a divided city and a hub of international intrigue in the first decade of the Cold War. As a result of central status and the fact that East and West spies worked in very close proximity in Vienna during the early Cold War, the British intelligence services believed that the city would be a critical venue from which to gather much-needed information on the Soviet Union and its Eastern European allies.

British intelligence sent Peter Lunn to Vienna in an effort to build a system through which the West could gather telecommunication intelligence from the communists.[49] Lunn discovered that the Soviet Union had not established a new, secure telecommunication systems but rather used the established Austrian phone lines as the foundation of their system of communication.[50] Furthermore, British intelligence discovered that Vienna's phone lines served as a central hub through which a majority of Soviet Red Army phone calls got routed as they were sent back to Moscow.[51]

This discovery led the British intelligence service to devise a plan that focused on building a hidden tunnel under a popular shop in order to conceal the real nature of the underground intelligence gathering activity.[52] Underneath the shop and a house, which the British intelligence service also owned, they built a seventy-foot tunnel that allowed their technicians to tap into the Red Army's communications network.[53] The Vienna tunnel, known as Operation Silver, provided valuable intelligence for the British and the West for the life span of its operations. The tunnel produced good intelligence for the British and eventually the United States as well, once they were read into the operation, until the tunnel collapsed in 1952.[54] Conflicting accounts detail how the tunnel collapsed, but the end result was that Operation Silver provided the inspiration for the United States and the British to try an even more ambitious tunnel project in Berlin, as the Cold War tension increased in the 1950s and the insatiable appetite for intelligence seemed to expand exponentially as well.

The quest for telecommunication intelligence grew ever more important during Operation Silver, as the Soviet Union switched from using radio transmitters to pass and convey information to the use of underground cables and landlines, which the West had a much harder time intercepting signals.[55] Based on the success of Operation Silver, the CIA and British intelligence had agreed to work together as a way to combine their efforts in an attempt to gather much-needed military intelligence on Soviet forces in Germany and Eastern Europe. The CIA's chief of Berlin Base, Bill Harvey, worked with intelligence experts Richard M. Bissell and Frank Wisner to establish a plan in which the CIA, working with British intelligence service, would construct a tunnel, much like in Operation Silver, but longer and with greater access to telephones lines that carried the vast majority of the Soviet army's messages.[56]

Much like Vienna, the Soviet Union used the telephone trunk lines in Berlin as a vital network through which to pass all sorts of information, as well as military, diplomatic, and political traffic. In fact, the Berlin lines served as the central hub from which all calls from Moscow to Eastern European nations got routed.[57] In essence, the telephone trunk lines in Berlin offered a fantastic opportunity for the United States and Great Britain to gain a wide spectrum of intelligence that most certainly could provide greater insight into the actions of the Red Army and its satellites throughout Eastern and Central Europe. However, before the CIA could benefit from the intelligence traveling through the trunk lines, a whole host of planning and cover had to take place in order to ensure that the conceived tunnel would work as well as the one on Operation Silver.

The primary task was to gather information on the telephone trunk lines and schematics on their layout within the various sectors in Berlin.

Obviously, the largest concern was finding blueprints and schematics for the lines that were in the Soviets' sector. For this vital piece of information, Harvey turned to Walter O'Brien, a former professional baseball player, Chicago lawyer, former infantry officer in World War II, and current CIA officer for assistance.[58] O'Brien spoke German fluently, and Harvey assigned him the task of cultivating contacts in the West German post office who were responsible for running the long-distance switchboards.[59]

The idea behind recruiting West German assistance was that they could potentially assist in identifying and pointing out East Germans who had the proper knowledge that the CIA needed to put their plan into action. In the waning months of 1952, the basic elements necessary to move forward with the operation started to solidify. The efforts to cultivate East German sources familiar with the telephone system and the specifics of which lines carried the important Soviet military traffic blossomed in late 1952 and early 1953. Two important sources produced the critical information for the tunnel project to move forward. The first source focused on a "*Nummer Maedchen*," or numbers girl, in the East Berlin post office.[60] This specific source, cultivated by West German contacts, had access to the "specific long-distance cables used by Soviet official sources"; the post office kept highly classified records of who specifically used each line.[61] Though this information proved to be valuable, it had to be cross-checked to make sure that it was authentic and also that the lines assigned to Soviet officials were oriented in a way that allowed the United States to access the trunk bundles in a clandestine manner.

In addition to the numbers girl, the CIA also benefited from the services of a "lawyer in the Ministry of Post and Telecommunications," who provided specific and technical knowledge of the East German telecommunication system.[62] As the CIA developed a more complete network and understood the intricacies of how the Soviet military used the East German telephone system, it also received valuable information on the technical capabilities and physical layout of the telephone lines, as well as the trunk bundles. By the summer of 1953, the CIA had acquired enough intelligence and background information to move forward with Operation Gold, which became the code name for the Berlin tunnel.

Throughout 1953, the CIA planned and contracted with various services to build the tunnel, while at the same time, it started to conduct initial test taps to make sure that the information that U.S. intelligence had was correct and that the lines available did indeed provide military, political, or diplomatic intelligence. Again using agents inside East Germany, the CIA used these intelligence assets to conduct test taps to phone lines, which also provided CIA technicians with the capacity to listen to and record the information to deem whether the information being carried on the lines were worth the enormous effort to move forward with the full-scale production of the tunnel.[63] To paraphrase a history of Operation Gold, "the good news was that Soviet Union left the lines in operation. The bad news was that a quarter mile long tunnel needed to be dug to reach them."[64]

With the proper background information in place, Harvey moved forward with the proposal to build the Berlin tunnel, even though the CIA had estimated that it would cost approximately $15 million. Allen Dulles, the director of central intelligence, was lukewarm toward spending a huge sum of money on a single operation, but Harvey assuaged Dulles's concerns about the cost by telling him that the West Germans had proposed that they could dig the tunnel for roughly $5 million dollars.[65] Though the Germans had quoted a much lower price for the cost of digging the tunnel, they were unaware of the true purpose of the tunnel. According to histories of the CIA, "Harvey convinced the mayor of Berlin that the United States wanted to so some geological work under the city because of fears that the Soviet Union might try to sabotage West Berlin's sewer system."[66] The Berlin mayor agreed and was later told that the United States was installing a "secret radar installation."[67] Nevertheless the Berlin tunnel's construction proceeded.

After assessing and analyzing all the background information, the CIA provided the final specifics of the Berlin tunnel. The tunnel would be built at Alt Glienicke, at the southern side of Berlin near an abandoned industrial complex near a U.S. radar site that was still under construction. The main telephone lines that the CIA focused on tapping were 330 yards inside the East German border and twenty-four feet under the soil.[68] To access the trunk lines, the tunnel had to be 1,400 feet long and 8 feet in diameter, in order to accommodate all the necessary equipment.[69] The actual construction of the tunnel, which was composed of prefabricated sections, began in November 1954, and the system was considered ready for operation in February 1955, a short four months after construction began.[70]

For the next fourteen months, the tunnel provided the United States and the British with good intelligence on the Soviet military and its satellites in Eastern Europe. However, on March 26, 1956, the tunnel was discovered by East Germans and Soviets, and the operation was compromised. Furthermore, the Soviet Union used this discovery as a propaganda ploy to demonstrate that the United States was actively involved in clandestine operations. It was interesting to note that in the official Soviet recommendations as to how to handle the public unveiling of the Berlin tunnel, the United States received exclusive blame for the project. Specifically, Soviet officials wired these recommendations back to Moscow for Khrushchev's approval:

1. The chief of staff of Soviet forces must protest in writing to headquarters of American forces in Europe, with this to be published in the press.
2. Invite correspondents accredited both to East and West Berlin to inspect the installation.

3. Give approval to German friends to speak out on this question, but not before publication of this in the press.
4. Send a group of our specialists to study the equipment.
5. Despite the fact that the tunnel contains English equipment, direct all accusations in the press against the Americans only.[71]

There is widespread recognition that the Berlin tunnel produced much-needed intelligence for the United States and Great Britain at a time when relying on human sources provided little in assessing the military balance in Europe. However, there are also alternative interpretations of the tunnel's discovery by the East Germans and Soviet Union that highlight the nature of the espionage game during the 1950s. One such variation argues that the KGB knew about the tunnel and willingly sacrificed intelligence in an effort to protect and keep in place George Blake.[72] George Blake was a British intelligence officer who secretly worked for the KGB and provided Soviet intelligence with information on the Berlin Tunnel and other Western intelligence operations and British agents working in the Soviet Union and Europe.[73] Blake's information resulted in the execution of many of the agents he identified to the KGB.

The Berlin tunnel demonstrates that during the Cold War, the espionage game between the United States and the Soviet Union was driven by the ever-increasing demand for intelligence. This demand, in turn, led to the proliferation of spying into a third dimension, as the traditional means did not provide the necessary intelligence to assess the strategic military balance. Only aerial spying could provide the West with critical strategic intelligence.

THE U-2 AND MAY DAY

At the start of the 1950s, the United States had improvised a series of aircraft that could be used for a wide variety of intelligence-gathering missions. These aircraft, such as the RB-36, RB-47, and B-57, were evolutionary adaptations from airframes used for other purposes, mainly bombing. However, as the United States lacked the hard intelligence to discern where it stood in the strategic nuclear balance, as well as the international military balance, Eisenhower and others in his administration worried about the possibility of a "nuclear Pearl Harbor."[74]

Since the United States started flying reconnaissance and intelligence gathering flights around the Soviet Union in the aftermath of World War II, the Soviet Union's air defense capabilities had improved dramatically. In fact, since 1951, the United States had lost ten aircraft on these highly classified missions.[75] Something needed to be done so that the United States could acquire the strategic intelligence it needed, but yet not lose aircraft and aircrew, which could result in international turmoil. High-altitude aerial reconnaissance became the answer to the dilemma faced by the United States in its contest with the Soviet Union.

Richard S. Leghorn, who had commanded aerial reconnaissance squadrons during World War II, led the push for the United States to develop and build high-altitude reconnaissance aircraft when he was recalled to active duty during the Korean War. Leghorn saw the major problem as being that Soviet interceptor aircraft could engage spy planes up to 45,000 feet.[76] Leghorn reasoned that aircraft flying above 60,000 feet could avoid Soviet Air Force interceptors as well as the potentiality of the Soviet Union's Air Defense radars.[77] To test his hypothesis, Leghorn, who was head of the Reconnaissance Systems Branch of the Wright Air Development Command, worked with British aircraft manufacturer English Electric to redesign their Canberra medium bomber as a high-altitude reconnaissance aircraft.[78]

By making significant adjustments to the airframe, wings, and engines in addition to removing armor plating and other nonessential materials, Leghorn and the engineers from English Electric designed a modified B-57 Canberra that could potentially reach altitudes of 63,000–67,000 feet.[79] Despite the promise of his design, Leghorn's proposal had to navigate the Air Research and Development Command bureaucracy, which demanded that the special-purpose aircraft had to encompass the same military specifications as all other combat aircraft.[80] The result was a B-57 that could not meet the original requirements as established by Leghorn. This bureaucratic obstacle did not deter Leghorn, who had since moved to work in the Pentagon for the USAF's Chief of Staff for Development. With this position, Leghorn could continue to push his ideas about high-altitude reconnaissance within the USAF.[81]

Parallel to Leghorn's work on the development of a high-altitude aircraft, the Eisenhower administration had become concerned about the strategic military balance between the United States and the Soviet Union. The primary concern for Eisenhower was the protection against a nuclear Pearl Harbor. To assist in stabilizing the strategic nuclear balance, it was imperative that the United States have good, reliable intelligence on the strategic nuclear delivery systems of the Soviet Union. While operations such as the Berlin tunnel could provide key insights into operational and tactical elements of the Soviet Armed Forces, the Unites States needed better and more exact intelligence on the strategic capabilities of the Soviet Union.

Eisenhower went so far as to establish the Technological Capabilities Panel (TCP) under the direction of MIT President James Killian. One of the major objectives of the TCP (or Killian Commission, as it became known) was to look at promising technologies that could provide advantages to the United States in its struggle against the Soviet Union. Of specific importance was the need to develop technologies that could provide the necessary intelligence on the strategic nuclear delivery capabilities of the Soviet Union. The TCP focused on satellites as well as high-altitude aircraft as two specific options that could fulfill the intelligence needs of the United States.

Throughout 1953 Leghorn, working with the Air Force's Wright Air Development Command, encouraged aircraft manufacturers to submit designs for high-altitude reconnaissance aircraft to the Air Force. Four companies submitted proposals to the USAF for aircraft that could reach altitudes between 65,000 and 70,000 feet, three solicited and one unsolicited.[82] The unsolicited proposal came from the Lockheed Aircraft Corporation and was known as CL-282, which had been designed by Clarence "Kelly" Johnson.[83]

Johnson's design was a radical proposal for a single-engine jet aircraft that had long, slender wings, more reminiscent of a glider than a jet aircraft of the 1950s. The design parameters calculated that the aircraft could fly at an altitude of 70,000 feet with a range of 2,000 miles. Johnson and Lockheed submitted their proposal to the USAF in March 1954. However, due to the unorthodox design, as well as the single-engine construct, the USAF rejected the proposal in June of 1954.[84] Though rejected by the USAF, Johnson's proposal had supporters within the United States Air Force who saw a need and potential for his aircraft, specifically Trevor Gardner, who happen to be Special Assistant to for Research and Development to the Secretary of the Air Force.[85] Gardner tried to convince Strategic Air Command (SAC) Commander Curtis E. LeMay of the benefit and potential of the project, but LeMay was not interested in aircraft that were not capable of fighting. Not to be deterred, Gardner sought support with the CIA, which had been working with the USAF in sending balloons with cameras attached to them over the Soviet Union. The CIA forwarded a proposal to the USAF, "asking them to take the initiative" in the development of CL-282. The Air Force again rejected the offer; however, the project was not yet dead.

The TCP became the venue in which Lockheed's CL-282 project received substantial support from Edwin Land, a member of the TCP and chairman of Project Three, which was one of three subcommittee working groups under the over purview of Killian and his committee. Seeing promise in the CL-282 design as a platform to carry advanced cameras for photographic intelligence over the Soviet Union, in November 1954, Land and Killian had briefed Eisenhower on the potential and need for high-altitude reconnaissance; though the president was receptive to the idea, the biggest problem was finding an agency or service component to support the program.[86] The prevailing consensus among the executive agencies was that the CIA, not the USAF, should preside over the program. However, it was recognized that while there would be a lead agency, support was of course necessary among service components, specifically the USAF, to assist the CIA in the planning and execution of the program.[87]

On November 23, 1954, Congress approved the program. On November 24, 1954, President Eisenhower gave his approval to start planning for the overflight of the Soviet Union with the high-altitude aircraft by the CIA with assistance and cooperation from the USAF.[88] With Eisenhower's approval, Allen Dulles, DCI, placed Richard Bissell in charge of the U-2 and overflight program.[89] With the necessary approvals, Johnson of Lockheed refined the plans for the U-2 and promised a first flight test by August 2, 1955 (only nine months after approval), as well as the delivery of four aircraft by December 1955 (thirteen months after approval).[90]

In parallel to the building of the airframe, the CIA had to develop the camera and other specialized electronics that collected signals intelligence onboard the U-2. Due to the high altitude of U-2 flights—70,000 feet and above—aerial cameras and lenses used by the USAF had to be evolved and developed for the new environment and new mission. The overflight program, under the direction of Richard Bissell, was given the code name Operation Aquatone, and the parallel programs worked toward completion. In August 1955, the U-2 flew for the first time, and over the next several months, the initial testing program worked out minor issues with the aircraft to ensure that the U-2 and its pilots could operate at the extreme altitudes demanded for overflights of the Soviet Union.[91] The testing and training of pilots took place in the Nevada desert at Watertown Strip, later known as Groom Lake and Area 51. As the Aquatone program came into being, the CIA and the USAF worked out the process by which USAF pilots interested in flying the U-2 would resign from the USAF and work as civilian contractors for the CIA, but on the books, they worked for Lockheed.[92] When pilots finished their contractual obligation (eighteen months) with the CIA, they could reenter the Air Force without loss of time in service or grade equivalent with their peers. Put more simply, they were not denied promotion and advancement for joining the U-2 program.

By April 1956, the CIA's U-2s began conducting test flights across the United States with cameras and equipment as a way to make sure that systems and crews were ready for their overseas intelligence-gathering missions.[93] As a way to preserve the secrecy of these flights, the CIA and USAF built a cover story that the U-2s were weather research aircraft employed by National Advisory Committee on Aeronautics (NACA) to collect data on global weather patterns. By May the first operational unit of U-2s deployed to the Royal Air Force (RAF) base at Lakenheath. However, due to a tense political climate between the British government and the Soviet Union, the British would not allow U-2s to fly into the Soviet Union from their bases. Therefore, the U-2s moved to Wiesbanden, Germany, to start their operational missions, which began in July 1956.[94]

President Eisenhower, though tentative about approving the secret overflights of the U-2s, believed that he had little choice, as the Soviet Union had rejected his "Open Skies" proposal roughly a year earlier.[95] The need to have a better understanding of the military and strategic capabilities of the Soviet Union drove Eisenhower to approve a limited number of overflights, which were focused on key regions of the Soviet Union where the United States suspected there might be military bases and needed confirmation. The growing concern of a "bomber gap" between the United States and the Soviet Union served as a rationale as to why the United States had to resort to secret high-altitude flights over Soviet territory.[96]

As U-2s flew from Germany, and later Japan, Turkey, Norway, and even Pakistan, they provided critical intelligence to prove that there was no bomber gap and that the Soviet Union's Intercontinental Ballistic Missile (ICBM) development was not as advanced as had been previously thought. In short, the program was providing the critical intelligence that it had been designed to procure. However, the process of flying over segments of the Soviet Union was not without issues.

Starting as early as July 1956, the Soviet Union started filing protests with the United Nations of aircraft flying over its territory. Within the Eisenhower administration, there was growing concern as to the capability of the Soviet Union to track and even shoot down a U-2 aircraft. The concerns persisted until May 1960, and they caused Eisenhower to authorize only a small number of overflights over the Soviet Union each year. Even though the president was concerned, with the Soviet Union's test of ICBMs in the summer of 1957 and the launch of Sputnik on October 1957, the administration still had a pressing need to maintain up-to-date intelligence on the strategic nuclear capabilities of the Soviet Union. These demands drove the May 1, 1960, mission of Francis Gary Powers, as he made a bold flight planned to cover a span across the Soviet Union. Previously, overflights had only ventured through sections of Soviet airspace, while Powers's mission required that he would spend hours deep within Soviet air space.[97]

On May 1, 1960, President Eisenhower approved Powers's flight, which would cover roughly 2,900 miles over the Soviet Union, with a total trip length of 3,800 miles with a flying time of nine hours.[98] Despite increased concern over the Soviet Union's ability to track the U-2, the United States needed more intelligence about Soviet military bases and capabilities.

Approximately four hours into his mission, the Soviet Union shot down Powers over their country. When he did not land at the assigned airfield in Norway, the White House issued a press release that a National Aeronautics and Space Administration (NASA) weather aircraft had strayed off course into Soviet airspace. Though this seemingly mundane press release raised some public interest, as Eisenhower and Khrushchev were both preparing for a summit in Paris, unbeknown to the White House, CIA, and USAF, Powers had escaped his wrecked aircraft and had been captured by the Soviet Union. Khrushchev used this opportunity to expose the White House's press release as a lie, which allowed the Soviet premier to state that the Soviet Union had the parts of the aircraft and the pilot, who was alive and well.[99]

Powers spent twenty-one months as a prisoner in the Soviet Union before he would be exchanged for Soviet Agent William Fisher (aka Rudolf Abel) in Germany.[100] The exchange of these two spies on the Glienicker Bridge between Potsdam and West Berlin in many ways represented the trajectory of the espionage game being played by the United States and the Soviet Union. While the United States invested in high-technology programs such as the U-2, the Soviet Union focused on the tried-and-true method of using human collection sources to produce intelligence. The quest for more and better intelligence continued to drive both sides toward a desire for more and better methods of collection. Though the U-2 overflight program stopped after the Soviet Union shot down Powers, it was widely acknowledged that the program did produce much-needed intelligence on the military capabilities of the Soviet Union. Though the Soviet Union had stopped the overflight of its territory by aircraft, the United States and Eisenhower had advanced technological means to maintain their need to know.

CONCLUSION

The period of 1950–1960 was a critical period in the evolution of the espionage game between the United States and the Soviet Union. First and foremost, one of the primary concerns was both nations' need to have up-to-date to information on the strategic military capabilities of their adversary. This need drove the United States and the Soviet Union in opposite directions in many regards considering the use of espionage. For the Soviet Union, the focus was on rebuilding its illegal network of human agents to provide critical intelligence on the military capabilities of the United States. By using William Fisher, aka Rudolf Abel, they attempted to keep track of military shipments and other strategic indicators as the United States supplied and fought the Korean war.

Though the KGB had had much success with building large networks of agents with the covers of businessmen, artists, and official diplomats, the Soviet Union struggled to get ideological converts from the diverse population of the United States. This was different from the 1920s and 1930s, when American citizens willingly spied for the Soviet Union due to a deep belief in the principles of communism; this ideological pool of agents withered with the close the 1940s as the Second Red scare took hold in the United States. As a result, the KGB had a much more difficult time building internal networks involving U.S. citizens. This forced the KGB to rely on and, in fact, emphasize rebuilding its illegal network as a primary means to provide intelligence on the United States and its political, economic, and strategic capabilities. By no means did the KGB reject the use of technology, but rather it chose to purpose a proven method from an earlier era that had been fruitful and extremely beneficial as outlined in the first chapter of this book, "Allies Become Enemies."

From the perspective of the United States, the espionage game had become even more difficult as access to the Soviet Union proved to be even more challenging, especially developing networks of agents to spy on the communist country and its allies. As a result of limited success with developing HUMINT sources inside the Soviet Union, increased reliance focused on the development of technological solutions to gain understanding of the military capabilities of the Soviet Union and its allies. From the start of using "ferret" aircraft in the middle of the 1940s to use of the ultrasecret U-2s flying over Soviet territory, the United States, and more specifically, President Eisenhower, saw technology as a means to offset the lack of intelligence coming from HUMINT sources. Furthermore, as the strategic nuclear balance become more of a critical issue for the Eisenhower administration, advanced technological means become a useful way to keep track of developing fleets of bombers and missiles produced by the Soviet Union.

Beyond high-flying aircraft, the United States, in conjunction with the British, also devised ingenious schemes such as Operation Silver and Operation Gold to listen and record Soviet telephone traffic within Central and Eastern Europe. Again, the focus on the collection of the data was the status and disposition of Soviet and, later, Warsaw Pact military forces. Within the tense period of global confrontation, the Eisenhower administration saw it as a national priority to improve the intelligence gathered by the United States on the disposition, capability, and numbers of Soviet and Warsaw Pact military forces. For this type of intelligence gathering, the technological means of wiretapping via tunnels and high-flying aircraft proved very useful and beneficial. In short, the period of 1950–1960 established a trend that would maintain itself through the duration of the Cold War and even into the 21st century, as the United States and the Soviet Union maintained their commitments to collecting intelligence on each other.

CHAPTER 4

Crisis and Response, 1961–1968

Though the United States came out of the 1950s with a palpable sense of general stability within the context of the global struggle against the expansion of communism, the turbulent period of 1961–1968 saw many crises that demanded a U.S. response. As the Soviet Union further solidified its control over the Warsaw Pact and further attempted to expand its influence around the globe, Presidents John F. Kennedy and Lyndon B. Johnson had to not only respond with overt military, diplomatic, or economic power but also maintain an even more robust espionage program to ensure that the United States continued to maintain a strong global presence and awareness of the communist threat.

Elaborating on the action-reaction paradigm established in earlier chapters, this chapter focuses on how the foundations of using the CIA as a paramilitary organization designed to roll back and hedge against the expansion of communism in Latin America and even Africa had to be adjusted based on the catastrophic failure of the CIA's support of the Bay of Pigs operation. As such, a discussion about the CIA's development of a plan to oust Fidel Castro from power in Cuba with a U.S.-trained and -backed invasion force served as a significant component in the way the Kennedy administration saw and approved other espionage missions after the fiasco that was the Bay of Pigs. Though the Kennedy administration organizationally altered NSC 5412 by appointing a "special group" of advisers to replace the need for the "advisory group" as stipulated in NSC 5412, the president also inserted himself into the intelligence and espionage process, which subverted Eisenhower's attempt to maintain plausible deniability of specific covert actions.[1]

Kennedy's adjustments to the bureaucratic structure focused on the president as being in the direct line of "approval and review" of covert operations.[2] Structurally, Kennedy replaced the 5412 advisory committee with a special group that was composed of two separate subcommittees: the "Special Group–Augmented" (SG-A) and the "Special Group–Insurgencies" (SG-I).[3] SG-A focused on covert operations, while the SG-I maintained purview over guerilla operations. Despite the seemingly different focus and the administrative split between the SG-A and SG-I, they were composed of the same members of the overarching "special group." The members of the special group were Robert F. Kennedy (attorney general), General Maxwell Taylor (military adviser to the president), McGeorge Bundy (national security adviser), General Lyman Lymnitzer (Supreme Allied Commander NATO and former chairman of the Joint Chiefs of Staff), and Allen Dulles (director of central intelligence).[4] After the Bay of Pigs operation, Kennedy replaced Allen Dulles as DCI with John McCone. As result of his new position John McCone also replaced Dulles on the special group as well.

The reason for this structural change in the bureaucracy of covert operations was to provide some additional executive-level control over the operations. As for covert operations, after the Bay of Pigs failure, any covert programs with a proposed budget of over $3 million had to be scrutinized and debated with the SG-A, which had established general criteria when considering operations. The criteria focused on "risk, possibility of success, potential for exposure, political sensitivity, and cost."[5]

The net result of these changes was that President Kennedy became much more directly tied to decisions regarding the use of use of covert operations. In addition to the use of the CIA, the time period covered in this chapter also focuses on the beginning of U.S. reliance on satellite technology for espionage, or more specifically, intelligence gathering and surveillance. With the Soviet Union's successful launch of Sputnik in October of 1957 and the subsequent first successful launch of the Discoverer 13 satellite by the United States in 1960, a new era in espionage had evolved.

The Discoverer satellite, described by NASA as a scientific and research satellite, was more than it appeared. The satellite was actually a joint CIA/ USAF program that used the cover of scientific research as a platform to build and develop spy satellites. The main objective of the Discoverer, or Corona satellites, as known by the CIA, was to gather photographic intelligence on the military and strategic capabilities of the Soviet Union and other communist countries.

Though Eisenhower had authorized the development of spy satellites in days after Sputnik, the USAF had been researching the mission objectives of using these new extraterrestrial resources to replace, or at least augment, surveillance aircraft. The CIA also saw the potential for the new technological capabilities as a means to gather critical information.

With the embarrassment of the U-2 fiasco in May of 1960, the impetus to use space-based intelligence-gathering means appealed greatly to Eisenhower and his later successors in office. The period of 1960–1968 saw the proliferation of the use of a wide variety of satellite capabilities to gather intelligence by both the United States and the Soviet Union. Therefore, in many ways, this chapter provides insights into how the espionage game went through a major technological revolution with the introduction of space-based assets.

Though the United States continued to develop aircraft such as the SR-71 to gather prompt intelligence, the use of space became a new domain in Cold War espionage as the United States and Soviet Union strove to get a better understanding of the strategic capabilities and intentions of their primary adversaries. Therefore, a major objective in this chapter is to not only highlight significant espionage operations between the United States and the Soviet Union in the period of 1960–1968 but also to capture the changing dynamics of the Cold War espionage game.

It is important to note that although both the United States and Soviet Union sought additional advanced technological means to gather intelligence, they did not abandon their traditional efforts of using human spies and agents to collect additional intelligence. The reality was simply that the United States had a more difficult time penetrating the closed society of the Soviet Union as a means to gather critical strategic intelligence, which drove U.S. presidents to rely increasingly on other advanced technological means to collect strategic intelligence. The Soviet Union, as highlighted in the previous chapters, had an easier time inserting intelligence-gathering officers and cultivating agents, but it still lacked access to key pieces of strategic intelligence that could be gathered by air and space-based assets.

CASTRO, CUBA, AND THE BAY OF PIGS

In 1959 Fidel Castro and his band of "Green Mountain men" finally overthrew the U.S.-supported regime of Fulgencio Batista in Cuba. This internal Cuban fight had significant implications for the Cold War, especially the espionage game between the United States and the Soviet Union. The major issue of concern for the United States focused on Castro's early declaration that he wished to ally the new Cuban regime with the Soviet Union under the tenets of Marxism.[6] For U.S. President Dwight D. Eisenhower, having a declared Marxist regime ninety miles off the coast of the United States was a major problem. Under the tenets of the containment policy, the United States could not allow a communist regime to sprout within its own backyard.

Almost immediately after Castro's declaration, Eisenhower authorized the CIA to begin planning covert means to overthrow the regime of Fidel Castro.[7] More specifically, the Eisenhower administration focused on two primary objectives. The first was to plan for the internal overthrow of Castro by providing support to the development of anti-Castro forces within Cuba.[8] In many ways the CIA had long practiced these types of missions in the late 1940s and early 1950s in France and Italy specifically, as detailed in the first chapter. In fact, through the use of covert means, Eisenhower and the CIA achieved a victory in Guatemala in 1954 using methods developed, honed, and evolved in Europe in the late 1940s and in the Middle East in the early 1950s. The success of the operation in Guatemala provided the confidence necessary within the CIA that they could again capitalize on recent operations as a means to achieve yet another victory in the clandestine Cold War.[9]

On March 17, 1960, the 5412 Committee met in the Oval Office to provide final approval for the plan to remove Castro from power.[10] Eisenhower approved the plan that outlined the insertion of "Cuban exiles to organize local insurgents and provide logistical support for anti-Castro political forces."[11] Though Eisenhower had personally approved the operation, he emphasized the need to maintain operational security throughout the operations as a means to ensure that the role played by the United States in cultivating the anti-Castro factions was obscured.[12] After a few months of conducting the operation to promote and assist anti-Castro political forces, the CIA admitted that the first phase of the plan to oust Castro was not working very well.

The second phase of the plan evolved as the first phase withered under Castro's tight control of his government and the population in Cuba. DCI Allen W. Dulles and Richard Bissell pushed for a more robust plan that moved beyond developing internal political dissidents in Cuba. The new plan called for the assembly, training, and support of Cuban exiles to launch an invasion of Cuba with the overall objective of encouraging spontaneous political support to assist the anti-Castro invading force in forcibly removing Castro from power. Dulles and Bissell charged none other than William King Harvey (of the Berlin tunnel fame) to head the program to recruit and train Cuban exiles for the eventual invasion of Cuba.

The overall concept of the operation was that Harvey would oversee the recruitment of Cuban exiles willing to participate in the operation while he marshaled personnel and equipment from other departments in the CIA to provide the actual training and support of the forces. Furthermore, based on his experience in collecting electronic intelligence, Harvey also had the mission to provide intelligence to the planners of the military operation.[13] The objective was to have a brigade-sized unit (1,500–3,200 soldiers) to land at the Bay of Pigs in Cuba and establish a beachhead from which they could build support for an eventual operation to defeat and remove Castro and his supporters from power. The date of the operation was scheduled for spring 1961, which was to be after the transition between the Eisenhower administration and the newly elected Kennedy administration. Though the Eisenhower administration, specifically Vice President Richard M. Nixon, wanted an early date for the operation, it was clear that an operation that involved recruiting, training, and supporting a brigade-sized invasion force would take some time to assembly and get ready for the operation, especially when it was done in secret.[14]

As Harvey had experience with hastily assembling complex organizations, he quickly developed the Task Force W (the name of the organization overseeing the operation) into a working operation in Miami, Florida, that grew to six hundred case offices, making it one of the largest CIA operations in the world at the time.[15] The Miami-based operation that oversaw the recruitment of Cuban exiles, called JM/WAVE, began interviewing and questioning up to 2,800 Cuban exiles a day.[16] It was a laborious task to ensure that the exiles were the proper and necessary people required by the operation.

In addition to the assembly, training, and support of the anti-Castro invasion force, Harvey received an additional set of guidelines from Richard Bissell, which called for Harvey to plan for and develop the capability to conduct "executive action," which was a euphemism for the assassination of Fidel Castro.[17] However, Bissel was explicitly clear that Harvey was not to talk to Dulles or Eisenhower about the plans that would be conducted by the ZR/RIFLE unit, which was a special unit within the bureaucratic structure of Task Force W.[18]

With the bureaucracy in place, the CIA went about enacting the first phase of the operation. Richard Bissell described the plan as approved by Eisenhower thus:

What was approved was a plan to take about twenty-five Cuban refugees, young and well-motivated, and train them in sabotage and communication techniques— to train them to be guerillas—then insert them into Cuba. In the first class there were twenty-five, and in subsequent classes there might have been thirty to forty-five, not more than that. The design was a classic World War II underground activity. Our operation was to train eventually up to seventy-five or more individuals who would first of all have communication techniques and equipment, and second have some skills in sabotage. Their primary function was to enter the country, join guerilla groups or resistance groups already there, and put them in direct communications with an external headquarters. Partly to exercise command and control and partly to enable them to receive logistic supplies by boat and aircraft.[19]

Borrowing heavily on their experiences, both positive and negative, in the 1940s and 1950s in Europe (specifically France and Italy), Latin America (specifically Guatemala), and the Middle East (specifically Iran), the

CIA's plan for Cuba followed an established model. Bissel explains the objective thus:

The original conception of training guerilla leaders and organizing communications for guerilla groups actually in Cuba grew a little bit into the notion that once we had developed a true underground on the World War II model, with the capability of receiving people and equipment in small numbers and amounts, and moving them around, we would detonate an uprising in a small way with possibly a hundred people or two groups of a hundred people landing at different points on the coast.[20]

However, despite the best efforts of the United States, as well as the actual insertion of a very limited number of trained guerillas into Cuba, by the end of 1960, the indication was that the effort to build an internal guerilla movement that could eventually challenge Castro for power in Cuba was not working. Although the first phase of the operation withered, the election of John F. Kennedy as president of the United States also had a significant impact on the operation.

Once Kennedy assumed the presidency, the training and planning for the first phase of the operation shifted toward a much more complex and dynamic operation that bore little resemblance to the idea outlined by Bissell. Instead of supporting and building a small guerilla force that could infiltrate Cuba and build a cohesive resistance movement, the Kennedy administration focused on training and supporting a covert invasion force that could challenge Castro's military for control of Cuba.

United States Marine Corps Colonel Jack Hawkins became the military adviser to the CIA for the landing operation, and Tracy Barnes became the CIA's supervisor of the overall project.[21] The objective of the operation focused on "La Brigada" or "Brigade 2506" landing on a specific beach in Cuba and establishing a beachhead, which would, in turn, allow the Cuban government-in-exile, waiting in Florida, to return to the island and wrestle control from Castro and his communist forces. Hawkins was committed to make sure that the operation focused on key tasks to ensure that the beach landing was a success. Prior to the deployment of troops ashore, the CIA focused on knocking out Castro's air force.[22] With the beach landings scheduled for April 17, 1961, the plan was to launch airstrikes starting on April 15, 1961, against the Cuban air force as a way to make sure that the landing force had freedom of maneuver when they came ashore. However, in the days immediately prior to the operation, President Kennedy altered the CIA's plans for the airstrikes and the overall operation.

On April 12, 1961, President Kennedy publicly stated that the United States "would not militarily intervene in Cuba."[23] As a result of this public announcement, Kennedy instructed the CIA that the air operations scheduled to suppress the Cuban air force prior to Brigade 2506's landing at the Bay of Pigs had to look like it was done by "defecting Cuban pilots, not exiles" trained in Central America by the United States.[24] This action was conducted with a full cover story by the CIA, but the original number of sorties designed to suppress the Cuban air force had been reduced by President Kennedy as Cuba's Foreign minister Raul Rao "denounced the story as a plot by the United States" to militarily intervene in Cuba.[25] Kennedy's cancellation of the air operations stemmed from the potential that further air operations in support of the landing could "seriously embarrass American diplomacy in Latin America."[26]

As a result, the landing force that moved toward its objective in the Bay of Pigs on April 17, 1961, went ashore without having knocked out Cuba's air force. The initial result was that the landing force lost two transports that contained the majority of operation's ammunition and three B-26 aircraft. Though President Kennedy agreed to allow U.S. Navy aircraft from the USS Boxer to fly in a show-of-force mission over the landing beaches in Cuba on Tuesday, April 18, 1961, they did not intervene to stem the loss of Brigade 2506. Simply put, the operation was a complete failure, and despite the best efforts of the CIA to construct a strong facade that Cuban exiles conducted the operation, it was a well-known fact that the CIA and the United States were behind the operation. Interviewed years later, Richard Bissell commented:

The fact of the matter is that the press had been full of stories that a landing was planned. There was no way it could have been carried out without ninety-nine people out of every hundred in the entire world attributing it correctly to the U.S. government.[27]

Furthermore, Bissell stated:

The first, most pervasive, and, I would argue, most damaging misconception was that the covert character of the operation could be maintained. . . . It was this misconception that gave rise to a whole sequence of requirements and limitations on operational flexibility in the interest of preserving the impression of the operation as a strictly Cuban affair. Thus there was to be no use of facilities, personnel, or up-to-date equipment which could have been made available only by the U.S. government and would, if revealed or captured, constitute proof of official U.S. sponsorship.[28]

The failure of the Bay of Pigs operation resulted in Allen Dulles and Richard Bissell resigning from the CIA. Furthermore, the botched operation provided the Soviet Union with an empowered sense that the new U.S. president was weak and unable to effectively use his covert forces to achieve Western objectives. Though the failure of this operation represented a significant failure for the CIA and for the espionage efforts of the United States, the intelligence-collection process was changing based on new technology. The United States would be at the forefront of these changes, whereas the Soviet Union still relied on traditional HUMINT sources, which it had used extensively to gather information on the planned invasion of Cuba.

THE SOVIET UNION AND CUBAN EXILES

Castro's revolution in Cuba helped to cement a much closer relationship between Cuba and the Soviet Union.[29] Having reached a low point in the goals of the worldwide revolution in the 1950s, the Soviet Union looked for an invigoration of the tenets of communism around the globe. Though, in many ways, Fidel Castro was not their immediate choice, the Soviet Union, and the KGB specifically, saw Castro as a new hope to erode the dominance of the capitalist United States.[30] The fiasco of the Bay of Pigs invasion caught the Soviet Union off guard.[31] As a result of this bolt from the blue, and as an additional way to build a closer relationship with Castro's government, the KGB, under directions from the Central Committee in Moscow, focused on gathering more information about additional or follow-up plans within the United States to launch another invasion of Cuba. The means to gather this information was the tried-and-true method of using human intelligence source to gain deeper insights into the plans of the United States to depose Castro.

Though the KGB did not have Soviet agents within the high levels of the national security apparatus, the intelligence service of the Soviet Union used the openness of the U.S. society to gain a different perspective of potential future plans. Using KGB's network of "legal residents" in the United States, such as Oleg Kalugin, the KGB worked to ensure that it would not be caught off guard again. Furthermore, the KGB worked with Cuban intelligence to make sure that all information was eventually passed on to Castro to ensure that he was well aware of any future attempts to invade his island.

In 1958, Oleg Kalugin entered Columbia University as a student in the journalism program. He had been selected by his professors at Leningrad University to participate in a Fulbright student exchange program.[32] Though by all appearances Kalugin was a young, optimistic, and eager journalism student, the reality was that he was a KGB spy who had been inserted into the United States with "legal" cover as a means to collect intelligence on the United States. At the end of his year of study under the Fulbright exchange program, Kalugin took a three-week trip across the United States to see the sights and gather intelligence as he could. Though this first foray into penetrating the United States for the purposes of gathering intelligence produced limited significant intelligence for the KGB, the program did establish basic credentials for Kalugin to return to the

United States in 1960, after briefly returning to the Soviet Union and KGB headquarters in 1959.

In 1960, Kalugin returned to the United States, specifically New York City, as an "official correspondent" for Radio Moscow.[33] His new "day job" granted him access to the United Nations and other governmental meetings, speeches, and gatherings around New York, not to mention access to the vibrant social scene that accompanied those in high society and government. Though Kalugin had the cover of being a reporter, his real task was to gather intelligence on the United States and send it back the Soviet Union. Additionally, an implied task was to cultivate a greater network of disaffected Americans who would be willing to spy for the Soviet Union.

Again, as we have seen in earlier chapters, the Soviet Union still worked hard to build the internal network of American citizens or even other expats residing in the United States who would be willing to provide secrets to the Soviet Union, but the KGB never achieved the success it predecessor organization had in the late 1920s and through the 1930s.

The CIA-backed invasion at the Bays of Pigs provided a greater impetus for the KGB to ensure that the Soviet Union had all the necessary information to support Castro, as well as gain critical information to improve the KGB's situational awareness that the United States was not planning another attempt to retake Cuba. Oleg Kalugin worked to gather the necessary information for the KGB and the Central Committee in Moscow. Kalugin's account of his actions to gather information about future invasions of Cuba provides keen insights into how the KGB used legal residents to build and gather information for the Soviet Union and its allies.

Kalugin recounts:

Lubyanka [KGB Headquarters in Moscow] immediately instructed KGB officers in the United States to strengthen ties with the Cuban exile community. A friend of mine—a New York City bookstore owner involved in Left-wing politics—introduced me to his daughter. She turned out to have a Cuban lover, who secretly ferried Cuban exiles and arms back and forth to the island as part of continuing to attempt to overthrow Castro. I never met the pilot, but the woman [bookstore owner's daughter] supplied in great detail about his work: what planes he and his cohort flew, where they landed, where the exiles' Florida bases were.[34]

Based on the simple use of personal networks with leftist sympathies, the KGB was able to gather and piece together critical details of ongoing operations. Though Kalugin was limited in his ability to travel outside of New York, as per diplomatic protocol, he was still able to use unassuming Americans as a means to gather necessary information on operations conducted by Cuban exiles to overthrow Castro. Most assuredly, the KGB shared its information with Castro's intelligence service.

Moving beyond the information gathered in New York and feeling confident based on the information he had received from the pilot's lover, Kalugin took his operation one step further in 1961, as Moscow clamored for more and more information on Cuba. Again his memoirs provide the best description of how the operation evolved:

The annual conference of American trade unions was being held in Miami and I received permission from the U.S. State Department to go there, ostensibly to cover the conference. Traveling with a KGB colleague, Mikhail Sagatelyan, who worked in the Washington Bureau of TASS. We attended a few sessions of the union convention, then fanned out to the bars and restaurants Cuban émigrés were known to frequent. Posing sometimes as Russian émigré journalists, we talked with numerous Cubans. Soon we heard about a group of Cuban exiles planning another invasion of Cuba.[35]

Having found out about the meeting of Cuban exiles and their plan for another invasion of Cuban, Kalugin and Sagatelyan hatched a plan to pose as Icelandic and Turkish correspondents, respectively.[36] Interesting to note that they picked their respective nationalities because they thought that the Cubans would not know the accents of Iceland and Turkey.[37] With their backstories straight, Kalugin and Sagatelyan made their made to the meeting and gained access based on their journalistic credentials. Once inside the meeting, the Cubans provided "leaflets, memoranda, and literature that described the planning for a second invasion of Cuba."[38] In addition to the material provided by the Cubans, Kalugin and Sagatelyan also received several speeches about how the "United States had abandoned the objectives of the exiles."[39] Kalugin recounted that the Cubans "sensed our real interest" and offered to stay in touch and provide further information as it became available.[40]

When the Cubans asked for addresses and phone numbers of Kalugin and Sagatelyan, the KGB officers provided ambiguous answers that raised the suspicion of the Cubans, as Kalugin and Sagatelyan did not provide address or phone numbers, as they forgot them. In short, when a group of the Cubans left to confirm the bogus information, Kalugin and Sagatelyan quickly and politely dismissed themselves from the increasingly tense situation.[41]

The net result of the infiltration of the Cuban exiles' meeting was that Kalugin and Sagatelyan quickly deciphered that the Kennedy administration was not supporting a second planned invasion of Cuba. Furthermore, Kalugin stated that "despite anti-Castro fever gripping Miami, there was little chance of his enemies toppling him soon."[42] Hence, Moscow was pleased with the intelligence.[43]

The events surrounding the Bay of Pigs operation and the Soviet Union's immediate interest in the potential for future covert military operations nicely portray the dynamic of the Cold War game of espionage. While the operations conducted by Kalugin and the KGB to gather additional information on U.S.-backed future operations was necessary to maintain the vanguard of what was thought to be a burgeoning Latin American communist foothold in Latin America, the KGB failed to become aware of the other plots to remove Castro from power. These CIA-backed operations focused on poisoning or assassinating Castro.[44] Though we tend to think of the espionage game as one of action and reaction, it is often much more complex and dynamic, which entails that the intelligence organizations on both sides have a vast and flexible ability to adjust to the constantly changing circumstances. In the case of the Bay of Pigs, the KGB quickly became obsessive about another such operation, and they eventually pieced together enough information to discern that Kennedy was not using the CIA to fund, train, and support another amphibious invasion. However, this did not mean that the Kennedy administration was content with Castro staying in power. Rather, while the KGB got the information they wanted concerning future U.S. invasions of Cuba, the intelligence service of the Soviet Union failed to realize that the Kennedy administration changed its tactics and used covert means, not to support a large-scale amphibious invasion of Cuba but rather to focus on removing Castro with more direct and targeted means.

Furthermore, the covert events focused on Cuba by both the United States and the Soviet Union demonstrate that despite the increased use of advanced technological means to gather and interpret intelligence, the use of human officers and agents still proved a vital necessity. As the Cold War saw the onset of the space race, the intelligence agencies of the both the United States and the Soviet Union increasingly sought to augment the use of humans with satellites and other advanced technological means of collection.

SPYING FROM SPACE: THE UNITED STATES

In stark contrast to the heavy reliance on people to conduct the espionage activities focusing on Cuba by both the United States and the Soviet Union, the 1960s saw the increased reliance on space-based assets to gather intelligence. Though the actual space race started much earlier in the Cold War, the 1960s saw the first use of satellites for photoreconnaissance by both the United States and the Soviet Union.[45] The use of satellites for collecting intelligence became critical for both sides as the strategic nuclear balance between the United States and the Soviet Union shifted and adjusted during the period of 1960–1970. As a result, the need to have more and more awareness of the capabilities and numbers of the strategic nuclear balance became an evolving component of the espionage game.

As covered in the previous chapter, U.S. President Dwight D. Eisenhower had used the U-2 spy plane as a means to collect intelligence over the Soviet Union. However, with the May 1960 downing of the CIA's U-2 piloted by Francis Gary Powers, Eisenhower was cautious about flying additional missions over Soviet and Warsaw Pact airspace.

However, Eisenhower only had to wait until August 1960 to again acquire much-needed intelligence over the Soviet Union—this time without risking the public embarrassment of the "May-Day affair." On August 19, 1960, the CIA, the USAF, and President Eisenhower received the first photographs from the new "Corona" photoreconnaissance satellite.[46] In fact, the first successful mission of the United States' new spy satellite provided much more significant photographic coverage of the Soviet Union than all of the U-2 flights combined.[47] It was clear that by the summer of 1960, the espionage game had expanded to outer space.

The path that led to the successful return of approximately 1.5 million square miles of photographic coverage over the Soviet Union by the U.S. spy satellites started earlier in the 1950s with the USAF's Weapon System 117L program (WS-117L).[48] Starting in 1946, the soon-to-be-independent Air Force, working in conjunction with a small think tank within the Douglas Aircraft Corporation, later known as the RAND Corporation, had identified photographic reconnaissance as potential missions for manmade earth-orbiting satellites.[49] Throughout the remainder of the late 1940s and early 1950s, the USAF worked with the RAND Corporation and the Lockheed Corporation to further refine and detail the engineering needs to build and launch a military satellite for intelligence-gathering purposes. "Project 409-09: The Satellite Component Study" evolved into the WS-117L program in July 1956.[50] Though the WS-117L program encompassed more than just a photoreconnaissance satellite, one of the top priorities had been given to the Corona program by the Eisenhower administration.

Furthermore, based on the successful collaboration between the USAF and the CIA on the U-2 program, Eisenhower mandated that the CIA also be included in Corona with the USAF.[51] The Corona program and its "Key Hole" (KH) satellites become operational in February 1959 with the first launch of the satellite. Though the KH satellite and the Corona program were highly classified, the CIA and the USAF ran into a problem dealing with how to conceal the launches of the satellites from the public. To overcome this problem, the CIA and USAF included the Corona program within the civilian Discoverer satellite program. Therefore, although the public would be aware that there was a civilian launch of a Discoverer satellite, they would not truly know the exact contents of the payload topic of the launch vehicle.

Overall, the Corona program lasted from February 1959 until May 1972 and provided the United States with "2.1 million feet of film and 800,000 photographs, covering a total of 557 Million square miles."[52] The CIA, in it is official history of the Corona program, characterized it thus:

The totality of CORONA's contributions to U.S. Intelligence holdings on denied areas and to the U.S. space program in general is virtually unmeasurable. Its progress was marked by a series of notable firsts: the first to recover objects from orbit, the first to deliver intelligence information from a satellite, the first to produce stereoscopic satellite photography, the first to employ multiple re-entry vehicles, and the first satellite reconnaissance program to pass the 100-mission mark. By March 1964, CORONA had photographed 23 of the 25 Soviet ICBM complexes then in existence; three months later it had photographed all of them.

The value of CORONA to the U.S. intelligence effort is given dimension by this statement in a 1968 intelligence report: "No new ICBM complexes have been established in the USSR during the past year." So unequivocal a statement could be made only because of the confidence held by the analysts that if they were there, CORONA photography would have disclosed them.[53]

Beyond the ICBM complexes, the overhead spy satellites associated with Corona also located "all the Intermediate Range Ballistic missile sites, all the anti-ballistic missile sites, all warship bases, all submarine bases, in addition to other important military and industrial complexes" associated with the strategic power of the Soviet Union.[54] Furthermore, Corona and its series of Key Hole (KH) satellites provided keen intelligence on the conventional military capabilities of the Soviet Union's land forces and air forces. In its total of 120 successful flights, the Corona satellite program provided successive U.S. presidents with necessary intelligence on the strategic nuclear balance as well as the conventional force balance as a time of increased tension and uncertainty in the Cold War.

SPYING FROM SPACE: THE SOVIET UNION

Much like the United States and its need to have the most up-to-date intelligence on the strategic forces of the Soviet Union, the USSR faced a similar need. Although the Soviet Union had tried to rely on human sources to provide the necessary intelligence on the strategic forces development of the United States, this method of espionage proved lacking. With the onset of the space race in the late 1940s, the Soviet Union looked to space as a possibility to gather intelligence on the United States and thus maintain the strategic nuclear balance.

Though the history of the Soviet Union's early interest in the exploration of space is well known, the Soviet Union's desire to use space as a platform to gather intelligence on the military capabilities of the United States and its allies is much less developed and less known. The path to the development of the Soviet Union's first spy satellite started in 1948 when "a group of engineers, led by Colonel Mikhail Tikhonravov, initiated studies on the feasibility of artificial satellites."[55] When the group presented its studies to the Soviet Union's High Command, the High Command demoted Tikhonravov, because he was not authorized to use government resources to investigate a scientific issues that was deemed militarily insignificant.[56]

Despite this setback and the Soviet military's lack of interests in the potential of satellites, Tikhonravov resumed his work with a cadre of officials in the research institutes of Ministry of Aviation and the Ministry of Defense, Experimental Design Bureau. Mstislav Keldysh and Sergei Korolev, from the Ministry of Aviation and the Ministry of Defense, respectively, proved vital for Tikhonravov to continue his work. Both Keldysh and Korolev worked on rocket research and petitioned the Soviet Academy of Science for permission to continue research on artificial satellites, which could ultimately be mated with their research on intercontinental ballistic missiles.[57] In 1954, the Soviet Union was fully committed to designing and building strategic rocket forces, but Korolev and Keldysh assisted in keeping Tikhonravov's interest in satellites alive and funded.

In January 1956 the Soviet Union "secretly authorized the development of an artificial satellite, known as Object D."[58] Despite his initial reprimand, Tikhonravov had rehabilitated himself by improving the success of his work, and by 1957 he was placed in charge of satellite development for Object D.[59] Object D had two different components. The first involved simple satellites "designed to beat the Americans into space," which the world came to know as Sputnik I and Sputnik II, launched on October 4, 1957, and November 3, 1957, respectively.[60] The second component of Object D was the design, engineering, and construction of a photoreconnaissance satellite.[61] Object D-1, as the photographic spy satellite become know, had very similar design parameters to the Corona program being developed secretly in the United States at the same time. The OD-1 program as designed, however, had a deficiency: the mock-up of the designed satellite was impressive and very advanced; however, it was too heavy to be lifted into space by the rockets in the Soviet Union's inventory.[62]

As a result of the need to develop boosters with greater capacity to lift satellites into space, Korolev stepped in and assisted in redesigning the satellite. To build upon redundancy, and as a means to not waste precious resources, Korolev sought to redesign the satellite "to be compatible with Object D-2, which was a space vehicle designed to carry Soviet cosmonauts into space."[63] In May 1959, Khrushchev and the government of the Soviet Union approved the redesign of the various space vehicles streamlined by Korolev.[64]

The new family of spacecraft and satellites that shared many common components, as well as basic engineering and design features, came to be called Vostok, with successive numbers (e.g., Vostok 1, Vostok 2, and Vostok 3) to denote the different variations.[65] The spy satellite program, which shared "reentry and service module" compatibility with Vostok 1 (the manned space program), came to be called Zenit 2, and satellite required original research, design, and engineering of the electronics, cameras, and other components needed to produce a working photoreconnaissance satellite.[66] The Soviet Zenit 2 program faced many of the same hurdles the CIA and USAF engineers faced in designing and building the Discoverer/Corona satellites in the United States.

The work toward the completion of the Zenit 2 program began in 1961 with ambitions of building a spy satellite that could not only produce photographic intelligence but also send "near real time image signals" back to the Soviet Union for a much quicker assessment of the rapidly changing strategic environment.[67] The timing of the Soviet Union's quest to build a spy satellite is significant because, starting in the late 1950s, U.S. President Dwight D. Eisenhower had worked to streamline the strategic nuclear forces of the United States. As part of this process, the Eisenhower administration, in conjunction with the military services, developed the strategic nuclear triad.

This force structure, which integrated land-based intercontinental ballistic missiles (ICBMs), submarine-launched ballistic missiles (SLBMs), and land-based strategic bombers, posed a significant concern for the KGB, the Soviet military, and the government of the USSR. Therefore, in order to keep abreast of strategic force numbers, bases, and even deployments, the Soviet Union had to ensure that it had a very good understanding of the strategic nuclear forces held by the United States. Spy satellites proved a good way to maintain this vital intelligence, as both sides sought to use spaced-based assets for "national technical means of verification."[68]

The Soviet Union's spy satellite program paralleled the Corona/Discoverer program of the United States in several ways. First and foremost, like the United States, the Soviet Union used a scientific program as a cover for the reconnaissance satellite. The Vostok series of satellites, which led to an initial Soviet advantage in the early space age, provided the overall coverage for their development of spy satellites, which basically was the Zenit 2 photographic reconnaissance satellite.[69] Furthermore, the use of the Vostok cover program allowed the Soviet Union to publicly announce the launch of each satellite, while at the same time concealing the true intentions of the spy satellites within the Vostok program. This provided the Soviet Union with two distinct benefits. First, it allowed the Soviet Union to maintain its lead in the space race, which had the added benefit of showcasing its impressive scientific and engineering abilities around the globe. As the Cold War was a contest for building strong alliances, this definitely played in the favor of the Soviet Union. Second, the obfuscation of the Zenit 2 program within the Vostok program allowed the Soviet Union to essentially hide the satellite in plain sight, as the boosters and vehicles looked very much alike but had vastly different internal components.

The design parameters of the four cameras on the initial Zenit 2 satellites provided the Soviet Union with the ability to cover 60 x 180 kilometers with one camera with each pass of the satellites.[70] With each of the four cameras loaded with approximately "1,500 frames of film" and the ability to fly multiple-day missions (typically eight to twelve days per mission), the Zenit 2 spy satellite could cover approximately 14,400 square kilometers, or "more than the entire territory of the United States."[71] The Fluorite 2R cameras on the Zenit satellite were not just designed for wide-angle coverage; they also had a reported resolution of 10–15 meters, which could easily provide the Soviet Union with the necessary means to decipher the location and number of the strategic nuclear forces of the United States.[72]

In addition to collecting photographic intelligence, the Zenit 2 program also possessed the ability to collect signals intelligence and electronic intelligence.[73] As mentioned in earlier chapters, the need to collect signals and electronic intelligence on communications and air defense radars was a primary mission of the espionage efforts by both sides during the Cold War. The inclusion of these capabilities on the Zenit 2 satellite effectively provided the Soviet Union with a primary spy satellite that could collect three types of intelligence needed to assess the strategic nuclear balance throughout the 1960s.

The means of retrieving the intelligence from the Zenit 2 program was relatively straightforward. Having worked out the issue with deorbiting and reentry with the Vostok program, the film pods from the Zenit 2 satellites were simply jettisoned and deorbited over the territory of the Soviet Union and retrieved once they had landed. The transmission of signals and electronic intelligence took place as the satellite passed over "ground control centers."[74] Although the Soviet Union had had success with recovering vehicles from space on August 20, 1960, the operational capability of the Zenit 2 spy satellite took roughly three more years of testing before the Soviet Union had its operational spy satellite.[75]

Although the Soviet spy satellite had some parallels with the Corona program, there was one major difference: the Soviet spy satellite program was a project that was entirely funded, engineered, and run by the military.[76] In fact, the military bureaucracy of the Soviet Union adapted and absorbed the spy satellites. The primary recipient of the intelligence was the Chief Intelligence Directorate (GRU) of the Soviet Armed Forces' General Staff.[77] The intelligence gathered by the Zenit 2 mission provided not only critical information but also the necessary information to build targets sets for the Soviet Union's strategic nuclear forces.

It is important to note that although both the United States and the Soviet Union tended to claim that the use of satellite-gathered intelligence was a means to maintain balance in the tense strategic environment, because it provided a means from which either side could assess the capabilities of their main adversary, each side also used the photographs to produce target sets and strategic nuclear war plans in the event that the Cold War turned hot. By the time the Zenit 2 family of Soviet spy satellites flew for the last time in May 1970, a second-generation Zenit 4 program was already in production.[78] By the end of the 1960s, both the United States and the Soviet Union actively used space for the purpose of gathering a wide variety of intelligence; the espionage game had definitely shifted into a new frontier. Interestingly enough, both the Soviet Union and the United States at times worked to ban weapons from space, but both saw the need to use space for espionage, as it provided a "constant monitoring of the rivals to learn and verify the real military potential of the opposite."[79] The great secrecy both sides used to hide their use of space for intelligence-gathering purposes eventually evolved into the use of the term "national means of verification," which provided the United States and the Soviet Union with confidence in their intelligence assets to embark on strategic arms control negotiations, because each side could use its "national means of verification" to ensure that the other was not cheating to gain a strategic advantage. Hence, the use of satellites for spying provided a stabilizing force of the strategic nuclear balance. However, as the espionage game expanded to included space-based assets, terrestrial issues still drove intelligence operations, especially in Southeast Asia.

INDOCHINA AND THE VIETNAM WAR

Although the Cold War had expanded into outer space, and the espionage game between the United States and Soviet Union followed suit, the 1960s also saw the apogee of the CIA's use of paramilitary forces. The French War in Indochina and the subsequent involvement of the United States in Vietnam from 1954 until 1973 also served as the apogee of the CIA's use of large-scale paramilitary operations, a role that had been expanding since the origination of the intelligence agency in 1947. The fiasco that Vietnam became had an immediate effect on the CIA, as in the immediate years after Vietnam, the agency moved back toward the collection and interpretation of intelligence and would only timidly embrace paramilitary roles in the last two decades of the Cold War.

As for the KGB, the Soviet Union had KGB officers in Vietnam, but it more or less saw Vietnam as a great opportunity to damage the international image of the United States by using the presence of the United States as an action to unite the Third World, which was the new focus of the Brezhnev Doctrine.[80] Also, the KGB saw the war in Vietnam as a great opportunity to gather battlefield intelligence on U.S. equipment, to pass on to the GRU in an effort to make sure that Soviet and Warsaw Pact military equipment was on par or better than their U.S. counterparts. The need for the Soviet Union to gather intelligence on the technical capability of the U.S. military was a mainstay of focus for the Soviet intelligence services.

It is interesting to note, however, that the relationship between the North Vietnamese and the KGB was fraught with tension, yet at the strategic level, the Soviet Union capitalized on the adventurism of United States against the Vietnamese people.[81] The ability of the KGB to recognize the opportunity to use Vietnam as a means to build great support within the Third World, specifically in Africa and Latin America, seemed to pay dividends for them in the 1970s and early 1980s, but it would ultimately collapse as the Soviet Union suffered from systemic social, economic, and political problems in the late 1980s.[82] From the position of the United States and the CIA, though, Vietnam had to be saved from succumbing to the encroachment of communism.

The CIA's involvement with Indochina and, ultimately, Vietnam started with the French colonial war in Indochina in 1945 and would last until after the end of U.S. involvement in 1973. It would finally wither with the North Vietnamese victory in 1975.[83] From its original concerns about the stability and longevity of the regime of Ngo Dinh Diem, the CIA focused on the ability of South Vietnam to stand as a stable, independent nation in Southeast Asia. Of particular concern through the Eisenhower administration was the growing power of the North Vietnamese military and the National Liberation Front in the South. Consistently, in national intelligence estimates presented to President Eisenhower and his national security staff, the CIA had "pessimistic analysis" about the potential for U.S. success in Vietnam.[84] Despite the concerns voiced by the CIA, by the time John F. Kennedy had been elected president, Vietnam became a much harder venue to for the CIA to divert Kennedy's attention away from.

Kennedy took a hard stance against the expansion of communism and saw South Vietnam as a vital ally in the context of the Cold War. However, neither the president nor Secretary of Defense Robert S. McNamara heeded the advice of the CIA. Peer de Silva CIA Station Chief, in Saigon recounted that after a briefing on the enemy and its capabilities in Vietnam, McNamara:

simply had no comprehension of the nature of the conflict in Vietnam, let alone any idea of how it should be handled. As time wore on, he [McNamara] demonstrated that he only believed in the application of military force.[85]

De Silva's observation focused on the imperative pushed by the Kennedy Administration that "it was time to go on the offensive," a position that was a fundamental change from the policies and ideas developed by the Eisenhower administration.[86] From an operational perspective, this meant that the CIA had an expanded mission in Vietnam that included moving beyond just "intelligence reporting on the operations and intentions of the Vietcong and later working within Operation Phoenix to suppress the influence of cultivation of Vietcong operatives."[87] From 1962 onward, this new move to be a stronger tool for the United States to achieve success in Southeast Asia meant that the CIA had to be increasingly involved in the development, training, and support of anticommunist troops and tribes in Laos and Vietnam.[88] Although the CIA had vast experience with training paramilitary forces in Central Europe, Eastern Europe, and Latin America, its role in Vietnam expanded well beyond its previous paramilitary endeavors. The CIA's support of and work with Hmong tribes in the mountains of Vietnam and the paramilitary forces in Laos in an attempt to shift the tide of the war toward the side of the United States and South Vietnam came to be a costly, demanding, and huge set of operations that stressed the abilities of the agency. Furthermore, under the direction of Admiral William F. Raborn Jr., who had become the new DCI in April 1965, the CIA increasingly became focused on how it could be a better asset to Lyndon B. Johnson and his Military Assistance Command Vietnam (MACV) and their efforts to "win the war."[89] The general consensus within the CIA was that the war was not going to be won; however, it became an active and willing participant in the U.S. war effort. This drove the CIA to further expand and embrace the paramilitary mission, which had always been a secondary mission behind intelligence gathering. By the end of U.S. involvement in Vietnam, the CIA had a tarnished reputation that took decades to repair.

CONCLUSIONS

In many ways the period of 1961–1968 represents a significant period in the evolution of the espionage game between the United States and the Soviet Union. First and foremost, the period saw the continuation of the use of the CIA as an intelligence-gathering apparatus, but it also saw the height of its expansion as a paramilitary force. The use of the CIA as the primary agency to plan, train, and conduct the operation at the Bay of Pigs in Cuba proved to be the high-water mark of the U.S. president using the intelligence agency as a paramilitary force. Though this function had been building and evolving since the first days of the agency in 1947, the apogee of its evolution culminated with the fiasco at the Bay of Pigs.

Even though the military failure in Cuba had an impact on the CIA, the agency and the successive U.S. presidential administrations under Lyndon B. Johnson and Richard Nixon could not completely break away from the paramilitary component of the CIA during America's involvement in Vietnam. Being involved in Vietnam, and especially in operations associated with the Phoenix Project, the CIA still toyed with paramilitary operations, but these would wither and assume a different character in the last two decades of the Cold War.

While the CIA toiled with its proper role in intelligence and paramilitary operations, the KGB stayed focused on building a more robust intelligence-gathering network in the United States. While still trying to recapture the long-lost networks of the 1920s and 1930s, the KGB had some success with placing both legal and illegal operatives within the United States. However, the effectiveness of these sources was questionable as they had limited access to the corridors of power and decision making within the U.S. government. The largest success the KGB extrapolated from the 1960s was that it could use the adventurism of both the CIA and the U.S. military as a way to bolster the KGB's appeal to third world countries. Though this propaganda effort paid some dividends in the late 1960s and through the early 1970s and likewise fit well within the tenets of Brezhnev's doctrine to cultivate support within Africa and Latin America, it did not provide the Central Committee and the commanders of the KGB with the keen insights they sought about the military and strategic potential of the United States within the context of the Cold War.

Though this action-reaction paradigm seemed to mimic the early days of intelligence operations in the 1940s, the 1960s also witnessed the developed and proliferation of the use of space-based assets to collect the very-much-obsessed-over strategic intelligence. During the 1960s both the United States and the Soviet Union developed and deployed a wide variety of space-based assets designed to collect photographic, electronic, and signals intelligence on each other. The use of space-based intelligence-gathering platforms transitioned the Cold War espionage game into a new era in which both the Soviet Union and the United States saw the value of investing and using space as a new domain from which they could collect much-needed strategic and military intelligence on each other. Even though both nations saw the use of outer space as an expansion of the espionage game, the way each nation integrated space based assets into its intelligence-gathering repertoire represented divergent paths that will be highlighted in following chapters, and they also had a profound impact on how the CIA and KGB would continue to play the espionage game for the duration of the Cold War.

Ultimately, the 1960s represents a series of almost paradoxical themes. First, the CIA fully embraced the paramilitary mission, which had been a serious point of debate within the agency since its inception, as well as within the minds of U.S. presidents since Harry S. Truman. At the end of the era, between the Bay of Pigs and Vietnam, the agency would move away from this flirtation with paramilitary operations.

The KGB, while still firmly committed to building a robust human-based intelligence-gathering network on its primary adversary, saw the usefulness of exploiting outer space and advanced technologies as potential ways to gain much-needed intelligence on the capabilities of the Western world. Hence, this transition demonstrated that the KGB and the Soviet Union were not just interested in exploiting human-based intelligence during the Cold War but also had the advanced technical capabilities and means necessary to also build spy satellites that could gather intelligence that, when combined with other means of intelligence, would provide a much greater picture and understanding of the United States. Despite the seemingly paradoxical nature between HUMINT and advanced techno-logical means, the espionage game continued to evolve through the culmi-nation of the Cold War.

CHAPTER 5

Détente and Ostpolitik, 1968–1976

By 1968 the Cold War was well into its third decade. As the United States and Soviet Union had already established well-defined spheres of influence around the globe, the intelligence agencies on both sides had continued to expand their capabilities beyond the use of officers and agents to collect intelligence. Space and electronic had become yet other sources for the ever-increasing demand for more intelligence as the Cold War evolved. However, the period between 1968 and 1976 represents a shift in the trajectory of the espionage game that had been evolving since the Soviet Union's success in penetrating the Manhattan Project. Within this period of reduced cooler tension between the superpowers, the espionage agencies of the United States and the Soviet Union faced very different obstacles and had very different perspectives on the nature of the espionage game.

From the position of the CIA, the sustained stress of the war in Vietnam and the continuous operations around the globe combating the forces of communism had begun to take their toll on the clandestine service. Moreover, as the 1960s transitioned to the 1970s, the growing youth culture in the United States became increasingly suspicious of secretive government organizations. Therefore, the CIA had to focus on its core mission, yet at the same time defend its clandestine nature as a means to pursue the overall policies and programs of the United States.

However, due the release of the Pentagon papers and the testimony of William Colby before congressional hearings into the practices of the CIA over the previous years, especially regarding plots to assassinate world leaders, by the end of the period, the CIA found itself in a position wherein it had to defend its actions and operations of the past. Furthermore, Congress and, to some degree, the American people wanted greater depth of knowledge of the operations and capabilities of the primary spy agency of the United States. The CIA was forced to provide some details of its operational past and make admissions that some of their operations had less than ethical components, but yet were designed to further U.S. national interests within the context of the fight against communist expansion.

This period for the CIA represents a low point from which the agency would have to regain its focus and the public trust slowly. U.S. President Gerald R. Ford characterized the beginning of this process in 1974, when he stated in his memoirs:

I met with Colby in the Oval Office and learned—for the first time—about what the agency executives referred to as the "family jewels." These were highly classified documents that provided details about unsavory and illegal CIA practices. In the 1950s and 1960s, the CIA had plotted to assassinate foreign leaders, including Fidel Castro. Although none of these assassinations had been carried out, the fact that government officials had even considered them was distressing. In the aftermath of Watergate, it was important that we be totally aboveboard about these past abuses and avoid giving any substance to charges that we were engaging in a "cover-up."[1]

Though the CIA had to suffer through a period of public scrutiny and some congressional investigations, the agency did not waver from its mission. Even when the CIA had to curtail some of its more "ambitious" missions, intelligence service still maintained a robust capability to gather the necessary political, diplomatic, economic, and social intelligence necessary to further the objectives of the United States in the global mission to contain communism. Of particular interest is that during this period, the CIA relied more on advanced technological capabilities to gather intelligence as a means to move away from the waning effect of using human officers and agents to collect strategic intelligence. Though the CIA never completely abandoned human intelligence-gathering practices, this period represents a crossover point when the agency focused its efforts on other means, especially from high altitude and space.

The perspective of the Soviet Union and the KGB was substantially different from the CIA's outlook. Based on the diminishing global influence of the United States in the aftermath of the Vietnam War, the KGB believed that the tide had turned and that the malaise of the United States represented a great opportunity to recast the Soviet Union's efforts in the global struggle. Believing that the "world was going their way," the KGB's leaders sought to capitalize on this opportunity and expand their clandestine operations into Africa and Latin America as a way to build greater partnerships in the global struggle.

Though the KGB had paralleled the CIA in the development of satellites and advanced espionage techniques, the Soviet Union in many ways saw the late 1960s and early 1970s as a prime opportunity to build on the perceived shifting dynamic within the Cold War espionage game, which appeared to be skewing against the capabilities of the United States. To benefit from this opportunity, the KGB once again invested in heavy

HUMINT capabilities that provided insights and intelligence that could only be gathered by traditional means.

Furthermore, the KGB had a series of U.S. citizens who brazenly offered unique military secrets to the KGB leaders in Moscow. Though the KGB believed itself to be in the midst of an espionage renaissance, the Soviet Union's intelligence service did realize that the technological capabilities of the United States had begun to outclass the capabilities of the Soviet Union. Therefore, this period of détente and Ostpolitik has a unique duality from the perspective of the KGB. The primary point was that the KGB believed that it had at least regenerated a robust intelligence-gathering network in the United States and around the globe, which seemed to coincide with the waning influence of the United States in the post-Vietnam and post-Watergate world. Second, and in many ways related to the first, was the recognition that the technology in U.S. weapons was becoming more advanced, which drove the KGB to focus its intelligence-gathering efforts on gaining insights into these new capabilities and advancements.

As in the 1930s and 1940s, the Soviet Union's obsession stayed fixated on using human resources as the best means to collect this vital information. This unique period in the context of the global Cold War provided the KGB with the opportunity to regain what it had lost in the late 1940s when communist intelligence networks inside the United States collapsed.

This chapter, therefore, provides an overview of how the CIA and the KGB viewed their respective positions and attempted to either rebuild their efforts or to maximize their capabilities in the period between 1968 and 1976. With this in mind, the underlying theme of the evolution of the espionage game will be woven into the dynamic history of this critical period of the Cold War.

THE CHANGING ENVIRONMENT AND SHIFTING THE OPERATIONAL ETHOS

In 1968 the CIA had developed and evolved well beyond its original capacity as envisioned in 1947. However, having reached the 20-year mark, the agency faced a rapidly changing domestic environment as well as a very different international security environment. Vietnam was, of course, a catalyst for at least part of this adjustment, but the strategic nuclear balance was yet another issue that affected the CIA in this new era of espionage.

Within the CIA, questions about U.S. involvement in Vietnam began to mimic the popular debate raging across the United States. John Ranelagh quotes a CIA officer who characterized the impact of Vietnam within the agency:

In the early 1960s, before we had a heavy involvement in Vietnam, there were more people who would have said that by a minimal effort we could have contained the situation. But the number of people who continued to believe that dwindled very rapidly once we had our own heavy involvement. Some were true believers, some were not. There was a breaking up of the consensus. People who followed the subject had their belief about it matured by events. In the Office of National Estimates in the late 1960s and early 1970s the people who actually worked the subject were themselves as passionate in their minds and in their instincts about it as the people demonstrating in the streets.[2]

The net effect was that CIA was suffering internal dissent while at the same time besieged by the increasing suspicion of a growing segment of the population in the United States that deeply distrusted the actions—especially covert actions—of the U.S. government. This growing distrust, which originated in the days and months prior to the Tet Offensive, only grew in the aftermath of the fighting in Vietnam.[3] However, the attacks did not just come from the outside; former CIA officer Philip Agee wrote a book wherein he stated his disillusionment with the goals, objectives, and operations of his former employer:

At last I am finding the proper course. Behind these decisions have been the continuation of the Vietnam War and the Vietnamization program. Now more than ever exposure of CIS methods could help American people understand how we got into Vietnam and how our other Vietnams are germinating wherever the CIA is at work. . . .

I have also decided to seek ways of getting useful information on the CIA to revolutionary organizations that could use it to defend themselves better. . . .

Increasingly, as the oppressed in capitalist society comprehend the myth of liberal reform, their ruling minorities have no choice but to increase repression and order to avert socialist revolution. Eliminate CIA stations, US military missions, AID Pubic Safety missions, and "free" trade-union program and those minorities would disappear, faster perhaps, than they themselves would imagine.[4]

Though Agee's sentiments represented a growing distrust of the U.S. government and especially the CIA due to its inherent covert nature, Agee's commitment to the United States had long been suspect. In fact, after his departure from the CIA, which is disputed as "being fired" or "disillusioned," Agee ended up in Cuba, which is where he wrote his book while also launching a crusade to publicize the names and operations of the CIA.[5] Some reports indicate that Agee ended up working for Fidel Castro's intelligence service, and Agee also allegedly received support and endorsements from the KGB.[6] Nevertheless, Agee's attack came at a time when the CIA was undergoing a major shift.

Prior to the transition between the administrations of Lyndon Johnson and Richard Nixon, Richard Helms assumed the DCI position in the CIA with the departure of William Radford. Helms ushered in a new era in the CIA. Helms had learned from his decades of experience in covert operations that the bold and rapid expansion of the CIA's paramilitary powers had significant drawbacks, especially within the shifting domestic mood in the United States.

Helms ushered in a new era of professionalism that saw the CIA deemphasize operations such as the Bay of Pigs in favor of more traditional missions of providing strategic intelligence to the president of the United States. This shift took the CIA out of the policy-advocating role into which it had slowly crept during the Eisenhower and Kennedy administrations. Helms saw to it that the CIA settled back into the policy support role, which had been an original mission of the organization in the aftermath of World War II. A necessary part of this transition process was to smooth over the ever-present tension between the CIA and Congress. Although Congress had at times tried to exercise greater oversight control of the CIA and its activities, the executive-level agency always had enough support to stifle any major adjustments to its independence. However, in the wake of growing distrust due to Vietnam, the U.S. Senate again tried to establish a "formal oversight committee."[7] However, Helms was able to subvert such a change, but he did offer a significant increase in the number of CIA briefings to congressional committees and subcommittees. This overture reinforced Helms's desire to reinforce the CIA's characterization as a professional, executive-level institution that supported the policies and strategic objectives of the United States.

Despite the renewed interest in reorienting the CIA toward its more traditional and professional position of collecting and analyzing information, the agency ran into in phenomena that can only be called institutional bias. As President Johnson initiated what would become negotiations with the Soviet Union centering on arms control agreements covering strategic nuclear weapons and ballistic missile defenses. These efforts eventually produced the Strategic Arms Limitation Talks (SALT) under President Richard M. Nixon in 1972, the CIA had to fight consistently with the Nixon administration as to its projections and assessments of the rapidly changing strategic nuclear balance between the United States and the Soviet Union.

The largest issues stemming from this period deal with the Soviet Union's interest in stabilizing the strategic nuclear balance, or even moving to shift it in their favor. The Johnson administration, and later the Nixon administration, became very focused on the intentions and capabilities of the Soviet Union to deploy new generations of ICBMs. Within the National Intelligence Estimates (NIEs), which provided the president of the United States a strategic overview of the global security environment, the CIA also forecast the future capabilities of the Soviet Union's strategic forces; however, there was growing concern within the Nixon administration that the CIA was soft-pedaling its estimates to the president in favor of promoting an "arms control bias."[8]

Secretary of Defense Melvin Laird and National Security Advisor Henry Kissinger worked to make sure that the NIEs provided the right trend, which synchronized with the Nixon's administrations idea that the Soviet Union was working toward shifting the strategic nuclear balance in its favor. The major point of contention over the intelligence that the Soviet Union had begun to move construction equipment and other indicators of building new missile silos within the Soviet Union focused on the whether or not these were "new" silos for new missiles, or if it was simply the case of hardening existing silos to provide the Soviet Union with an increased deterrent force of existing land-based missiles.

As the CIA faced yet another series of questions about its professional ability to provide reliable intelligence to influence and shape U.S. strategic policy, Albert Wohlstetter, academic and noted nuclear strategist, presented a paper that provided the Nixon administration, as well as outside academic experts such as William T. Lee and William R. Van Cleave, the firm evidence that they needed to prove that the CIA was indeed underestimating the capabilities and future intentions of the Soviet Union.[9] Combined with congressional interest with the CIA's actions in Vietnam in the very late 1960s and very early 1970s, the CIA seemed to be falling from its once-vaulted position.

The onslaught against the CIA did not stop at future ICBMs; it also centered on the Soviet Union's ability to produce and deploy multiple independently targetable reentry vehicles (MIRVs) and multiple reentry vehicles (MRVs) on the ICBMs. The Department of Defense (DOD), Laird, and Kissinger strongly held that the USSR was moving toward MIRV technology and warheads. The CIA was not convinced and suggested that the other agencies were mistaking MRV for MIRV. A passage from the national intelligence estimate of the period highlights this internal debate. The assessment was as follows:

We believe that the Soviets recognize the enormous difficulties of any attempt to achieve strategic superiority of such order as to significantly alter the strategic balance. Consequently, we consider it highly unlikely that they will attempt within the period of this estimate [1969–1973] to achieve a first strike capability, i.e., a capability to launch a surprise attack against the U.S. with assurance that the USSR would not itself receive damage it would regard as unacceptable. For one thing, the Soviets would almost certainly conclude that the cost of such an undertaking along with all their other military commitments would be prohibitive. More important, they almost certainly would consider it impossible to develop and deploy the combination of offensive and defensive forces necessary to counter successfully the various elements of U.S. strategic attack forces. Finally, even if such a project were economically and technically feasible the Soviets would almost certainly calculate that the U.S. would detect and match or overmatch their efforts.[10]

This assessment—that the Soviet Union was not moving toward a more aggressive first strike posture—contradicted the belief of Melvin Laird,

Henry Kissinger, and even civilian academics like William R. Van Cleave.[11] Yet the CIA was portrayed as an agency that was not in line with the administration's read of the strategic environment.

The reality was that in the early 1970s, the CIA was in a massive adjustment period, and it had to refocus its priorities and redefine how it wanted to continue to provide strategic intelligence to the United States. Although, from an internal perspective, the intelligence agency seemed to be suffering from the changes as a result of Vietnam as well as the shifting political environment within the United States, the CIA still had strong national technical means that continued to provide sound and good intelligence for the United States. The interpretation of what the intelligence meant was the reality of the debate.

However, despite the apparent withering of the CIA, the spies in Langley still had jobs to do. In a nod to its original operations in Europe under the tenure of Harry S. Truman, the CIA refocused on its ability to shape internal international elections when President Richard M. Nixon was concerned about Chile and the leftist direction the nation seemed to be heading. Having learned valuable lessons from earlier operations in Guatemala, Iran, and Cuba, the CIA embraced older techniques, tactics, and procedures from France and Italy in order to shape the outcome of elections in Chile.

PRESIDENT NIXON, THE CIA, AND CHILE

Harkening back to its earlier successes in operations in France and Italy in the years immediately after World War II, the CIA during the Nixon administration moved away from the paramilitary activities that had garnered it far too much public attention since the Bay of Pigs fiasco and embraced a more nostalgic role in influencing elections, specifically in Chile.

Within the first year of his presidential term, Richard Nixon had received intelligence that the nation of Chile in South America had been receiving covert support from the KGB in an effort to make sure that the Marxist Salvador Allende Gossens would be the next president of Chile.[12] Now, the Nixon administration did not know that the KGB had in fact been cultivating a relationship with Allende since his showing of some national political promise in the late 1950s.[13] However, the Soviet Union had some reservations about Allende because he was not a member of the Chilean Communist Party and would run for the presidency of Chile within a coalition of leftist parties, which encompassed communists, socialists, and populists, under the banner of the Unidad Popular (UP) party.[14] The KGB understood, however, that in 1970 Allende stood a good chance to win the election. Therefore, although he was just a "contact," never a full-fledged "agent," the KGB decided to lend its covert support to his election campaign.[15]

Allende's Marxist past and his leftist leaning, backed by intelligence of his association with the KGB, was enough to convince the United States and especially President Nixon that the Soviet Union was making a play in Chile, and therefore, the United States had to act.[16] However, Nixon faced a dilemma. Earlier in his first year in office, Nixon supported the democratic efforts of Chile largely advanced by Eduardo Frei, who had won the 1964 presidential election in Chile, with substantial fiscal assistance from the CIA.[17] As such, Nixon publicly announced he would support "Chilean problems being solve by Chile," believing that the people of Chile would sustain their support of Frei.[18] The crux of the dilemma was that Nixon did not want the socialists to win power in the election of 1970, as recent intelligence seemed to indicate was likely. Even though the Nixon administration authorized the use of approximately $500,000 dollars to assist in covertly supporting nonsocialist parties to defeat Allende in the national election, the efforts of the CIA failed. Interestingly enough, as the United States used the CIA to try and sway the 1970s elections in Chile, the KGB and the Soviet Union were doing the same.[19]

The two primary intelligence agencies were not the only interested parties in the political election in Chile. The International Telephone and Telegraph Corporation (ITT) and Anaconda Copper were two U.S.-based international businesses that were very concerned about a socialist victory in Chile and had the contacts to approach the U.S. government.[20] The primary concern of ITT and Anaconda was that a win by Allende would be followed by a "nationalization of assets," and hence, each company would lose all of its infrastructure and access to Chilean markets.

Therefore, each company offered assistance to the U.S. government in the run-up to the election. Anaconda, through channels and connections in the State Department, offered the U.S. government $500,000 U.S. dollars to assist in the support campaign activity to defeat Allende.[21] ITT, on the other hand, had a connection with the CIA, as John McCone, former DCI (1961–1965), was a member of its board of directors.[22] McCone approached DCI, Richard Helms, and offered $1 million to assist in the CIA's efforts to sway the elections away from the socialists.[23] Although private U.S. corporations offered direct assistant to the CIA and the State Department, Richard Helms, relying on an NIE from 1968 that held that "forces of social reform in Chile are too strong to be manipulated from outside influence," suggested that McCone and ITT use their money directly with other corporations and contacts in Chile, which he supplied to McCone.[24] The efforts did not fare any better than the CIA's own attempts covertly to persuade Chileans to vote against Allende. On September 4, 1970, Salvador Allende Gossens won the popular election in Chile. However, the both United States and the Soviet Union were not fully satisfied with the outcome, as Allende still had to win a "confirmation election" by the Chilean Congress on October 24, 1970.

From the position of the Soviet Union, and specifically Yuri Andropov, head of the KGB (1967–1982), there was still concern about the need to maintain covert support for Allende. Andropov reported in September 1970 to the Central Committee of the Soviet Union:

As the question of the election of the President will finally be decided by a vote in Congress on 24 October, Allende is still faced with a determined struggle with his political opponents, and substantial material resources may still be required for this purpose. With the aim of strengthening confidential relations with Allende and creating conditions for continuing cooperation with him in the future, it would be expedient to give him material assistance amounting to 30,000 dollars if the need arises.

At the same time, the Committee of State Security [KGB] will carry out measures designed to promote the consolidation of Allende's victory and his election to the post of President of the country.[25]

Hence the KGB wanted to make sure it saw its support for Allende through to the final confirmation vote, as the Soviet Union's spies believed they were very close to a victory.

From the perspective of President Nixon, the popular election results in September were a disaster and demanded even great attention from the United States. In fact, the election of Allende was such a surprise that Henry Kissinger later remarked:

Had I believed in the spring and summer of 1970 that there was a significant likelihood of an Allende victory, I would have had an obligation to the President to give him an opportunity to consider a covert action program of 1964 proportions, including the backing on a single candidate. I was resentful that this option had been foreclosed without even being discussed.[26]

The simple fact was that President Nixon and key members in his administration were shocked at Allende's victory in Chile and focused intently on trying to correct this significant issue that they had not been able to influence in the months prior to the election. As such, Nixon demanded action. The administration, with the help of the CIA, devised a two-track strategy to evict Allende from power. The first track aimed at "making the economy scream."[27] By using this phrase President Nixon meant that through diplomatic, business, and covert means, the United States would attempt to influence the Chilean economy. Nixon's thinking was that with a poor economy, the Chilean Congress and people would remove Allende from power. This also allowed Nixon to stay true to his pledge that he would allow Chileans to solve Chile's problems, at least in the public sphere. The main effort of the first track would be the purview of the State Department using the U.S. Ambassador to Chile Edward Korry, along with business connections such as ITT and Anaconda Copper, to pursue an improvised attempt to portray Allende's presidency as bad for the Chilean economy and its people.

With his objective, and in line with the tenets of Track I, Ambassador Korry mentioned to outgoing President Frei and senior military commanders that "if Allende was allowed to become president of Chile, all military aid would stop and that not a nut or bolt would be allowed to reach the country."[28] Again, this track aimed at "allowing" Chileans to make their own decisions, albeit with significant encouragement from the United States as the CIA attempted to break the Chilean economy and remove Allende from power.

Track II had a much more forceful objective. Nixon wanted the CIA to build a plan for a coup d'état against Allende and asked Richard Helms to put the agency's best men on the job.[29] Furthermore, Nixon did not want the any details of Track II to be leaked to the State Department or Ambassador Korry. They were to be kept totally in the dark that the CIA, with the express approval of President Nixon, was also working to directly overthrow Allende.[30] The CIA, and Helms specifically, were not happy with the president's plans for Track II.[31] The reality was that the CIA had a much better understanding of the internal dynamics of Chilean politics and the military specifically. The first problem was that the CIA could not find an ideal candidate to lead the coup, as the top two primary leaders, President Eduardo Frei and General Rene Schneider, were known to be "constitutionalists who were unwilling to take illegal action" to derail Allende's presidency.[32] The second major issue faced by Helms was that he did not want the CIA to conduct, or even support, any indigenous assassination operations against Allende.[33]

The CIA had very limited options and even less time to achieve its objective. The men identified by the CIA for this sensitive operation were retired Chilean General Robert Viaux and General Camilo Valenzuela.[34] However, both Viaux and Valenzuela had limited support within the Chilean military, so long as General Schneider still remained true to his constitutional principles.[35]

To move forward with the operation, Viaux communicated back to the CIA that his plans for a coup would first start with a kidnapping of General Schneider, and with this obstacle removed, the full-blown coup could move forward. The CIA was deeply skeptical that the plan would work. Based on his assessment of the success of Viaux's plan, the CIA's officer in charge of the operation, Thomas Karamessines, met with Henry Kissinger and Alexander Haig to discuss the lengths to which the United States would go to continue to support Viaux's coup plans. After this consultation, which happened on October 15, the CIA sent the following message to Viaux:

We have reviewed your plans and based on your information and ours, we come to the conclusion that your plans for a coup at this time cannot succeed. Failing, they may reduce your capabilities in the future. Preserve your assets. We will stay in touch. The time will come when you with all your other friends can do something. You will have our support.[36]

Despite the message from the CIA, Viaux and Valenzuela moved forward with their plans to kidnap Schneider and initiate a coup. The first attempt to kidnap Schneider failed on October 19. The second attempt took place on October 22 and ended badly when General Schneider defended himself from the kidnappers with a pistol, for which he was subsequently shot.[37] Due to the botched operation, Viaux and Valenzuela were arrested, tried, and sentenced. However, more importantly, the CIA had not been implicated, as the October 15 message clearly indicated that the CIA did not authorize the coup. The result of the events in September and October 1970 was that no further coup attempts were carried out, as the CIA believed that the conditions had at least been set for the Chilean military to follow a path forward, if they so choose.[38] In September 1973 General Augusto Pinochet led a junta that launched a coup against Allende and finally achieved the end state that President Nixon had wanted three years earlier.

Though the Nixon administration's obsession with Allende going communist dwindled with Pinochet's coup, the Soviet Union was indeed making a play to ensure closer ties with Allende and Chile. In fact, as was noted earlier, the KGB had provided assistance to Allende as he ran his campaign. Furthermore, the support to Allende did not dry up after his election.[39] Reports from KGB officers in Chile writing back to Moscow stated that:

In a cautious way Allende was made to understand the necessity of reorganizing Chile's army and intelligence services, and of setting up a relationship between Chile's and the USSR's intelligence services. Allende reacted to this positively.[40]

Knowing that Nixon and the CIA had a two-track plan to derail Allende's elections enticed the KGB to maintain a closer relationship with Allende. The KGB cultivated this position by passing on information of the CIA's support of the two tracks.[41] Also, the KGB made sure that Allende was well aware of the CIA's work to support a coup against his regime. The overall objective by the KGB and Moscow was to increase the presence of the Soviet Union at a time when the United States seemed most vulnerable. Allende and Chile represented a great opportunity for Andropov and the KGB to establish a big win for the Soviet Union, though it had to been done in a deliberate manner, so as to not arouse the suspicions of Nixon and the CIA.

The need to be discreet in the KGB's operations to cultivate allies in Latin America was reinforced by Andropov in 1972 when he wrote:

The main thing is to keep our finger on the pulse of events, and obtain multifaceted information about the situation there [Chile and Peru], and about the correlation of forces. It is necessary to direct the course of events, and make sure that events do not catch us unawares, so that we don't have any surprises, and will be aware of the very first tremors of approaching changes and events-thus enabling us to report them to the leadership in a time manner.

There is one particular question which perhaps does not affect us [The KGB] directly, but which cannot be avoided, and that is the interpretation that the events in Chile and Peru have received in our press, and the emphasis that has been placed on the role of the Soviet Union there. One gets the impression that the [Soviet] press is doing too much boasting and bragging.[42]

Based on Andropov's written comments, the Soviet Union had to be much better at not boasting so much about seemingly besting the United States in Chile, as the political situation in Chile was leaning toward, but was far from being stabilized and firmly committed to, the Soviet Union. Andropov's advice to his officers in Chile was as follows:

Do not permit anything that would cause complaints about our activity in Chile and Peru.

Do not force the establishment of liaison with the [intelligence] service in Chile. Arouse their interest by passing them intelligence of a topical nature.[43]

In essence, the Soviet Union's head spy, Yuri Andropov, simply instructed his officers in Chile to only provide the Allende regime with intelligence about the CIA's efforts to topple the regime as a means to build increased trust between the Soviet Union and Chile. Andropov and the KGB knew that Allende could be spooked easily; therefore, they had to be slow and cautious about building a strong, reliable relationship. As the CIA continued to press the Chilean economy throughout 1972, Andropov and the KGB made sure to keep feeding Allende intelligence about the CIA's actions as they attempted to break his regime.

The KGB was also focused on the upcoming parliamentary elections in the spring of 1973 and began to make arrangements yet again to provide Allende with fiscal support, starting with $100,000 as a means to demonstrate the KGB's willingness to maintain and even strengthen the relationship between the USSR and Chile.[44] Since his election, the KGB had been happy with its success, and as the elections of 1973 appeared on the horizon, it maintained that its delicate approach with Allende was paying off.[45]

However, despite the optimistic assessment provided by the KGB, Allende's position at the head of the Chilean government was tenuous at best. In the parliamentary elections of March 1973, Allende's Unidad party only secured 44 percent of the popular vote, whereas the majority of the vote went to the rival opposition parties. The KGB and Andropov failed to explain to Soviet Premier Leonid Brezhnev why their support for Allende and his party did not produce better results. Yet, in fact, Andropov and the KGB submitted additional requests for more money and greater numbers of operatives to continue cultivating the Soviet Union's relationship with Allende, and Brezhnev approved.[46] However, as the KGB considered spending much more money and manpower to bolster the seemingly worsening conditions of Allende, Andropov called a meeting at KGB headquarters to assess the reality of the situation. In a parallel to Richard Helm's assessment earlier to his CIA officers, Andropov and his staff concluded that additional money and efforts in Chile would have minimal impact on Allende's ability to hold onto power.[47] They would simply have to make do with their current operations and budget.

OPERATIONAL CHAOS AND PROBLEMS WITHIN THE CIA

The CIA seemed to be floundering in the 1970–1973 period as it attempted to adjust not only to the significant changes in the strategic security environment but also to the internal domestic situation in the United States. The Vietnam War had driven a portion of the U.S. population to become increasingly suspicious of the actions of the U.S. government, specifically the CIA. Though some of these feelings were based on misunderstood actions of the clandestine service, the actions of the agency nevertheless did not always work to suppress and alleviate these outside concerns. Operation Chaos, which the CIA ran starting at the behest of President Lyndon Baines Johnson in 1967 and which President Richard Nixon continued on into his tenure, was an example of the type of operation that caused the CIA to face even greater public and congressional scrutiny.

Under the control of the CIA's focused and driven counterintelligence chief, James Jesus Angleton, Operation Chaos started as an attempt to determine whether the Soviet Union or other international forces had been unduly influencing and supporting the growing antiwar sentiments within the United States.[48] While at its most basic level, the objective of the operation seemed well within the purview of the CIA's mission, as well as the U.S. president's executive authority, the practice of the program operated on the fringe of legality. As part of the original charter of the CIA, one of the central tenets of the operational ethos of the agency was that it was not allowed to operate within the United States. Hence, as long as its operations were directed outside the United States, there would be no issues. However, to get the information needed to ascertain if communist nations were cultivating the peace movement within the United States, the CIA had to focus its operation both outward toward communist nations and inward to focus on U.S. citizens, groups, and even media outlets were may be under the undue influence of the communists. Specifically, Angleton issued the order to all overseas stations that this operation had the highest priority and required the CIA to also look and investigate the "U.S. Peace Movement, members of the New Left, University Radicals, and Black Nationalists."[49] The process involved spying on and investigating U.S. citizens within the United States who had been known for protesting not only the policies of the U.S. government on Vietnam but also racial and other political issues. This type of operation was certainly well within a gray area of the CIA's charter.

Knowing that the act of spying on American citizens within the United States was highly problematic, especially if any of the details of the operation were ever leaked to the press, Angleton and the CIA made the operation a joint endeavor with the FBI.[50] By working with the FBI, the CIA had access to files and research on many of the individuals they were focusing on. However, the partnership with the FBI was not just about access to information; it was also about giving the appearance of "legitimacy" to the operation.[51] Despite the efforts of Angleton and the officers involved in Operation Chaos, the CIA was unable to prove any connection to foreign entities "manipulating or financing" the antiwar movement in the United States.[52]

However, this did not stop the operation, as the CIA once again turned the operation to international antiwar movements to ensure that there was no greater collusion among international radical groups that could pose a threat to the stability of the United States.[53] The internal concerns within the CIA about spying on U.S. citizens and about the legitimacy of the operation culminated in 1972 when DCI Richard Helms reoriented Operation Chaos to international terrorism, an endeavor much more in line with the traditional tenets of the CIA.[54]

Pressure for this reorientation came from within the CIA as CIA Inspector General William Broe, during the period of Operation Chaos, wrote an official internal report in which he stated:

Even though there is general belief that CIA involvement is directed primarily at foreign manipulation and subversion exploitation of U.S. citizens, we also encountered general concern over what appeared to constitute a monitoring of the political views and activities of Americans not known to be suspected of being involved in espionage. Occasionally, stations were asked to report on the whereabouts and activities of prominent persons . . . whose comings and goings were not only in the public domain but for whom allegations of subversion seemed sufficiently nebulous to raise renewed doubts at the nature and legitimacy of the program.[55]

Interestingly enough, DCI William Colby shut down Operation Chaos in 1973 after an article in the U.S. press focused on "illegalities" of the CIA.[56] Starting with the tenure of Richard Helms as DCI and carrying over into the tenure of William Colby, the CIA as an institution was growing increasingly concerned that the U.S. presidents (e.g., Lyndon B. Johnson and Richard Nixon) were increasingly using the CIA as a personal political tool, not as a strategic asset in the context of the Cold War.[57]

Despite concerns of successive DCIs as well as many CIA officers about the agency abusing its authority, the successive investigative committees (the Rockefeller Commission and the Church Committee) into the operations of the intelligence service found that Operation Chaos did not violate the charter of the CIA and that, indeed, the operation was within the operational purview of the agency. However, both the Rockefeller Commission and the Church Committee recommended that the CIA should not be used as a tool to "perform what were essentially internal security tasks."[58] Despite the official findings that Operation Chaos did not technically violate the charter of the CIA, the public's perception of the CIA was still wary, especially after the shenanigans at the Watergate Hotel complex. From the perspective of the Soviet Union, the 1970s were a period when the United States appeared weak, and the KGB believed that it could exploit this era as a means to get ahead in the global confrontation with its main adversary.[59]

AN OPPORTUNITY FOR THE KGB

Détente was a unique period in the Cold War in which the United States and the Soviet Union enjoyed a much more normalized relationship.[60] Though both sides had their continued suspicions, the overall tension between the two primary Cold War powers eased. With the United States struggling in the aftermath of Vietnam, and the further actions by President Richard M. Nixon in relation to his reelection campaign in 1972, the Soviet Union and the KGB saw the potential to exploit this period of eased tensions. As such, the KGB emphasized the cultivation of human resources who could divulge critical defense and political secrets that would benefit the Soviet Union. The KGB's First Directorate (FCD) was the department within the Soviet Union's intelligence service that controlled and ran foreign operations. Vladimir Aleksandrovich Kryuchkov became head of the FCD in 1974 and quickly reinforced the KGB's sense that the détente provided ample opportunity to gain key intelligence about the United States. As earlier chapters have outlined, the KGB had been striving to rebuild its legal and illegal intelligence networks since the FBI and Venona had broken the KGB's vast network of spies in the 1920s–1940s. However, in light of the growing discontent within the United States, as well as the international economic and political issues, the major difference in recruiting agents in the era of détente from the earlier era was that people were no longer simply motivated by ideology.[61] Rather, money and other material demands seemed to drive agents of the new era. In a reaction to the changing dynamics in the identification, cultivation, and productivity of spies, Kryuchkov issued new guidance to his FCD. In 1976 one of the memoranda outlined the era by stating:

Operational experience in recent years has shown that many intelligence tasks related to capitalists and developing countries can be successfully covered from the territory of the USSR by close cooperation between Residencies and the appropriate components of the central apparatus of the Service.

Having at their disposal the necessary agent resources of Soviet nationals, as well as a variety of operational-technical facilities, the components of the central apparatus are in a position to carry out on Soviet territory of foreigners who are of intelligence interest, and are able to exert on them influence which will work in our favor; they can also carry out complex checking measures, and obtain operational information on the targets through the deployment of agents. Moreover, the components of the Centre can dispatch to foreign countries officers and agents to carry out intelligence tasks, and to extend help to the Residencies for the realization of their specific operational agent requirements.[62]

Though the above memorandum outlines cultivating agents with significant assistance from the embedded KGB officers with the Diplomatic Residencies of the Soviet Union, the KGB also offered broad guidelines for Soviet intelligence officers as a means to capitalize on the new wave of U.S. citizens willing to offer intelligence to the Soviet Union. Kryuchkov's guidance focused on developing a "Psychological Personality Portrait" as a means to reduce the time it took to identify, cultivate, and exploit a foreign agent.[63] The essence of the new protocol focused on "personal qualities, intellectual qualities, emotional qualities, attitude toward other people, Self-appraisal, and other personal qualities of operational significance, and personal habits."[64] Within each of these categories were additional definitions of "positive" and "negative" traits that were designed to build a quick profile that the FCD could rapidly exploit.

By the middle of the 1970s, Kryuchkov and the KGB were well on their way to building a system that allowed the KGB the potential to build intelligence sources around the globe. Though the FCD worked hard on this operation, it was merely codifying and streamlining a process that the KGB had been developing for some time.

KGB officer, and later double agent, Oleg Kalugin recounts in his memoirs an operation in 1971 in which he flew to New Delhi, India, to influence a CIA officer named "Mr. Leonard" who had been performing sloppy spycraft in an attempt to cultivate agents within the Indian government, military, and security agencies.[65] Through KGB agents and contacts in India, Soviet intelligence targeted Leonard as someone who could be used. Kalugin recounts how he simply arranged a meeting with Leonard and presented him with a dossier of his sloppy spycraft and let Leonard know the social, political, and international ramifications of his ineptness.[66]

Having Mr. Leonard in an awkward and very damaging situation, Kalugin offered a solution. The Soviet Union would like to have Leonard provide information "about CIA's activities in India," and in return the KGB would not only suppress the gross violations of Leonard's work but also provide him with information on the Soviet Union that would cultivate the CIA's confidence in Mr. Leonard's espionage abilities.[67] In addition to bolstering his professional reputation as a spy, the KGB also offered Mr. Leonard monetary compensation for his efforts.[68]

Though the operation did not work out as planned, as Mr. Leonard never appeared at the follow-up meeting, Kalugin and the KGB went ahead and sent their information to the Indian press as a means to once again demonstrate that the CIA was up to its old tricks.[69] This operation, which took place in the 1970s, demonstrated how the KGB began in the 1970s to become much more flexible and responsive in trying to cultivate more and more intelligence sources, without the years of tedious and deliberate background work. These are the exact characteristics that Kryuchkov aimed to exploit during his tenure in the FCD.

In the early and mid-1970s, the KGB worked to cultivate two major elements of its intelligence-gathering network: the first was trying to exploit new agents within the United States, and the second was the development of "illegal" spies who lived under fake names and had very detailed backstories. By the 1970s, the KGB was thinking about how to best use second-generation illegals who had been born and raised in the United States.[70] However, government officials and even high-ranking officers in the KGB, who had not lived, and in some cases never visited, the United States or even Western nations, fundamentally misunderstood the organization of democratic states. Soviet Diplomat Arkadi Shevchenko noted:

Many are inclined to the fantastic notion that there must be a secret control center somewhere in the United States. They themselves, after all, are used to a system ruled by a small group working in sorcery in one place.[71]

This cultural assumption helped drive the KGB to obsess over getting access to government elites, military officers, and any other corridors of power that could help them gain insightful intelligence on the United States. Even though the quest for intelligence was logical, the KGB continued to build networks of intelligence that focused on a false assumption about the United States.

An example of the fusion of the KGB's assumptions about the United States and Kryuchkov's work within the FCD are exemplified in the actions of KGB illegal Dalibar Valoshek, who was a 33-year-old Czechoslovakian border guard when he was recruited by the KGB with the assistance of Czech allies.[72] The KGB built an elaborate backstory for Valoshek, his wife, and their young son. Assuming the name of a Sudeten German who had died in World War II, Valoshek become Rudolf Albert Herrmann, and his biography detailed that he had survived the war and ended up in East Germany, only to escape in 1957 to the West.[73] Likewise his wife also received a new identity and lived her life as Ingalore Noerke [Inga Herrmann], even though the real Ingalore Noerke had been killed during an Allied air raid during World War II.[74]

The couple infiltrated Toronto, Canada, in 1957 under the auspices of oppressed anticommunists. Once in Toronto the couple bought a deli that happened to also be a "popular gathering spot for members of the Canadian Broadcast Corporation (CBC)."[75] The Herrmanns (Valosheks) befriended their frequent customers, and Rudolf (Dalibar) used these contacts to get a job with the CBC, after he sold the deli.[76]

Initially hired as a sound engineer, Rudolf (Dalibar) took night classes in filmmaking to bolster his ability to secure a better position within the CBC. By 1968 the Herrmanns had become Canadian citizens and had firmly positioned themselves as secure, stable spies for the KGB. Based off this great success, the KGB moved the Herrmanns to New York as a means to penetrate and gain intelligence on the United States. Based on his success as a filmmaker for the CBC, Rudolf got a job with the Hudson Institute in New York, which was a think tank that handled strategic and defense-related issues. However, by 1970 this position failed to produce any great intelligence, as Rudolf was a photographer and cameraman, which barred him from access to any of the strategic or defense-related work by the Hudson institute.

However, though Herrmann's bright star had faded, there was another opportunity that could greatly benefit the KGB. The Herrmanns' son, Peter, by 1972 was of college age, and his father had confided in him his true identity and essentially recruited Peter for the KGB. Rudolf reported back to the KGB on his personal operation, and the Soviet Union's intelligence agency agreed to train and pay for Peter's university.[77] Peter started studying at the McGill University in Canada before he transferred to Georgetown University in Washington, D.C., in 1976.[78] Peter's handlers in the KGB instructed him to "report on students whose fathers had government jobs, especially if they had character flaws which could be exploited."[79]

This last clause in the KGB's directions is the direct link to Kryuchkov's ideas about exploiting character flaws as a means to exploit agents. With potential access to U.S. government workers and elected officials, the KGB saw Peter's position as a second-generation illegal as a potentially rich foundation on which to build and generate access to more and better intelligence on the United States. Furthermore, the KGB also demanded that Peter work at Georgetown's Center for Strategic and International Studies as yet another way to gain access to the corridors of power in the United States.[80]

The FBI dashed the hopes of the KGB in May 1977 when they arrested Rudolf (Dalibar) on espionage charges.[81] The FBI offered Rudolf a deal by which he could provide the FBI with information on his spying activities, as well as information on the KGB's programs, or he, his son, and his wife would all face charges of espionage.[82] Dalibar spent two years working as a double agent for the FBI before he and his family were "moved to an undisclosed location," presumably for their own protection.[83]

The actions of Herrmann and his son demonstrate that the KGB was very successful at inserting and building some illegal networks of spies.

Furthermore, the case of the Herrmanns shows that they were even successful in building a second generation of illegals who had the potential to gain access to the government of the United States. However, it is important to note that despite the success of inserting and cultivating these illegal networks, the KGB generally failed to gain access to the exacting intelligence it obsessed over.

CONCLUSION

The period between 1968 and 1976 was a watershed moment in the historical continuum of the espionage game between the CIA and the KGB. On the side of the KGB, the Soviet Union saw the social and political pressures that faced the United States as a result of Vietnam and Watergate as a great opportunity to revisit and increase the KGB's consistent obsession with both legal and illegal networks within the United States. In addition, the credibility damage that the United States sustained within the international community as a result of Vietnam further empowered the Soviet Union to seek opportunities in Latin America, Africa, Asia, and the Middle East. The aim of this expansion was to improve the overall position of the Soviet Union within the context of the Cold War's strategic balance.

The Soviet Union's involvement in Chile is a great representation of the KGB's initiatives to improve the Soviet Union's position in the global balance of power. The uniqueness of the KGB's support and loose connection to Allende was that the KGB overlooked Allende's lackluster Marxist credentials and rather sought to merely provide him intelligence on U.S. operations designed to discredit his power. It is interesting to note the deliberate and methodical way in which the KGB operated within the context of its operations in Chile, as compared to the KGB's desire to work more diligently on operations with illegals.

From the KGB's perspective, this meant that they needed to compress its standard, deliberate protocol in developing and cultivating agents, specifically in the United States but also around the globe. The directives and actions taken by FCD head, and later head of the KGB, Vladimir Kryuchkov directly reflect the sense of urgency and promptness that the KGB wished to exploit in this window of opportunity. An additional and concurrent action that evolved in this time period was the KGB's desire to penetrate further into the U.S. government with second-generation illegals.

The case of Rudolf Herrmann and his infiltration into the United States with his family demonstrates how the KGB used and planned to expand the illegals program as the families become more integrated into American society and culture. The development of Peter Herrmann as a very young spy sent to Georgetown University to cultivate relationships with students whose parents worked for the U.S. government clearly demonstrated that the openness of the U.S. culture held certain vulnerabilities that could be exploited by the KGB. Furthermore, the KGB not only pushed Peter Herrmann to exploit personal relationships, but it also directed him to get a job at the University's Center for Strategic and International Studies as a way to gain potential access to governmental policy makers and staffers with an aim toward building access to greater insights on the actions and plans of the United States.

The KGB's use of second-generation illegals such as Peter Herrmann foresaw that as first-generation illegals integrated into the United States, which always posed some significant risk. With the use of second generation illegals this risk was negated to a certain degree because these spies grew up and matured as "standard" American citizens. Spies like Peter Herrmann offered the KGB and the Soviet Union a way to place agents with the U.S. government and not risk the same issues that came with the first-generation illegals such as Rudolf Herrmann.

The CIA, however, was not in a position to seek an expansion of opportunity or power. Due to the changing political and social climate in the United States, the CIA became a central target for reform and greater openness, especially after Watergate. Under Ford's administration the CIA faced greater scrutiny and calls to testify about its operations. The serving DCI of the period, William Colby, openly obliged and provided testimony to the Commission to the President on CIA Activities, which was chaired by Vice President Nelson Rockefeller. The objective of establishing this panel, according to President Ford, was to "look into allegations, determine the extent to which the agency had exceeded its authority, and make recommendations to prevent such abuses in the future."[84]

Colby, unlike previous DCIs who had tended to be quite professional and who maintained the CIA's commitment to the president, provided open and honest testimony, to the point that many within the CIA and the executive branch of the U.S. government, including Nelson Rockefeller, believed that he was being too honest and open.[85] Though the commission found that the CIA's Operation Chaos, in which the CIA opened U.S. citizens' mail and spied on them within the United States, was improper, the final report of Rockefeller's commission said:

the great majority of the CIA's activities comply with its statutory authority. Nevertheless, over 28 years of its history, the CIA has engaged in some activities that should be criticized and not permitted to happen again-both in light of the limits imposed on the agency by law and as a matter of public policy. Some of these activities were initiated or ordered by Presidents, either directly or indirectly. Some fall within the doubtful area between responsibilities delegated to the CIA by Congress and the National Security Council on the one hand and activities specifically prohibited to the agency on the other. Some of them were plainly unlawful and constituted improper invasions upon the rights of Americans. The agency's own recent actions, undertaken for the most part in 1973 and 1974, have gone far to terminate the activities upon which this investigation focused.[86]

Generally content with the findings of the Rockefeller commission, Colby and the CIA also had to contend with an investigatory committee from the U.S. House of Representatives and the U.S. Senate. The most notable was the committee headed by Senator Frank Church (D, Idaho). Church used the public's mood and growing distrust of the U.S. government as well as the media's interest in the Rockefeller commission, to investigate the past deeds of the CIA. The most hyped part of the committee's investigation focused on the agency's use of assassination. In the report of the committee, *Alleged Assassination Plots against Foreign Leaders*, Church and his colleagues highlighted past efforts to assassinate foreign leaders by the CIA.

Though the committee members found that the CIA had indeed conducted operations to try to assassinate Fidel Castro and other foreign leaders, they softened the blow that these operations were not conducted by a rogue intelligence agency but rather that the CIA conducted these operations with the direct "authorization of the president or senior government officials."[87] Having conducted various investigations with information on the CIA's past deeds, Colby, in his quest for openness and to maintain the CIA as a standing, important, and credible part of the national security apparatus of the United States, provided the secrets of the CIA, knowing that they would inevitably be leaked to the public.[88] The changing dynamics in the social and political culture of the United States drove Colby's decision, yet at the same time, he saved the agency by convincing a hostile Congress and public that the CIA had since cleaned up its operational ethos and still served a vital role in the war against the Soviet Union. Under the presidential administrations of James E. Carter and Ronald W. Reagan, the CIA rebuilt its reputation and strove to assist in winning the Cold War against the Soviet Union.

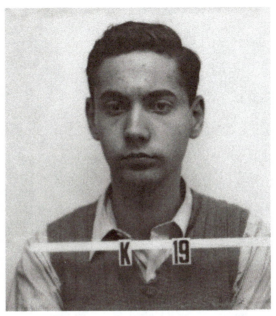

Manhattan Project Identification Badge for Theodore Hall (Atomic Heritage Foundation and Los Alamos National Laboratory, https://www.atomicheritage .org/profile/theodore-hall)

Manhattan Project Identification Badge for Klaus Fuchs (Atomic Heritage Foundation and Los Alamos National Laboratory, https://www.atomicheritage .org/profile/klaus-fuchs)

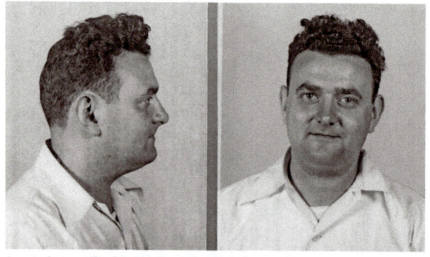

Arrest photograph of David Greenglass, Manhattan Project Worker and brother of Ethel Rosenberg (Atomic Heritage Foundation, https://www.atomicheritage .org/profile/david-greenglass, and United States Department of Justice, Federal Bureau of Investigation, https://www.fbi.gov/history/famous-cases/atom-spy -caserosenbergs)

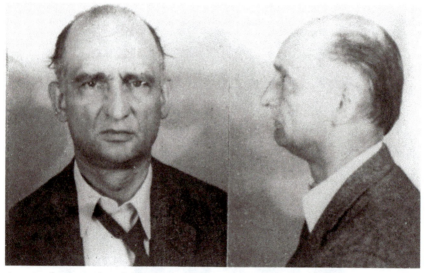

Arrest photograph of William Fisher, a.k.a. Rudolph Abel (United States Department of Justice, Federal Bureau of Investigation, https://www.fbi.gov /history/famous-cases/hollow-nickel-rudolph-abel)

Crude map showing the Berlin Tunnel and its penetration into the Soviet Sector (CIA, https://www.cia.gov/news-information/featured-story-archive/the -berlin-tunnel-exposed.html)

Photograph of the interior of one section of the Berlin Tunnel (CIA, https://www
.cia.gov/news-information/featured-story-archive/the-berlin-tunnel-exposed
.html)

Early USAF U-2 aircraft (https://www.cia.gov/news-information/featured
-story-archive/2015-featured-story-archive/area-51-u-2-and-the-accidental-test
-flight.html)

Later version of U-2 in flight (CIA, https://www.cia.gov/news-information
/featured-story-archive/2010-featured-story-archive/cia-and-u-2-a-50-year
-anniversary.html)

U-2 pilot Francis Gary Powers poses with a U-2 (CIA, https://www.cia.gov
/news-information/featured-story-archive/2015-featured-story-archive/francis
-gary-powers.html)

Corona imagery of Soviet Runway (National Reconnaissance Office, Center for the Study of National Reconnaissance, http://www.nro.gov/Portals/65/images /corona/highres/cor1h.jpg?ver=2018-04-30-144015-230)

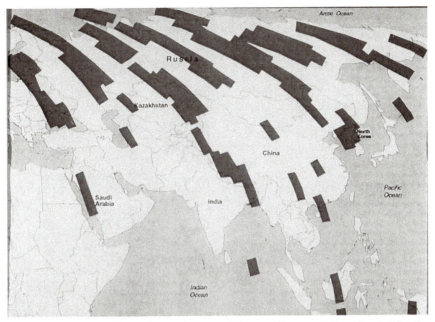

Map of Corona satellite coverage (National Reconnaissance Office, Center for the Study of National Reconnaissance, http://www.nro.gov/Portals/65/images/corona/highres/cor18h.jpg?ver=2018-04-30-144016-480)

USAF C-119 aircraft snags a Corona film canister (National Reconnaissance Office, Center for the Study of National Reconnaissance, http://www.nro.gov/Portals/65/images/corona/highres/cor13h.jpg?ver=2018-04-30-144015-917)

Corona satellite prepares for launch (National Reconnaissance Office, Center for the Study of National Reconnaissance, http://www.nro.gov/Portals/65/images /corona/lowres/cor19.jpg?ver=2018-04-30-144045-637)

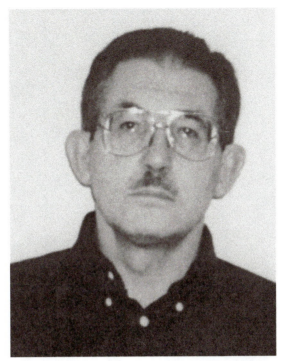

Arrest photograph of Aldrich Ames (United States Department of Justice, Federal Bureau of Investigation, https://www.fbi.gov/history/famous-cases /aldrich-ames)

Photograph of FBI's arrest of Aldrich Ames (United States Department of Justice, Federal Bureau of Investigation, https://www.fbi.gov/history/famous-cases /aldrich-ames)

CHAPTER 6

Carter, Reagan, and the Denouement of the Cold War, 1976–1988

The last, long decade of the Cold War was a very dynamic and active period for the espionage game between the United States and the Soviet Union. By 1976, both the CIA and the KGB had well-established tactics, techniques, and procedures to ensure that their respective nations had the necessary intelligence in the ideological struggle between these two superpowers. However, the geopolitical environment that had characterized the earlier decades of the Cold War had changed, especially for the United States in the wake of Vietnam and the Watergate scandal. Though the CIA had to adjust to the new reality of widespread general and public skepticism of their actions, it still had a primary mission to provide intelligence to the President of the United States. However, Presidents James E. Carter and Ronald W. Reagan viewed the CIA from two very different perspectives.

President Jimmy Carter had a "visceral dislike" of the CIA and the covert nature of its actions, especially after the hearings from the Church committee.[1] However, as the Soviet Union strove to take advantage of the perceived weakened state of the United States in the immediate aftermath of Vietnam, Carter overcame his initial reaction to the CIA and saw the benefit of using the intelligence agency as a means to exploit weaknesses in the Soviet political and social system.

The Soviet Union since the late 1960s had been dealing with substantial economic issues, as well as social and political turmoil both within the Soviet Union and within the Warsaw Pact. Though the leaders of the Soviet state recognized the fundamental issues within their system, they simply could not overlook the opportunity to capitalize on their perceived shift in the geopolitical balance of the Cold War in this last decade. They firmly believed that the late 1970s and early 1980s was a time for them to gain allies in Africa, Latin America, and even Europe.

Therefore, as we saw in Chapter 5, the KGB stepped up its attempts to build an even greater legal and illegal network of agents that could provide critical intelligence for its worldwide agenda. However, in focusing their zeal on besting the United States, the KGB and the leaders of the Soviet Union did not fully recognize the fact that they were increasingly vulnerable due to social and humanitarian issues.

Jimmy Carter and his national security team saw the use of the CIA as a way to exploit this new vulnerability of the communist state. However, the use of the CIA was to be focused on more traditional means of using "influence" and "propaganda" as compared to paramilitary activity. Carter, using the Helsinki Accords as an ideological pulpit to further his international policy for advancing human rights and civil liberties for all, saw the Central Intelligence Agency as a tool that could be used to advance his democratic and high-minded agenda. Using the CIA for the winning and advancement of freedom around the globe, but especially with the Soviet Union and the Warsaw Pact, was an objective that Carter saw as worthy of the CIA.

Though President Ronald W. Reagan maintained many of Carter's covert operations, he had a very different fundamental understanding of the CIA and its value to the United States. Unlike Carter, Reagan saw the Central Intelligence Agency as a tool that could be used more assertively to challenge and even wither the Soviet system. Reagan's use of the CIA, therefore, focused on a two-phase approach that saw the CIA return to its paramilitary past.

Specifically, Reagan did not shy away from the use of the CIA as a tool for spreading propaganda about the ills of the communist system. In this regard, his first phase of the use of intelligence services was merely a continuation of the policies and programs started under Carter.[2] In stark contrast to Carter's vision, however, Reagan also saw the CIA as a very valuable tool that could combat communist expansion in Latin America, Africa, and more directly in Southwest Asia.

Under Reagan and his DCI, William J. Casey, a former Office of Strategic Service officer, the CIA recaptured some of its swagger as it once again was called to be much more active in its use and gathering of intelligence with an aim toward directly confronting and even rolling back communism around the globe.

From the perspective of the KGB, the last, long decade of the Cold War was a productive period amid significant internal change. This period saw the KGB gain a very valuable agent in Aldrich Ames, who provided significant intelligence that the KGB quickly acted upon. However, at the same time, the failing health of Leonid Brezhnev led to a rapid succession of leaders from former KGB head Yuri Andropov to Konstantin Chernenko and finally to Mikhail Gorbachev, all within the span of November 1982 to March 1985.

Starting with the election of Ronald Reagan as president of the United States in November 1980, the KGB become obsessively focused on the potential and planning of a preemptive nuclear first strike on the Soviet Union by the United States. As head of the KGB, Yuri Andropov obsessed over this possibility and directed the intelligence agencies of the Soviet Union to follow new protocols that provided critical intelligence on when the attack would come. This required the KGB to double down on building its legal and illegal networks, not only within the United States but also within NATO. This was not a major adjustment for the KGB, as we have seen that building based intelligence networks had always been a strong priority for the KGB. However, the difference now was that these networks would know how to focus on very deliberate signs that could provide indications of an eminent nuclear attack from the United States.

In addition to fixating on the potential for a world war, the KGB and the Soviet Union also recognized that the West, and particularly the United States, had excelled in advanced technologies such as computers, lasers, composite construction, and radar-absorbing materials. Therefore, they also had to ensure that they collected good intelligence on these technologies as a way to ensure that the military balance did not swing in favor of the West, which became yet another obsession with the KGB after Reagan made his Strategic Defense Initiative speech in March 1983.

This last chapter, focusing on the lead-up to the end of the Cold War, details how the espionage continued to evolve, yet it still maintained traditional tenets. Even at the end of the Cold War, the espionage game was strong and continuing despite the eventual collapse of the 50-year struggle. It is significant to note that the essence of the game merely expanded during this final phase, yet the CIA and the KGB did not deviate from the traditional mission that had been established in the months after the end of World War II.

CARTER, TECHNOLOGY, HUMAN RIGHTS, AND THE CIA

In August 1975 the Helsinki Accords, also known as the "final act" of the European conference on security, concluded and provided some definitive agreements, though they were not treaties in the traditional sense. The agreements that evolved out these talks included roughly thirty-five countries, of which the United States and Soviet Union were two. From the perspective of Leonid Brezhnev, the Helsinki Accords were the solidification of political objectives that the Soviet Union had been working toward since the Stalinist period.[3]

First and foremost, the conclusion of the meetings allowed Brezhnev and the Soviet Union to finally get general recognition across Europe of the boundaries that they had secured and held fast to in Eastern and Central Europe since the end of World War II.[4] Second, the split of Germany was acknowledged as two distinct spheres and therefore two distinct states, which again had been a primary objective since the onset of the Cold War in the 1940s.[5] Finally, and most significantly, these two agreements solidified the western edge of the Soviet Union's sphere of influence well away from the actual border of the Soviet State. Brezhnev therefore believed that the international community's recognition of these geopolitical points provided the Soviet Union, as well as the global community, a certain degree of "stability," which of course went hand in hand with the tenets of détente.[6]

U.S. President Gerald Ford went along with the tenets of the Helsinki agreement to maintain the spirit of détente as well as to maintain some degree of continuity in U.S. foreign policy after the resignation of Richard Nixon. However, within the United States, a group of Senators led by Henry "Scoop" Jackson (D–Washington) began to focus on the Soviet Union's heinous human rights record. The issue that fueled this movement with the United States was the inability of Russian Jews to emigrate to Israel, in addition to the basic lack of civil rights and civil liberties of citizens of the Soviet Union.

The issue of human rights was significant because, as part of the final act of the Helsinki Accords, the participants agreed to three broad "baskets," which focused on issues that were important and timely in the context of the era. The first basket focused on the "inviolability of existing European borders."[7] This is the basket that most appealed to Brezhnev and the leaders of the Soviet Union, as it allowed them to finally rest easy that there would no longer be great disputes over the Warsaw Pact satellites and their borders with the Soviet Union. Though this was not an official recognition of the legitimacy of these borders, the agreement merely sought to suppress and end any open and hostile tensions over border disputes.

The second basket focused on increased trade and information across Europe, which not only benefited the West but was also a key plank in the concept of Ostpolitik.[8] Seeing that the Soviet Union was having significant economic issues and believing that it was falling well behind the West in high technology, more open and free exchange of trade and information would greatly benefit the Soviet Union, and its leaders quickly and firmly supported this position. However, the West also wanted to make sure that human rights received some attention, but the first and second baskets did not allow for this. Also, Brezhnev and the leadership of the Soviet Union were in no mood to rehash old issues, as they had been wrestling with these concerns since the Soviet Union's draconian intervention in Prague, Czechoslovakia, in 1968.

However, the Western nations pushed the idea of human rights, as they believed that it was significant and that the Soviet Union had already had its success with the first and second baskets. Therefore, the third basket of the Helsinki Accords focused on human rights. Specifically, it stated that all parties signing onto the accords must:

respect human rights and fundamental freedoms, including freedom of thought, conscience, religion, or belief . . . promote and encourage the effective exercise of civil, political, economic, social, cultural, and other rights and freedoms all of which derive from the inherent dignity of the human person.[9]

The leadership of the Soviet Union strove to suppress and dilute these key tenets, but in the end, they could not convince the other nations that protecting freedoms and rights was an insignificant action. After consultation among themselves, the Soviet delegation, largely led by Brezhnev, concluded that the victories won by the acceptance of baskets one and two greatly outweighed the acceptance of human rights conditions in basket three.[10]

Furthermore, they concluded that the tenets of basket one, which focused on national boundaries, provided them with some insulation as they believed that the spirit and intent of the agreement mandated that other nations would not interfere within the domestic confines of other states. Hence, Brezhnev thought that the Soviet Union would not have to adjust its stance on human rights and civil liberties, as it was an internal matter, and under the agreement of the Helsinki Accords other signatories would not interfere with internal domestic matters. Brezhnev's assumption and interpretation were wrong.

When Jimmy Carter won the election in 1976 over Gerald Ford, the CIA was in for some changes. First and foremost, Carter replaced sitting DCI George H. W. Bush with Admiral Stansfield Turner, who was currently serving in a NATO command assigned in Europe.[11] George H. W. Bush had wished to remain as head of the CIA because he believed that the agency needed continuity after a rough couple of years; however, Carter disagreed.[12] After enduring a Senate confirmation hearing, Turner assessed his new agency by reflecting and stating:

I found Bush to be tops for CIA people. They loved him. He was just the kind of director they want [sic]. He did exactly what they wanted him to do. They run the agency. That's what I came up against. But I can't run something without being in charge. The place was a shambles in administration and needed somebody to take charge of it, and they didn't want that.[13]

Within the first year of his tenure, Turner had boldly seized the reins of the CIA to demonstrate that he was indeed in control and would not allow the agency to continue to be a disgrace.[14] Internally, the CIA had its own opinions about the new DCI.

The long-serving officers in the CIA believed that Turner did not understand the nature of the espionage game and only wanted to firmly command the intelligence-gathering means of the United States.[15] This represented to significant shift in the way that the CIA did business. Rather than employing a robust human intelligence-gathering network that entailed complex and dynamic nations that were not easy to control, Turner transitioned the CIA away from HUMINT sources and made the agency focus on more technical means of gathering intelligence.[16] The ethos of the CIA had been that the agency was made up of professionals "who went to specific places for specific purposes, made personal friendships, through which in large part they operated, and had a 'feel' for their jobs."[17] From the internal perspective within the CIA, the officers believed that Turner was shattering this long-held and solidified operational ethos.

Turner defended his actions, which did indeed call for a greater reliance on satellites, or other advanced national technical means, for intelligence collection as a safer, steadier, and more dependable means of intelligence collection. He justified his changes to the operational reality of the CIA because he believed that "in times of crisis, it was very hard to rely on HUMINT source."[18]

Turner further defended his position by stating:

The human people have not understood the revolution in intelligence collection brought on by the technical systems. It means that we have got to change. You can't have this enormous flow of data coming into the system without changing the way you go about all this intelligence.[19]

Even though Turner clashed with the CIA over the long-term use of HUMINT, he still believed that there was a need for this type of collection, but made the argument that HUMINT was important as a means to "fill in the missing pieces."[20] The emphasis on satellites would be the priority, and HUMINT would be used to provide clarity and context to the intelligence operations. This was a shift that others in the CIA were not fully comfortable with, as they believed that HUMINT was every bit as valuable as national technical means.

Turner and President Carter were not just obsessed with technology, but rather they believed in the abilities of the CIA's newest spy satellite, the KH-11. On the administration's first day in office, January 21, 1977, the CIA held a short briefing with the new president of the United States to showcase the latest technology in spy satellites. Acting (and interim) DCI E. Henry Knoche met with Carter and brought with him near-real-time photographic intelligence taken from space.[21] The photographs that the CIA briefed to President Carter represented a new age in spying in that the capabilities of the KH-11 far surpassed previous spy satellites.

The KH-11 satellite was a costly, but valuable, piece of hardware that allowed the CIA to present prompt intelligence that could be relayed to the president within ninety minutes.[22] The CIA, with the assistance of the TRW Corporation, had designed the KH-11 satellites to stay in orbit approximately 770 days, as compared to the life span of previous spy satellites that lasted less than a year.[23] Beyond expanding the operational life span of this new intelligence source, the resolution and capabilities of the camera far surpassed older space-based assets used by the CIA and the military services of the United States. The daytime resolution of the KH-11 has been calculated at two inches, with a similar capability at night based on the latest infrared and computer imaging technology of the era.[24] This meant that the CIA would deploy two KH-11s, one dedicated to daytime surveillance and the second dedicated to nighttime surveillance. This ability provided the United States with the ability to have prompt intelligence and global coverage day and night, which synchronized with Turner's comments about using HUMINT to provide complementary intelligence advanced by national technical means.

Beyond the advanced capabilities of the KH-11, which was used later in Carter's tenure as president to locate the American hostages in Iran, the satellite came with an additional cost that both Carter and Turner were willing to underwrite.[25] The reality was that the Carter administration had witnessed the espionage game evolve as primarily human-based endeavors, whereby technical means were used to collect and even support HUMINT. However, with the capabilities of the KH-11, the CIA had invested a tremendous sum of money that would hamper the human side of the espionage game.

In fact, an argument can be made that this capability, as stated by Turner, now placed satellites as the primary means of collecting intelligence, and HUMINT would be used to refine and contextualize the electronic means. This did not ease the tension between the CIA and the Carter administration, though it did provide Jimmy Carter with a more defined sense of the role of the CIA. However, the covert-actions advocates and HUMINT supporters still believed in their abilities and role in collecting intelligence for the United States.

The discord within the agency was further exacerbated by President Carter's initial pangs about the use of covert intelligence operations by the United States. In essence, Carter did acknowledge the value of having an executive-level agency that could provide much-needed intelligence on the global strategic balance, but he did not want to violate the legal or ethical norms that the Church committee had taken the CIA to task over in the closing years of Ford's tenure as president. As the tension within the agency seemed to reflect the general mood of the United States in the second half of the 1970s, President Carter came to see the advocacy of human rights as a valuable mission for which the CIA was uniquely positioned.

Using the tenets of the Helsinki Accords as a foundation, Carter recognized that the CIA could be used to spread "covert propaganda" into the Soviet Union.[26] Though the CIA had used various means in its past to spread pro-democratic information designed to combat the expansion of communism, this time it was a bit different. The Carter administration, especially Secretary of State Cyrus Vance and National Security Advisor Zbigniew Brzezinski, saw the marrying of the Helsinki Accords tenets and the use of covert propaganda operations as a uniquely tailored method of pressuring the Soviet Union.

As the Soviet Union wrestled with increased economic turmoil and instability, the Soviet's government also had a growing issue with dissidents. Since the agreements in Helsinki, the ailing Brezhnev had a problem that he could not simply suppress in the traditional Soviet manner. Though he assumed that the human rights basket of Helsinki left him alone to deal with his own internal issues, he did recognize that the Carter administration had linked the tenets within the baskets at Helsinki and came to see human rights as a strong plank on which the United States could seek to reassert its influence on global affairs and, more specifically, the Soviet Union's poor record of human rights.

Using the CIA to advance this agenda fit well within Carter's ideas about the legal, ethical, and just use of covert action. The CIA would merely become a mechanism to advance an agenda that upheld human rights and civil liberties as basic rights for all people. With the recognition of this position, both the CIA and the Carter administration at least came to a workable solution for the agency in the twilight of the 1970s.

As we have seen in the 1940s and 1950s, the CIA had extensive experience in using propaganda and covert means to promote pro-democratic messages. Once again, under Carter's tenure, the CIA relied on its historical experience to push a more universal, democratic agenda that focused exclusively on human rights. More specifically, the CIA would advance the objectives of this agenda as a means to combat Soviet propaganda, in an effort to leverage human rights as a critical vulnerability from which the Soviet Union could be attacked.[27]

Carter gave his approval to start operations in March 1977, just two months after his inauguration as president. The focal point was not just the Soviet Union but also the spread of communism around the globe. Hence, this effort by the CIA became a worldwide endeavor composed of many separate operations all driving toward the same objective. Advocating human rights and using the tenets of The Helsinki Accords as a foundation, President Carter quickly overcame his aversion to using covert operations.

The first portion of these operations focused on producing and distributing "the political writing of dissidents within the Soviet Union."[28] This material, known as samizdat, was suppressed and very tightly controlled in the oppressive Soviet state. Therefore, the CIA assisted in the reproduction of political tomes, essays, and critiques of the Soviet system. As the Soviet regime had a very restrictive control on typewriters, printing presses, and copy machines, the mere mass copying of these underground messages could have an impact on the people of the Soviet Union and their ideas about their totalitarian regime. Furthermore, the CIA expanded its actions to reach a wider market.

Not content to just serve as a copy house for underground Soviet and Eastern European dissidents, the CIA used the growing Soviet émigré community in Western Europe, the United States, and Canada as a means to advance an even wider network of anti-Soviet publications. The agency supported and opened publishing houses and academic journals through which they actively sought the works of dissidents, which could then be covertly sent and distributed back into the Soviet Union and the Warsaw Pact region.[29] The Carter administration saw this use of covert operations as advancing the "freedom of the press" ideas and firmly believed that people, regardless of their national origin, had a right to voice their opinions about their social, economic, and political conditions. Furthermore, it was a covert way to showcase the inherently oppressive nature of the Soviet regime without directly confronting Soviet Union's leadership; after all, the Soviet Union also had agreed to the tenets of the Helsinki Accords.

In a related set of operations that were, again, directly tied to the tenets of the Helsinki Accords, the Carter administration also used the CIA as a means to promote "nationalities programs, aimed at keeping alive the culture, history, religions, and traditions of non-Russian minorities."[30] The CIA, having developed decades of regional experience, was very good at promoting these soft programs. The nationalities program, combined with the support of dissident writings, was producing significant soft and quiet pressure on the Soviet state, but this was not apparent until several years later when the real fissures of the Soviet system presented themselves in the late 1980s.

THE KGB IN THE LATE 1970s

As the CIA worked to undermine the Soviet Union on the human rights front, the KGB, which believed that the 1970s were a time of great opportunity for the Soviet Union, also worked covertly to influence international public opinion. Interestingly enough, they too were working with propaganda in an attempt to capitalize on the post-Vietnam period as a way to sway more people toward the Soviet position. Using the Soviet concept of "active measures," the KGB outlined its operations as disinformation campaigns. Specifically, the KGB saw these "progressive" operations as:

designed to mislead not the working people but their enemies—the ruling circles of capitalism—in order to induce them to act in a certain way, or abstain from actions contrary to the interests of the USSR; they promote peace and social prog-ress; they serve international détente; they are humane, creating the conditions for the noble struggle for humanity's bright future.[31]

These actions were not just perpetuated by the intelligence services of the USSR but also the intelligence services of the Warsaw Pact. The objec-tive of these operations was to present news stories, letters to the editor, and other publications that showcased the racial issues within the United States, the failed attempts of the United States and hence the CIA to inter-vene in the business of other countries, and the any other issues that portrayed the United States in a hypocritical and negative light. a Czech intelligence officer summarized the objectives and nature of these anti-American operations as:

Anti-American propaganda campaigns are the easiest to carry out. A single press article containing sensational facts of a "new American conspiracy" may be suf-ficient. Other papers become interested, the public is shocked, and government authorities in developing countries have a fresh opportunity to clamor against the imperialists while demonstrators hasten to break American embassy windows.[32]

Understanding the nature of the Brezhnev doctrine, whereby the Soviet Union declared the right to intervene in socialist countries when it per-ceived threats to the stability of socialism at stake, the active measures described above could be synchronized as a way to ensure that the tenets of socialism in the second and third worlds were supported and maintained.

By planting fabricated news stories, with an eye toward inciting civil unrest and protests against the United States and its capitalist allies, the KGB saw these actions as maintaining and even reinforcing the tenets of Brezhnev's doctrine. It is interesting to note that although the KGB and the leadership in the Soviet Union proclaimed that these actions were designed to promote peace and social progress, elements reinforced within the Helsinki Accords; the KGB's actions were direct and overt inter-ventions into the social and political spheres of other countries, as action directly prohibited within the Helsinki Accords. At the time of agreeing to the Helsinki Accords, Brezhnev and the political leadership of the Soviet Union had greatly worried about the United States and its Western allies not respecting the sovereignty of the USSR and the Warsaw Pact, yet the communists had no issues in meddling in the internal affairs of third-world nations, as long as the intent was to sway more nations toward the orbit of the Soviet Union.

While the KGB sought to ensure that the image of the United States was further eroded in the immediate years after Vietnam, the KGB also recognized that the election of Jimmy Carter as president of the United States represented something of a problem for them, because he was a Washington, D.C., outsider. Yuri Andropov, head of the KGB, in the period immediately before the 1976 elections in the United States, "personally approved operations to get inside the inner circles of well-known and prominent American political figures."[33] To gain access and insights into the new Carter administration, the KGB used Georgi Arbatov, the head of the Soviet Union's U.S. and Canada Institute and advisor to Soviet premiers from Brezhnev through Gorbachev, to befriend Cyrus Vance.[34] When Carter nominated Vance to be Secretary of State, the KGB believed that that the Soviet government would gain access to inside information within the presidency as Arbatov tried to solidify and expand a relationship with Vance.[35] Despite the optimistic hopes of this opportunity, the access to inside of the administration never materialized. Not wishing to accept failure, the KGB also tried to use the Soviet Union's Ambassador to the United States Anatoli Dobrynin as yet another way to access the inside thinking of the Carter administration. Yet again the grand scheme of the KGB penetrating the inner sanctum of the White House never materialized.

When the KGB's plan to cultivate agents within the executive branch of the federal government failed, Soviet officers resorted to the easiest means in the espionage game: discredit your enemy.[36] As previously mentioned, the KGB's "active measures" program was not just confined to the third world, but also was used to fabricate and leak news items and publications on Carter's cabinet.[37] While this would not gain access to valuable intelligence, it was at least an attempt to smear the reputations of the Foreign Policy and National Security teams in Carter's administration. Not wanting to admit failure, the KGB's head of the FCD V. A. Kryuchkov submitted a report that instead focused on internal threats to the Soviet Union. Kryuchkov stated in his report that he believed:

Today American intelligence is planning to recruit agents among Soviet citizens, train them and then advance them into administrative positions within Soviet politics, the economy, and science. The CIA has drafted a program to subject agents to individual instruction in espionage techniques and also intensive political and ideological brainwashing. . . . The CIA intends that individual agents working in isolation to carry out policies of sabotage and distortion of superior's instructions will be coordinated from a single center in the US intelligence system. The CIA believes that such deliberate actions by agents will create internal political difficulties for the Soviet Union, retard development of its economy and channel its scientific research into dead ends.[38]

Though the KGB's head took this report seriously and forwarded it to his political masters in the Politburo and Central Committee, the reality was that an operation as described was inconsistent with Jimmy Carter's views on covert operations. However, Kryuchkov was correct. The Carter administration and the CIA were attempting to influence Soviet citizens, but they were going about it by using the dissidents' networks and the tenets of the Helsinki Accords. Though not as grand as the conspiracy operation outlined by Kryuchkov, the effects had ramifications for the long-term stability of the Soviet Union.

As the KGB struggled to gain a stronger understanding of the internal dynamics of the Carter administration, the Soviet government still believed that the Cold War struggle was turning in the favor of communism. Therefore, in addition to the numerous traditional espionage and propaganda operations that KGB conducted during the 1970s, the Soviet Union also made sure to invest and update nation's satellite surveillance capabilities, which started earlier in the Cold War. By the time Carter's administration was firmly in office, the Soviet Union was on its third generation of reconnaissance satellites.[39] The major mission of these systems was to provide photoreconnaissance and signals intelligence on the United States and western allies. Though the technology of the Soviet Union's spy satellites lagged behind those of the United States, the method and style of employment made up for these shortcomings.[40] Rather than deploying a single or even two satellites, the Soviet Union deployed a constellation of satellites that provided global coverage.[41] In essence, the Soviet Union's approach to spying from space focused on using proven spacecraft such as the Soyuz module and reconfiguring spacecraft's internal compartment to house the necessary hardware to collect the required intelligence.

Rather than designing whole new vehicles and spacecraft, the Soviet Union used proven technology and simply built more and longer-serving satellites that did a good job of providing intelligence for assessing the Cold War contest. As the decade of the 1970s yielded to the 1980s, the space-based capabilities of the Soviet Union become even more significant as the Soviet Union become obsessed with a nuclear attack from the United States under the direction of U.S. President Ronald Reagan.

THE SOVIET UNION'S OBSESSION

As mentioned previously, the election of Ronald Reagan as president of the United States in November 1980 created yet another crisis and years of concern for the leadership of the Soviet Union, as well as the KGB. In May 1981 the KGB, under the direction of Brezhnev, shifted focus from the idea that the Soviet Union was winning the Cold War and seriously began to grow concerned about the significant possibility that the United States was preparing and would eventually launch a nuclear attack against the USSR. The first major part of this shift led to the KGB and the Soviet Union's military intelligence agency, the GRU, to work closely together across the globe to ensure that no indicators of an imminent war were missed.[42] Though through their interesting histories, the KGB and GRU had always harbored suspicions of one another, in the early 1980s, they both suppressed their natural paranoia and joined forces for the first time to work toward this new important objective.[43]

The new intelligence operations consumed a large percentage of the KGB's capability were called Operation RYAN, which was an acronym for *Raketno-Yadernoye Napadenie* (nuclear missile attack).[44] Andropov, the KGB's head, characterized the perceived situation as "explosive as it has been since the end of the Second World War."[45] Unbeknown to Andropov in May 1981, in just seventeen months, he would be Brezhnev's successor as the general secretary of the Soviet Union. Andropov maintained his obsession with RYAN as he transitioned from head of the KGB to general secretary of the Communist Party of the Soviet Union. For Andropov, Reagan's interest in being tough on communism and rebuilding the conventional and nuclear capabilities of the U.S. military were indicators that the newest president was a serious concern who merited close observation.

However, despite the intelligence service's fixation with nuclear war, others in the service of the Soviet Union did not see the same indicators. In fact, the long-serving Ambassador Anatoli Dobrynin believed that the Soviet Union's assessment of Reagan was a "paranoid interpretation."[46] Furthermore, the Soviet Union's Embassy in London was much less "alarmist" about the immediate potential for a first strike from the United States.[47] Though others throughout the international diplomatic and intelligence bureaucracy held similar views about the unlikelihood of a surprise missile attack by the United States, no one was willing to question the leadership's views and demands for intelligence on a potential nuclear attack from the United States or a NATO country.

The obsession with RYAN also brought with it new instructions from Kryuchkov, as the KGB now had to prioritize its intelligence-gathering capabilities to focus on indicators of a nuclear attack. According to Kryuchkov, the justification for RYAN was:

The main adversary has stepped up the tempo and scale of military preparation, the need to deal with the central assignment of the KGB's foreign intelligence service at the present stage- not to overlook the immediate threat of a nuclear attack on the Soviet Union-has acquired an especial degree of urgency.[48]

To further reinforce the need for the KGB and the FCD to reorient its assets toward this new and important objective, Kryuchov elaborated further on the overall objectives and the types of intelligence the KGB need to fulfill its mission to the Soviet state. He stated:

The need to discover specific plans and actions by our adversary connected with his preparation for a surprise nuclear missile attack on the USSR and other socialist countries is now of particularly grave importance. In this context, the primary task is to obtain reliable documentary and other advance information on all aspects and details of military, political, and strategic activity of the main adversary, revealing his secret preparations for war.[49]

Having established the justification and the aim of Operation RYAN, Kryuchov explained to his officers that the KGB would direct it resources toward gathering information within the "political, economic, military, and civilian defense sectors," while the GRU, which was for the first time in Soviet history working in close coordination with the state's intelligence service, would focus on more military-specific objectives such as "operational readiness of the strategic and tactical nuclear forces of the United States and NATO."[50]

After explaining the rationale for the operation and providing a quick overview of how the alliance between the GRU and the KGB would work toward the ultimate objective as a means to safeguard the Soviet Union, Kryuchov provided his officers and agents with a much more detailed list of targets and specific intelligence indicators that the agency wished to collect.

The primary categories of intelligence that the KGB sought to gather in an attempt to foil any Western plans for a surprise nuclear missile attack can be largely synthesized into two groups. The first are more traditional items that indicate that the large military and political bureaucracies that controlled the U.S. and NATO military forces were preparing for war. As such, Kryuchov outlined that observations of parking lots used by government and military workers in the United States, as well as across Europe, needed to be watched to detect that no irregular patterns of late hours and more workers emerged. Any indicators of abnormal hours or a heightened workload could provide critical intelligence that the preparations for the preemptive nuclear strike were imminent. Furthermore, the KGB also paid closer attention to the defense conditions and operational readiness exercises of U.S. and NATO forces. This first category of sources had always been part of the collection program for the KGB and the GRU, but the major difference within the context of Operation RYAN was that the reporting mandates from officers in the field and agents working for the KGB and the GRU became much more stringent. Also, the KGB watched and gathered intelligence on CIA activity in Europe, and more importantly, Eastern and Central Europe as they believed that an increase in operations in these regions were indicators of preparations for postattack resistance and insurgency movements. Therefore, an increased indication of CIA activity could be vital in understanding the intentions of the United States.

The second piece of this process used satellites to gather and collect information on military forces and strategic nuclear forces. Much like Stansfield Turner had emphasized for the CIA a few years earlier, the KGB used satellites to gather the large-scale indicators of a potential attack, while the HUMINT sources provided additional context and lower-order indicators. Hence, when the KGB and the GRU combined the two streams of intelligence, they received a more detailed understanding of the strategic situation; at least, this was the idea behind the significance of Operation RYAN. The reality was that by 1983, the obsession over a surprise nuclear attack reached a crescendo and quickly faded by 1984 as the leadership of the Soviet Union rapidly changed and the officers and agents within the KGB lost their obsession with a surprise nuclear attack from the West.

However, before Operation RYAN waned, the KGB maintained its steadfast fixation. First, in March 1983, when U.S. President Ronald Reagan made his Strategic Defense Initiative (SDI) speech, the KGB took this message as an attempt "to psychologically prepare the American people for nuclear war."[51] Yet this was far from the truth, as Reagan had serious concerns about the tenets of the concept of Mutual Assured Destruction (MAD) associated with a nuclear exchange between the United States and the Soviet Union and wanted to begin a research program to shift the United States away from this dangerous concept.[52] His speech was not an indicator of an imminent nuclear attack, but rather a shift in the fundamentals of the strategic environment and ultimately the Cold War. However, due to their obsession over a surprise attack, the KGB missed the reality of this moment.

Two additional factors sealed the fate of Operation RYAN. The first was the death of Yuri Andropov in September 1983, who even from his deathbed maintained a vigilant watch over potential indicators of an imminent nuclear attack from the West while he also encouraged the KGB to maintain its steadfast commitment to uncovering the truth about the West's, and specifically Reagan's, intentions.[53] In November 1983, the KGB finally believed that its suspicions were being confirmed with the initiation of the NATO's Able Archer exercise. This relatively high-profile military exercise was designed to practice and simulate nuclear release procedures throughout NATO and even involved parts played by Reagan and other high-profile cabinet members. However, after a very few tense days in which the KGB and the GRU believed that NATO was indeed preparing for a surprise attack, the exercise and all associated alerts in Europe and the United States stopped. The KGB had been caught off guard and, despite its best efforts, failed to provide advance warning for the Soviet homeland. This was indeed a major intelligence failure that quickly led to the demise of Operation RYAN. After the end of the Cold War, former KGB officers commented that the KGB "would have gained a far more accurate insight into American policy by reading the *New York Times* or *Washington Post*."[54]

NEW CONCERNS FOR A NEW ERA

With the passing of Andropov and the ascension of Mikhail Gorbachev, the Soviet Union went through one of its most significant evolutions since the 1917 October Revolution. Gorbachev was well aware of the internal social and economic dynamics and had to deal with these systemic issues. In short, the chronic problems centered on economic and political issues that plagued the Soviet system since the middle of the 1970s and were exacerbated by the Soviet Union's invasion of Afghanistan in December 1979. As former British Ambassador to Moscow Rodric Braithwaite stated, the viability of the Soviet system had become questionable; "with or without the war in Afghanistan the Soviet Union was collapsing."[55]

A fundamental flaw in the Soviet system had long been the centrally planned economy, by which the production schedule of industry was established by a central committee, regardless of the real demands required by the nation and the people, which were often in overt competition. By the time the Cold War had entered the late 1960s, this problem had come to manifest itself within the context of détente. Also, the development of the Warsaw Pact, which encompassed a significant economic component, contributed to the overt complexity of the precarious and deeply flawed system. However, before the collapse of the Soviet system in 1992, it is necessary to review the economic history of the Soviet Union for a firm understanding of how the stresses of the Afghan war helped to acerbate an already crumbling economic infrastructure.

In fact, economist Richard Allen makes a very strong case that, historically speaking, from 1928 until the mid-1960s, the Soviet Union's economy appeared to be one of the most robust systems on the planet.[56] However, the impressive growth statistics and production schedules masked significant and fundamental flaws in the nature of the Soviet Union's economy.

In a system that emphasized production and growth numbers, the state provided little incentive for industry to reinvest in updating machinery, streamlining production methods, and researching new technologies.[57] Therefore, by the late 1960s and early 1970s, Leonid Brezhnev faced a significant economic crisis as the Soviet economy began to stagnate and the leaders of the Soviet Union faced the dilemma of updating old factories or investing in new ones that encompassed newer technology. Though the Soviet Union chose to invest in new plants and production facilities such as steel, they encountered a decline in access to cheap and easy-to-access raw materials such as iron ore.[58] Hence, the price of extracting raw materials compounded the cost of investing in new factory and industrial facilities and increased the strain on the already overburdened economic system, which focused on keeping prices artificially low.

Therefore, though the Soviet Union had invested in new plants and facilities, which was a capital-rich endeavor, the Soviet government faced the unforeseen consequences of having to spend more money to extract and mine raw materials while not being able to pass the costs on to the people. This problem is exemplified by the Soviet Union's selling of cheap gas to its Warsaw Pact allies, such as Poland, which was not an issue until the price of extracting petroleum and then refining it increased in the early 1970s. As a result of a spike in the cost of production and refinement of petrol, the Soviet Union had to maintain its artificially low prices for its Polish ally. By the mid-1970s, every barrel of gas "sold" to Poland from the Soviet Union lost money.

Leonid Brezhnev recognized these systemic issues, but he lacked the necessary insights to make the significant, wholesale reforms necessary across the Soviet Union and the Warsaw Pact. As a result, the issues manifested as the Soviet Union encountered a leadership crisis when Brezhnev died and Andropov and Chernenko served short leadership terms due to poor health and old age. By mid-1985, when Mikhail Gorbachev assumed the leadership of the Soviet Union, the economic issues that first came to bear in the late 1960s and early 1970s still plagued the system. Throughout this period, it was not uncommon for the people of the Soviet Union to face shortages in consumer goods, as the government typically favored investing in industrial or military production over consumer goods. By 1987 Gorbachev attempted to reform the stagnating system via his policy of perestroika, which means reforms and restructuring. The idea was that the Soviet Union could make the necessary adjustments to its economic system in a way that would recapture the heady growth of the period from the 1920s through the 1960s. However, the entrenched issues within the economic system created additional demands on the people of the Soviet Union as they faced additional shortages and production slowdowns as the corrections were made. This additional stress happened as the people of the Soviet Union became increasingly aware of the costs of its adventurism in Afghanistan. Therefore, it is easy to see that the war in Afghanistan did not directly contribute to the economic decline of the Soviet Union, but rather the system collapsed due to systemic issues that increasingly placed more and more hardship on the people of the Soviet Union, while its leaders attempted to correct systemic economic flaws.

Compounding economic issues, the Soviet Union also faced inherent political problems, only exacerbated by the Soviet-Afghan war. In fact, as Gorbachev strove to make the necessary political adjustments, he realized that they would have a profound economic and social impact. To understand the need for Gorbachev to reform the political system of the Soviet Union, it is easiest to look at four fundamental problems that captured Gorbachev's attention.[59] The first was an attempt to make the Soviet system more pluralistic. This meant that Gorbachev and a group of reform-minded Communist Party members believed that the Soviet political system, which, in the 1920s and early 1930s, allowed for a controlled, yet limited debate among political parties, had atrophied in the Stalinist and post-Stalinist era. Gorbachev believed that by allowing a wide range of debate on political topics, the Soviet political system could recapture the vitality and intellectual stimulus of the early era of the nation.

The specific actions identified by Gorbachev as needing political reform focused on "competitive elections, freedom of group organizations, and the establishment of representative assemblies."[60] The problem was that the Soviet system saw these radical reforms as problematic as they ran counter to the entrenched ideas about the need for the Communist Party to keep tight control of the political process, while at the same time making sure that the regime remained in power. One can come to appreciate the ideas of Gorbachev and his reforms, but he was bucking a stagnant system that had only become more rigid under the leadership of Brezhnev, Andropov, and Chernenko, as this troika of Stalinist-era leaders suppressed any efforts at liberal reforms.

According to prominent Gorbachev historian Archie Brown, Gorbachev, on assuming power after the short-term and lackluster leadership of Andropov and Chernenko, took the opportunity in 1986 to emphasize the overt need for the Soviet Union to restructure its political and economic systems. Using the terms perestroika and *democratizatsiya*, Gorbachev advanced an agenda that aimed to readjust and improve the "bitterness and lack of respect" he saw taking hold of the younger generation of Soviet citizens as they suffered under the pains of a stagnating economy and an oppressive and secretive political system.[61]

Yet, despite the need for reforms, Gorbachev had to overcome the inertia of a lumbering Soviet political and economic bureaucracy. This was no easy task. In fact, Gorbachev, in an effort to outline his ideas and justify their need, wrote *Perestroika: New Thinking for Our Country and the World* as a means to demonstrate that reform was within the ideological parameters of Lenin's vision for the Soviet Union. Throughout the book, Gorbachev skillfully identifies the tenets of perestroika as they applied to the social, political, economic, and ethical spheres of Soviet life.

The central problem facing Gorbachev and his attempts at reforms focused on not destroying the structure of the Soviet system in a way that threatened the old-guard Stalinists. His process, therefore, became a slow, deliberate attempt to liberalize the Soviet Union, while staying within the parameters of V. I. Lenin's vision. However, a paradox arose that cautioned against the attempts at democratization because the system feared that any loosening of the tight grip held by the Soviet bureaucracy on the political process could result in a dwindling of power.

The reform efforts by Gorbachev had a slow, cumbersome start but were beginning to be adopted by the end of the 1980s. However, the problem was that as Gorbachev attempted to initiate economic, political, and social reforms, he found that the three spheres of Soviet society were deeply interconnected. Therefore, reform and adjustments in the economic arena had profound impacts on the need for adjustment made to the political system, which necessitated that the government of the Soviet Union had to be more open with its citizens. The result was that although Gorbachev attempted a slow, cautious reform, he encountered the realization that once the forces of liberalism and democracy were unleashed, they were very hard to control. Hence the allowance of multiparty elections, openness in the press, and small adjustments to the economic system resulted in the unintended consequence of diminishing the power and structure of the Communist Party's bureaucracy and power. Though Gorbachev eschewed the radicalness of his ideas, Archie Brown has aptly stated that "he played a decisive role in moving the system from party to state rule and from monism to pluralism."[62] This allowed for the forces that would eventually dismantle the Soviet Union in December of 1991 to take hold and overcome the decrepit Soviet Union.

In addition to these vast systemic issues, Gorbachev also had to contend with a war in Afghanistan, a strong anticommunist West, and major technological changes. The combinations of these forces also worried the KGB's leaders, as they further had to contend with the need to reorient their missions away from the objectives outlined in the fruitless pursuits of Operation RYAN. The new focal point for the KGB would be the science and technology being used by the West to build the next-generation weapon systems that relied on advanced technologies, composite construction techniques, and advanced computing power. By capturing this intelligence, Directorate T of the KGB could save the sagging Soviet economy countless rubles by stealing these high-tech secrets.

Much like its predecessor in the 1930s, the KGB, in the early and mid-1980s, became fixated on infiltrating and gaining access to American firms that worked in a variety of high-tech fields. The focus was not only on military hardware but also on agriculture and other specialties that could benefit the lagging home front of the Soviet Union. Placing officers and generating agents within these firms, universities, and think tanks was a goal that the KGB believed would greatly benefit its aims. Based on intelligence received from Christopher Boyce, an employee for the TRW Corporation, which had contracts with the U.S. military and CIA for intelligence satellites, the KGB believed that security in these American firms was sloppy and easy to circumvent.[63]

To further reinforce this perception, the KGB also relied on reports from John Walker, a U.S. Navy senior NCO who had been providing the KGB with reams of intelligence on U.S. and NATO submarine and naval operations for years. Walker once boasted that "K-Mart had better security than the U.S. Navy."[64] Based on these insiders' assessments, the KGB believed that cultivating a network of agents within defense contractors, the military, and even U.S. universities was the surest way to gain access to the latest research and development on a wide variety of issues.

The 1980s saw the pinnacle process and built on the success of the KGB in the 1970s when it had acquired valuable information on NASA rockets, such as the Saturn V, and a host of U.S. military missiles, including the Honest John, Poseidon, Redeye, Roland, and even the Boeing 747.[65] These early successes fueled the KGB's quest for great access to more advanced technology as the West was going through the beginning stages of the computer and later information revolutions. Knowing that the Soviet Union's economic and industrial infrastructure was withering, the KGB believed that this renewed commitment to economic and industrial espionage could assist in ensuring that the Soviet Union was not left behind in the global struggle against the United States.

The list of corporations was impressive, as it included IBM, Texas Instruments, Westinghouse, Honeywell, and Monsanto, as well as the standard military defense contracts.[66] Furthermore, the KGB also sought to use university students as agents to gather intelligence from major U.S. universities. Again, the universities targeted by the KGB was top-notch and included MIT, Columbia, Cornell, Harvard, Princeton, American, Catholic, Georgetown, and George Washington on the East Coast.[67] Not just fixating on the East Coast, the KGB also sought to place students in Stanford, University of California Berkeley, University of Southern California, and the California Institute of Technology.[68] The process designed by the KGB was not just about haphazardly planting agents and spies through these universities and corporations but rather designing a robust plan that allocated intelligence-gathering resources to specific needs of the Soviet Union. Therefore, the scheme focused on general area topics such as "agriculture, metallurgy, power-generation, engineering and advanced technologies and defense industries."[69] Based on the internal assessment of the capabilities of the Soviet Union, the KGB and the government of the Soviet Union believed that they were at least "ten years behind" the West and therefore had to redouble their efforts to catch up.[70]

The KGB had success in gathering intelligence on industrial, agricultural, and defense capabilities of the United States. On defense matters, the KGB defined the Soviet Union's priorities as:

Military technology measures taken by the Main Adversary to build up first-strike weapons: the quantitative increase in nuclear munitions and delivery means (MX missile complexes, Trident, Pershing 2, cruise missiles, and strategic bombers); replacement of one generation of nuclear missiles by another (Minuteman, Trident 2), the development of qualitatively new types of weapons (space devices for multiple use for military purposes, laser and pencil beam weapons, non-acoustic anti-submarine defense weapons, and electronic warfare weapons.[71]

Though the Soviet Union's obsession with first-strike nuclear weapons was still a major priority, a major objective of the KGB's industrial and defense-related operations was stealing research and development that could save the country money as it worked to improve its industrial, agricultural, and defense-related capabilities.

Practically, the ability to gather information on the U.S. F/A-18 fighter aircraft, the B-1B strategic bomber, and the Airborne Early Warning and Control aircraft used by the United States, as well as NATO, saved the Soviet Union's defense industries millions of dollars.[72] From the perspective of the KGB, the Soviet Union was reaping great success with the information gathered through these sources. It is important to note that the KGB, during this period, also leveraged its Warsaw Pact allies and their respective intelligence services as additional assets to gain this vital information. Therefore, it was a full-force blitz by the communist world to make sure that they did not get outclassed and outgunned by the West as their economies were stagnating and suffering.

From a military force perspective, the Soviet Union developed roughly 150 weapons systems that were directly based on Western technologies gathered during the late 1970s and through the 1980s.[73] Using this significant benchmark as an indicator of success, the KGB believed that it was making great headway in the struggle against the main adversary. However, the success of stealing secrets to bolster the agricultural, industrial, electronic, and defense sectors of the Soviet Union's economy did not fix the systemic problems found in the Soviet Union's economy and social sectors, which were the major issues that plagued Gorbachev as he tried to make adjustments to a crumbling system. The CIA and Ronald Reagan saw these vulnerabilities and exploited them both overtly and covertly.

THE CIA, THE SOLIDARITY MOVEMENT, AND THE MUJAHIDEEN

The Reagan administration, not known for its similarities with the presidential administration of Jimmy Carter, used the CIA to continue and even increase the pressure on the Soviet system by expanding two primary programs started under Carter. The first was the support of the Solidarity movement in Poland, which began with Carter and his commitment to human rights, as outlined by the Helsinki Accords. The second action was the support of the Mujahideen in Afghanistan as a way to embroil and stress the weakening Soviet system. Additionally, Reagan's appointment of William Casey as DCI moved the agency away from some of the more technological foci that had evolved in the years since the end of the Vietnam War. As a veteran of the OSS, Casey brought back a passion for covert missions that were hell-bent on smashing communism and the Soviet Union. In the cases of supporting the Solidarity movement in Poland and the Mujahideen in Afghanistan, Casey saw both operations as vital in the war against communism. For Casey, the CIA was a critical tool to "reduce Soviet power in absolute terms."[74] Both the Solidarity movement and the Mujahideen were efforts that Casey saw as critical in assisting the United States in achieving its overall Cold War objective.

In the summer of 1980, workers at the Lenin shipyard in Gdansk, Poland, formed a labor union to advance their rights as workers in the beleaguered Polish economy. The initial strike that spawned the Solidarity movement was called based on the firing and dismissal of leaders in what would become the Solidarity union and an international movement. Based on his record of supporting human rights, and encouraged by Brzezinski, Jimmy Carter authorized the CIA to assist the workers in Poland by providing some copying and basic propaganda assistance to get their message to a wider base within Poland as well as the Warsaw Pact.[75] Furthermore, Brzezinski, in December 1980, "briefed a senior emissary from Pope John Paul II about the US support of nationalist movements in eastern Europe."[76] With the transition to the Reagan administration in January of 1981, the U.S. covert support for the Solidarity movement expanded significantly.

Levering the CIA's satellite technology, Casey allied with the Mossad in an effort to gain internal intelligence on the social and political situation within Poland.[77] Simply, Casey wanted on-the-ground information from the Mossad's agents in Poland, and in exchange he would provide the Israelis with satellite photographs and other intelligence on Iraq and Syria.[78] The Israelis agreed to the work with Casey and the CIA. Additionally, the CIA, with the expressed support of Reagan and Casey, used both international and domestic parties to increase the covert support of the Solidarity movement. First, on the international scene, the CIA used the Catholic Church as an avenue to encourage the budding relationship between Lech Walesa, leader of Solidarity, and Pope John Paul II, who met in January of 1981.

Casey and other Catholics in Reagan's administration appealed to the Pope's staff to encourage support for the workers in Poland. However, Pope John Paul II and his staff were very careful not to play into the hands of the Soviet Union by making overt and careless statements that highlighted their clear support and cooperation with the United States.[79] Rather, the Catholic Church provided information for Casey on the political and social situation in Poland based off the efforts of Cardinal Wyszynski, who had gained a strong reputation in Poland for mediating between the Polish government and the Solidarity movement.[80]

In addition to using the Catholic Church, the CIA also used the AFL-CIO as a means to build a greater awareness within the United States for the Solidarity cause, as well as within Europe. Again, Casey saw the international labor movement as an avenue through which the CIA could gain keen insights into the political and social situation on the ground. Even though the AFL-CIO had overtly rejected offers to work with the Reagan administration due to the union's strong and longtime affiliation with the Democratic Party in the United States, the union did provide "advice, training, and financial" support to the Solidarity movement, in addition to great assistance in printing and preparing propaganda for their international brothers in Poland.[81] Casey welcomed this support, as did the president.

Building on this foundation, the CIA solidified its plan in the aftermath of the declaration of martial law in Poland on December 12, 1981. The CIA's support of Solidarity now served a greater purpose, and Casey wanted to ensure that the "first anticommunist organization aboveground in the Soviet bloc survived."[82] Additionally, the CIA's support and backing of Solidarity could also "shatter the myth of Soviet invincibility," which had long persisted in the Warsaw Pact and the third world.[83]

The CIA's operation to support and assist the Solidarity movement in Poland was driven by four central actions:

To provide critical funds to Solidarity to sustain the Movement. These could take the form of cash, both U.S. dollars and Polish zlotys.

Supply advanced communications equipment to organize an effective Command, Control, Communications, and Intelligence (C3I) network for the Solidarity underground. This would enable the movement to communicate even under martial law.

Offer training to a few select individuals in the movement to use advanced communication equipment that would be provided.

Use CIA assets to serve as the eyes and ears of Solidarity, sharing critical intelligence when appropriate.[84]

By May 1982, in the National Security Strategy of the United States, as outlined in National Security Decision Directive (NSDD) 32, the Reagan administration solidified its covert actions to support political movements that "attempted to throw off communist rule" by providing clandestine support and broadcast operations for these freedom fighters.[85] For the duration of Reagan's administration, the CIA maintained and increased its support of the Solidarity movement. With the success of the operations in Poland, the CIA also continued to support the Mujahideen in Afghanistan with an aim to further weaken the Soviet Union.

The CIA's involvement in Afghanistan, which has been traditionally associated with the Reagan administration's agreement to send stinger missiles to the Mujahideen, actually started with the Carter administration. President Carter and his national security staff began covert operations to "oppose the Marxist government in Kabul."[86] The objective of these operations was to highlight the Soviet Union's increased activity in Afghanistan while also making sure that resistance groups were not suppressed and unheard.

Maintaining his commitment to the tenets of the Helsinki Accords, Carter authorized the CIA to conduct covert operations that provided "indirect financial assistance to insurgent groups, direct finance to Afghan émigré groups, anti-regime activities, and non-lethal material assistance."[87] Also within these broad objectives, the Carter administration provided weapons and training to support the various anti-Soviet groups throughout Afghanistan.[88] Though these operations were important in the context of Carter's stance against the Soviet Union and communism, they were funded at very low levels.[89]

The significance of these operations increased when the Soviet Union invaded Afghanistan in December 1979. With the U.S. presidential election of 1980 months away, which resulted in the election of Ronald Reagan as fortieth president of the United States, the CIA's involvement in Afghanistan skyrocketed as the new administration saw a great opportunity to impact the Soviet Union directly.

Under the direction of William Casey, the CIA worked a complex program that included the assistance of Pakistan, Saudi Arabia, Egypt, Great Britain, Israel, and even China as partners that aided in expanding the support, training, and assistance to the Mujahideen.[90] From the perspective of CIA, they saw the issue in Afghanistan different from the Carter administration. Not content with just providing a basic level of support, Reagan and Casey realized a great opportunity to expose the weakening Soviet system. They saw the Mujahideen as a low-grade insurgency that needed more assistance, arms, and financing as a way to make sure that the Soviet Union began to accrue a higher level of losses, which would have vast effects within the Soviet state as well as within Afghanistan and even within the greater international community.[91] To advance the objectives of the United States, the CIA, with great effort by Casey, expanded its support, training, and financial assistance to the Mujahideen.

The CIA's operations in Afghanistan were not just the typical covert operations supported by black budgets and the traditional cloak-and-dagger business of the espionage world. The Reagan administration codified its commitment to these operations in National Security Decision Directive (NSDD) 166 entitled "U.S. Policy, Program, and Strategy in Afghanistan," signed by President Reagan March 27, 1985. In the introduction of the document, the Reagan administration stated:

The two principle elements in our Afghanistan strategy are a program of covert action support to the Afghan resistance, and our diplomatic/political strategy to pressure the Soviet Union to withdrawal its forces from Afghanistan and to increase international support for the Afghan resistance forces.[92]

Having established the elements of the operations in Afghanistan, the CIA worked with international partners to make sure that the Mujahideen had the arms, resources, and training needed to inflict a great level of pain not only on the Soviet army but also on the Soviet Union at large. The CIA believed that by substantially expanding the scale and scope of the support started by Carter, the policy goals outlined in NSDD 166 could be achieved and would have a significant impact on the Soviet Union and its image in the international community. The goals of the administration, which would be achieved by the CIA's actions, were:

Demonstrate to the Soviet Union that its long-term strategy for subjugating Afghanistan is not working.
    Deny Afghanistan to the Soviets as a base.
    Promote Soviet isolation in the Third and Islamic worlds on the Afghanistan issue.
    Prevent the defeat of an indigenous movement which is resisting Soviet aggression.
    Show firmness of purpose in deterring Soviet aggression in the third world.[93]

Recognizing that the Soviet strategy in Afghanistan was focused on grinding down the Mujahideen by using the Soviet's advantage in conventional forces as well as airpower, the CIA knew that the characterization of the Mujahideen as a "band of ragtag guerillas fighting against a modern conventional foe" had to be changed.[94] Therefore, the quality and quantity of weapons had to be improved with an aim toward balancing the lopsided force ratio. In addition to the qualitative adjustments, the CIA also worked with the intelligence service of Pakistan (ISI) to ensure that the Mujahideen had more and better training in tactics, techniques, and procedures to increase their lethality against the Soviet ground and air forces.[95] The infusion of more and better small arms, light artillery, and man-portable surface-to-air missiles provided the results the CIA desired.

Casey, however, was not content with just fighting the Soviet Union through the Mujahideen in a proxy war in Afghanistan; he wanted to expand the operation directly to include pushing fighters into the Soviet Union.[96] Though this idea had support within the administration, including the president, it was a complex and difficult operation that would not be able to be enacted before the Soviet Union left Afghanistan in 1989.

Therefore, the traditional narrative that the CIA's contribution was centered on providing stinger missiles to the Mujahideen is only a small part of the much greater vision Casey and Reagan had of the role of the CIA as being vital in ensuring that the United States was winning the Cold War. In this last era of the Cold War, though the espionage game had evolved and expanded, it still focused on using covert and clandestine services to weaken the enemy. The CIA and its support of the Mujahideen in Afghanistan fulfilled this mission and achieved the desired outcomes outlined in NSDD 166.

CONCLUSION

The years between 1976 and 1988 were a very dynamic, and at times very tense, period in the Cold War. In the context of the espionage game between the United States and the Soviet Union, this period saw the continued evolution of technology as a means to provide a greater level of intelligence; however, what is also significant in this period was the continual reliance on the use of human agents and officers in the spy craft business by both the KGB and the CIA.

Under President Carter and his DCI Admiral Stansfield Turner, the CIA began a significant adjustment through which satellites and other electronic and high-technology means were used to collect and gather intelligence. The traditional use of human agents and intelligence officers was reserved to provide background and contextual information that was needed to provide deeper insights into the signals or photographic intelligence collected by other national technical means.

In the wake of Vietnam and the congressional hearings on the past operations of the CIA, this technological adjustment toward a greater reliance on satellites made some sense, as it attempted to demystify the role, purpose, and to some extent the operations of the CIA. However, as the global political mood shifted from détente and the European community debated the merits of the Helsinki Accords, the Carter administration saw the opportunity to once again mobilize the CIA in a capacity that paralleled its first missions in the late 1940s in Europe. The objective was to highlight the poor human rights record of the Soviet Union and use this as a way to pressure the Soviet system. The CIA worked to produce books, articles, and monographs by Soviet dissidents that highlighted the repressive nature of the system with an aim toward weakening the regime.

Using the tenets of the Helsinki Accords therefore became a main method identified by President Carter's administration through which the CIA could slowly rebuild its operational confidence. It also helped that President Carter saw these covert operations as benefiting the greater good of people around the globe. The Reagan administration, though it had a much different philosophical idea about the use of covert operations, maintained the basic mission and operations started by Carter, but they would become more aggressive and assertive as the administration sensed an opportunity to shift the tide in the Cold War power struggle.

From the perspective of the KGB leadership, they were coming off the years in which they strongly believed that the "world was going their way."[97] However, they quickly began to realize that they were vulnerable to two significant forces. The first was the human rights problem they had with their repressive system. The KGB could only submit counter-propaganda and attempt to build intelligence on members of the Carter administration, as they were not the traditional Washington, D.C., insiders. However, beyond the push to get more intelligence during the late 1970s, the KGB quickly realized that with the election of Ronald Reagan in November 1980, the Soviet Union faced a new era in the Cold War.

This era was characterized by the Soviet Union's obsession with a potential first nuclear strike from the United States. This obsession within and outside the KGB drove the Soviet Union's intelligence service to focus its intelligence-gathering activities in an effort to predict when a first strike was imminent. To further increase its ability to provide critical intelligence, the KGB partnered with the GRU to build a larger and more robust capability to collect intelligence. By the mid-1980s, this obsession faded as Brezhnev and later Andropov died, and their fixation to focus a large number of their intelligence assets on this limited, but important, objective passed as yet another phase of the late Cold War.

By the time Mikhail Gorbachev assumed power in the Soviet Union, the KGB had recognized that the Soviet Union's science, research, and technology was years behind that of the West. Hence, the KGB focused its attention on espionage that could allow Soviet industry to short-circuit long and costly research and development programs. As a result of its industrial espionage efforts, the KGB focused on not just military technology but also computer and a whole host of advanced agricultural and industrial capabilities as well. Even though this type of "industrial espionage" may seem a diversion from the general trend of the Cold War, the intelligence services of the Soviet Union had a history since the 1920s of actively seeking to acquire industrial and commercial secrets that would allow the communist nation to maintain pace with Western nations. However, unlike in the past, by the 1980s, the economy of the Soviet Union was on shaky ground and could not be sustained, even though Gorbachev tried.

As the Reagan administration saw critical vulnerabilities in the Soviet and Warsaw pact political systems, they used the CIA as an active measure to push the communist system to their internal breaking points. Ironically, Reagan is often given credit for winning the Cold War; however, the policies of using the CIA to support both the Solidarity movement in Poland and the Mujahideen in Afghanistan started during the Carter administration. The major difference was the DCI, William Casey. Casey, as a former OSS officer, saw the CIA as an agency that could again take the fight to the Soviet Union in a grandiose move to "roll back" the communist tide. Casey's penchant for activist covert operations led him to expand the Carter-era ideas of supporting Solidarity in Poland and the Mujahideen in Afghanistan. The biggest alteration to these operations was that the Casey-era CIA had larger budgets and robust support from the DCI and the president to support these operations, as Casey and Reagan both saw them as critical opportunities that the CIA could use to weaken, if not break, the Soviet Union and the communist nations in the Eastern bloc. Even though these operations did have an influence on the final fall of the Soviet Union, they were compounded by the internal political, economic, and social issues within the Soviet system. Even as the Cold War drew to an end, the espionage game continued.

CHAPTER 7

The New World Order and Beyond, 1989–2014

The tearing down of the Berlin wall in November 1989 and the collapse of the Warsaw Pact and Soviet Union in 1991 served to officially end the Cold War. However, for the intelligence services of the United States and the Soviet Union, these significant events posed a serious problem. In the case of both intelligence services, their primary mission had been focused on gathering intelligence and running operations against one another for the duration of the 50-year struggle. Even though both the CIA and the KGB had other nations and functions, form the period 1945–1991, the main focal point of both institutions had been on each other. The larger question, as the Soviet system collapsed, was how the KGB would restructure and adjust its security services to meet the changing international security environment. From the CIA's perspective, the United States also had to adjust to a new operating environment.

Prior to these momentous changes, both the KGB and the CIA had to deal with major defectors who exposed the twisted and interesting history of intelligence operations during the Cold War. From the vantage point of the Soviet Union, the KGB not only had to deal with the collapse of the Soviet its state system, economy, and social structure, but also the fact that one of the intelligence service's stars, Oleg Kalugin, had become disenchanted with the whole system—and especially the ills of the Soviet security bureaucracy. As a result, he became an outspoken critic of the Soviet system and eventually immigrated to the United States in 1995. Kalugin's knowledge and openness to tell his story provided keen insights in the operational ethos as well as the overall operational capabilities of the Soviet Union's intelligence service. In the context of the emerging new world order, there were general questions about how the future intelligence service would operate in the world, and Kalugin's insights provided a glimpse into understanding how the Russian's saw and use espionage as a key component of national power.

As the Cold War concluded, the CIA had to deal with its own internal issues. First and foremost, since 1985 the CIA had been very concerned over the loss of agents within the Soviet Union. This was a problem because Gorbachev instituted glasnost as a way to open the social and political spectrum within the Soviet Union. Though people did still have to fear the internal security forces, in theory, the conditions within the Soviet Union were ripe for developing and exploiting agents. However, the CIA faced the problem that the vast majority of its agents in the Soviet Union had been getting arrested and detained by the Soviet authorities. The CIA could not understand how the internal security forces of the Soviet Union were breaking their agents and, hence, their access to intelligence. This issue became a major problem with which the CIA wrestled until the end of the Cold War, when longtime CIA officer Aldrich Ames was arrested by the FBI for espionage in 1994. Ames was the piece of the puzzle that the CIA had overlooked.

Only after the demise of the Cold War did these long-standing espionage professionals yield their secrets. Therefore, the espionage game that typified the Cold War did not just evaporate with the termination of the ideological struggle between the United States and the Soviet Union, but rather the espionage game continued into the post–Cold War security environment as the globe tried to figure out the demands and nature of the new and seemingly unstable security environment. In the midst of this turbulence, other insights into front organizations emerged. In the early 1990s, the World Peace Council, an organization that had been a fixture for the advancement and recognition of third world issues since the late 1950s, was exposed as a front organization to advance the foreign policy objectives and ideals of the Soviet Union. Also, just a year prior to the exposure of the true aims of the World Peace Council, the U.S. Congress and executive branch wrestled with the espionage activities that came to be known as Iran-Contra.

The collapse of the Cold War opened a floodgate of information on the espionage activities on both sides of the proverbial iron curtain. In the spirit of the era, government agencies, think thanks, and academic institutions became fixated on the operations, technologies, and spies of the Cold War era. Furthermore, since the Cold War ended and the Soviet Union ceased to be a state, the archives in the Warsaw Pact, as well as the Soviet Union, opened for brief periods of time to provide even more insights into the 50-year-long espionage game played between the CIA and the KGB.

The brief and euphoric period immediately following the Cold War quickly evaporated as the 1990s and the early 2000s demonstrated that the global security environment was a more dangerous and complex construct requiring intelligence services to be even more vigilant against threats. The threats in the new world order could come from traditional militaries, transnational terrorist groups, or even domestic terrorist activities.

Therefore, the CIA and the new intelligence service in the Russian Federation (the FSB) maintained their Cold War ways. Though the ideological tension between the Russian federation and the United States was gone, by the end of the 1990s, Russia's quest to regain its regional and international status once again highlighted old friction points left over from the Cold War. Outside of Russia, a series of outspoken critics of Russia and Vladimir Putin suffered unexplainable poisonings. Also, as the 21st century blossomed, "sleeper cells" of Russian agents had been uncovered and exposed as operating in the United States. Lastly, as of 2018, there is an ongoing investigation into Russian influence into the U.S. elections of 2016, as well as Russia's connections with the president of the United States. As we move forward to explain the end of the Cold War and how it affected the espionage game between the United States and Russia, we find that the 21st century maintains many of the same tenets that the CIA and the KGB developed and expanded over the course of the Cold War.

THE KGB AND OLEG KALUGIN

In 1987 Kryuchkov accompanied Gorbachev to Washington, D.C.; the trip was significant because it was the first time the head of the KGB's FCD visited the West.[1] The significant honor for Kryuchkov had come about due to the massive amounts of science and technological intelligence that the KGB's officers and agents had stolen in the West. Furthermore, the KGB had been cultivating a very productive and useful mole within the CIA. During his trip to Washington, D.C., Kryuchkov had a low-key dinner with Deputy Director of Central Intelligence Robert Gates. Later Gates recounted:

It is embarrassing to realize that, at this first high-level CIA-KGB meeting, Kryuchkov smugly knew that he had a spy—Aldrich Ames—at the heart of the CIA, that he knew quite well what we were telling the President and others about the Soviet Union, and that he was aware of many of our human and technical collection efforts in the USSR.[2]

As the last years of the Cold War passed, and despite the efforts of the CIA to assist the Mujahideen in Afghanistan and support the Solidarity movement in Poland, the KGB believed that its efforts to focus on science and technology as well as neutralizing Soviet citizens who were betraying their country were making great strides. An indicator of Gorbachev's satisfaction with the KGB's efforts was not only the offer for Kryuchkov to travel with him to Washington, D.C., but also that, in October 1988, Kryuchkov become head of the KGB.

As head of the KGB, Kryuchkov embraced the glasnost and perestroika spearheaded by Gorbachev. At the close of the 1980s, as the Warsaw Pact was crumbling from within, Kryuchkov still remained aware of the potential for a surprise first strike by the United States or NATO, as he had been during Operation RYAN, but by 1989 he presented a more "open climate toward East-West relations."[3] While remaining true to his inner suspicions of the West, publicly, Kryuchkov evoked a different image when he declared, "The KGB should have an image not only in our country but worldwide which is consistent with the noble goals I believe we are pursuing in our work."[4] Though Kryuchkov had publicly acknowledged the tenets of Gorbachev's new openness and systemic reforms, he steadfastly remained a dogmatic KGB officer who was still obsessed with the long-standing conspiracy theories cultivated and perpetuated by Andropov. The reality was that Gorbachev did not adhere to these same traditional myths and sought a different course for the Soviet Union that focused on a closer relationship with the West and specifically the United States. However, Kryuchkov was still committed to the preservation of the old Soviet State and still firmly believed that the ultimate goal of the United States was to "eliminate the Soviet Union as a united state."[5]

Kryuchkov was correct that the United States still focused on breaking the communist state. However, the reality was that the increased pressure of outside forces coming from dissidents, the Solidarity movement, and the Soviet Union's poor record on human rights compounded the catastrophic internal economic, social, and political issues facing the Soviet Union. As Gorbachev strove to make necessary corrections to preserve and update the Soviet system, the reality was that the KGB remained committed to an outdated and misinformed understanding of the rapidly shifting security environment. Kryuchkov represented the old way of thinking, and there were others in the KGB who had a very different understanding of the new geopolitical realities facing the Soviet Union. KGB General Oleg Kalugin was one such voice within the Soviet Union's intelligence service.

As recounted in earlier chapters, Kalugin was a rising star in the KGB and had spent years living and working in the United States and abroad, which gave him a much greater sense of the international security environment than the apparatchiks and leadership of the KGB. However, based on his experience and, having spent so much time living abroad, he also ran the risk of being suspected of being sympathetic toward the main adversary of the Soviet Union. In 1980, the KGB promoted Kalugin and moved him to Leningrad to serve as a first chief deputy to KGB Leningrad Chief Daniil Nozyrev.[6] Though this new position had the appearance of a promotion, Kalugin had no real power and was tasked with handling low-level intelligence matters. Furthermore, Nozyrev wanted Kalugin to know that he would not tolerate any obstructionist or insubordinate behavior.[7] Within the first few months of the new assignment, Kalugin had been tipped off by a "friend," Rear Admiral Sokolov, within the KGB that the KGB had suspected him of being a double agent for the CIA.

As a career KGB officer who had made significant personal and professional sacrifices for the Soviet Union, Kalugin found this assumption difficult to accept. In his memoirs he recounts the moment the reality of this new situation struck him:

The system to which I had devoted my life, the system to which I had been boundlessly loyal, now suspected me of betrayal. I had been sullied by unproven allegations, allegations so amorphous that I didn't even know how to fight back. I increasingly began to feel like millions of other Soviets who had been unjustly accused of crimes, though most of them had experienced a far worst fate. In our system, everyone was a suspect, including someone as fantastically loyal as myself. From that day forward, something changes inside me, for I realized that the system was essentially vicious.[8]

As he went about his professional duties, Kalugin maintained and developed a friendship with Sokolov, who had assisted him in his first day in Leningrad; however, years later he found out that Nozyrev had used Sokolov as an informant to keep track of Kalugin and his ideas.[9] For Kalugin this was yet another glaring example of the ills of the Soviet system.

Kalugin became even further alienated during his time in Leningrad, as the emphasis was on catching Soviet citizens who were thought to be working with the CIA. Yet Kalugin came to realize that the system was flawed and only mainly concerned with maintaining the power of the apparatchiks and party members who aspired for more prestigious positions and more power. In September 1989, the KGB retired Kalugin as a means to make sure that this "troublemaker" was suppressed and isolated from the corridors of power.[10]

In June 1990 Kalugin made a public speech at the conference of the Democratic Platform of the Communist Party, which was a liberal reform party designed to take advantage of the political openness of the late Soviet period. Kalugin knew that the base of the party would be skeptical of a career KGB officer in their ranks, but he started his speech by saying:

Some people may think that I have jumped on the democratic bandwagon with evil intentions. I understand that there may be suspicion in your minds, but let me tell you that you're wrong. I am from the KGB. I worked in that organization for more than thirty years, and I want to tell all of you how the KGB works against the best interest of democratic forces in this country.[11]

Any suspicions from the floor of the rally that Kalugin was an agent sent by the KGB to gather intelligence and report on the democratic platform evaporated with his opening statement. Kalugin knew that with his open and public address, he was making a significant change in his professional life. The essence of his speech was that the KGB needed to be transformed fundamentally if political reforms had any real chance of having a permanent impact of the Soviet system. In the body of his speech, Kalugin stated:

We cannot begin a serious restructuring of our society until we rid ourselves of the restraints imposed by an organization which has penetrated every sphere of our lives, which interferes with all aspects of state life, political life, the economy, science, arts, religion, even sports. Today, just as ten or twenty years ago, that hand of the KGB is everywhere. And any real talk of *perestroika* without reforming the KGB is nothing but a lie. All the much-ballyhooed changes in the KGB are cosmetic, a disguise upon the ugly face of the Stalin-Brezhnev era. In fact, all elements of the old dictatorship are still in place. The chief assistant and handmaiden of the Communist Party remains the KGB. In order to secure genuine changes in our country, this structure of violence and falsehood must be dismantled.[12]

Kalugin's address created a stir across the Soviet Union and especially within the KGB. Days after his address, by orders of Gorbachev, Kalugin was stripped of his rank as major general, stripped of his awards, and stripped of his pension.[13] The KGB's official statement was that "it is very unfortunate when an officer embarks on the path of illegal actions, behaves immorally, or commits treasons."[14] Simply, they were "not at all sorry they got rid of Kalugin."[15]

The KGB's actions reaffirmed Kalugin's point. However, despite the KGB's action against him, Kalugin's politically charged statement synchronized with a rapidly growing reform movement within the Soviet Union that was organizing around the newly elected chairman of the Russian parliament, Boris Yeltsin, in June 1991. In this rapidly changing and reform-minded era, Kalugin was asked to fill a vacant seat from Krasnodar in the USSR Congress of People's Deputies. He agreed to run for the seat, but he also knew that the KGB would use its vast resources to harass and defeat his campaign. Nevertheless, Kalugin persisted.

The KGB followed him, planted false newspaper articles, threatened him with arrest, and even planted questions that tried to paint him as a traitor during his campaign speeches.[16] However, despite their best efforts to intimidate and counter his message, Kalugin won the election and thus sent a message that there was a groundswell of the Soviet population that "resoundingly rejected the old order."[17]

The elation and hope for a new Russia took a brief step backward on August 18, 1991, when Kryuchkov and other hardliners attempted to launch a coup against Gorbachev and the reformers taking place across the Soviet Union. Kalugin had been identified for arrest by the KGB, as had others whom the KGB deemed traitors to the old system, but there were factions within the KGB that supported and agreed with Kalugin's thoughts about the need to reform the KGB. In the aftermath of the coup, and in the spirit of reform, Kalugin went back to the KGB as an advisor to reform the institution as the Soviet Union crumbled. In December 1991, the Soviet Union ceased to be, and the KGB entered a new era in which Kalugin tried to influence the organization for the benefit of Russia and the Russian federation.[18] However, as the immediate post–Cold War security environment evolved, the new intelligence service for the Russian Federation, the Federal Security Service (FSB), maintained some of its old habits.

ALDRICH AMES, THE CIA, AND MOLES

Sometime in 1988 Dimitri Fedorovich Polyakov, a general in the Soviet army's GRU, was shot in the head and buried in an unmarked grave by State security officials.[19] Prior to his execution, Polyakov had been detained since January 1985 and had been tried as a spy in secret and found guilty of betraying the Soviet Union. Polyakov was a career GRU officer who had served the Soviet Union since 1951 in various overseas intelligence operations. Since 1974 he had served in Moscow at various important positions within Soviet military intelligence bureaucracy that focused on war plans and use of nuclear, biological, and chemical weapons.[20] On the outside, Polyakov was a model military officer and a stalwart citizen of the Soviet Union. However, he harbored a secret.

Polyakov had been deeply disgruntled with his salary and the Soviet system since 1959, which was at the height of Khrushchev's effort to de-Stalinize the Soviet Union.[21] Because of his disillusionment with the communist system, U.S. intelligence sources within the FBI identified Polyakov as a potential agent. By 1962 the CIA had made contact with Polyakov and convinced him to be a spy for the West.[22] For the next 23 years, he worked as a double agent; in his day job, he remained committed to the GRU and the Soviet Union, while at the same time, he was covertly providing the CIA with vast intelligence on the Soviet Union and its military forces as well as communist allies in the Warsaw Pact. Simply, Polyakov was a treasured agent within the Soviet military who greatly benefited the United States.

However, after being a valuable asset for the CIA for over 20 years, Polyakov's disappearance was a great shock to the intelligence communities of the United States. To compound the loss of Polyakov, in the mid-to-late 1980s, the CIA had a stretch of very bad luck where the vast majority of its agents within the Soviet government and the armed forces went quiet. The counterintelligence officers in the FBI as well as the CIA were perplexed by this seeming spate of very bad luck. At first the CIA fixated on two potential explanations for the loss of well-placed agents within the Soviet Union. The first suspect was Edward Lee Howard, and later the CIA suspected Clayton J. Lonetree.

Edward Lee Howard was a citizen of the United States who had started with the CIA in 1981 and had been identified to join the Agency's

SE section, which was designed to cultivate and place CIA officers within the Soviet Union and the Warsaw Pact with the express purpose of developing and running agents, as well as collecting valuable military and political intelligence for the United States.[23] Despite the promise he showed in being selected for the SE section, Howard was an alcoholic, and yet the CIA still had him slated to go to Moscow for his operational assignment after his initial training. During his work on the Soviet desk, while he completed his initial training, Howard had access to the lists of the CIA's agents in the Soviet Union, as well as the various operations being run by the United States in the USSR.[24] Having completed his training, Howard only needed to sit and pass a polygraph test prior to his departure for his first assignment. He failed the polygraph and was quickly and summarily fired by the CIA after only working for them for roughly fifteen months.[25]

Disgruntled over his release from the agency, Howard concocted an elaborate plan to provide intelligence to the KGB while on a secret trip to Vienna, Austria. However, Howard did more than just provide the KGB with intelligence; he also defected to the Soviet Union in 1986 with valuable insider information on the CIA's SE operations.[26] Howard's defection led the CIA to believe that he may have been responsible for the loss of its agents in the middle of the 1980s; however, the timelines compared to Polyakov's arrest did not square with Howard's release of information to the KGB. Howard, though a suspect, was not the only intelligence leak that the CIA identified.

The second potential explanation for the loss of its agents in the Soviet Union was United States Marine Corps Sergeant Clayton J. Lonetree. Lonetree was an USMC embassy guard in Moscow in 1984 when he was seduced by Violetta Seina.[27] Lonetree and Seina had a long affair, during which Seina introduced Lonetree to her "Uncle Sasha."[28] The reality was that "Uncle Sasha" was a skilled KGB officer who used Lonetree's affection for Violetta as a lever to pressure him to provide information to the KGB. In 1986, the United States Marine Corp transferred Lonetree from the U.S. Embassy in Moscow to the U.S. Embassy in Vienna, Austria.[29] Despite Lonetree's move, the KGB kept him on the hook by promising him that his continued compliance would be best for himself and Violetta.[30] In 1986, at a party in the U.S. Embassy in Vienna, Lonetree confessed his actions to CIA officer and was promptly arrested and tried for espionage. The CIA believed that Lonetree had compromised 20 agents in the Soviet Union, but the reality was that the information he passed to the KGB was of little value.[31] Therefore, Lonetree's actions still did not explain the loss of agents by the CIA. The CIA still had a leak that frustrated them until the end of the Cold War. Aldrich Ames was the mol the CIA had been hunting, but they unaware of this traitor in their organization in 1986.

Aldrich Ames joined the CIA in 1962, following the path of his father, Carlton Ames, who was a counterintelligence officer in the CIA.[32] Carlton Ames, after a brief stint working undercover for the CIA, had a lackluster career in the intelligence agency. However, Carlton's career and time abroad had a significant impact on his son and seemed to be one of the compelling forces that drove Aldrich to join the CIA in 1962. After his initial training, Ames was sent to Ankara, Turkey, on his first operational assignment. Though he had high hopes of making a significant contribution to the agency, as well as to the Cold War objectives of the United States, his first overseas assigned was undistinguished. After five years abroad in Turkey, the CIA transferred Ames back to headquarters, and in 1972, he began focusing on analyzing top-secret material.[33] His next "field" assignment after returning to United States was to be posted in New York as a CIA officer identifying Soviets affiliated with the United Nations who were potential agents that could be turned by the United States as a way to get additional intelligence on the political objectives and operations of the Soviet Union. However, Ames's assignment to New York came at a critical time for the CIA and also happened to be a watershed era in his outlook and professional timeline.

From 1975 until the 1980s, the CIA was at a nadir, as discussed in Chapter 6. At this same time, Ames was becoming increasingly frustrated with his lack of professional advancement; his first marriage was failing, and he was drinking more and more.[34] Yet Ames was not a failure as a CIA officer; he just was not progressing as quickly as he expected he should. Furthermore, he believed that he should be having a much larger impact on intelligence operations than he actually was. However, despite his own personal assessment of his dismal professional success, the CIA kept providing Ames with good assignments, which he completed adequately. In 1981, the CIA sent Ames to Mexico City to again focus on recruiting Soviet agents.[35] While in Mexico City without his wife, Ames began an affair with Maridel Rosario Casas Dupuy, a cultural attaché in the Columbian embassy, who was also an agent for the CIA.[36] In 1983, the CIA brought Ames back to the United States, and he worked as chief in the Soviet counterintelligence branch for Southeastern Europe.[37]

While starting his new posting, Ames went through a bitter divorce with his first wife and then quickly married Maridel, who then in turn became a citizen of the United States.[38] This information about Ames's personal life may seem insignificant, but in reality, the process of his divorce and the new marriage stressed his financial resources. The growing sense of financial despair weighted heavily on Ames.[39]

Professionally, Ames's new position provided him with access to information on CIA agents in the Soviet Union who had been productive for the CIA. Furthermore, as part of his duties as chief of the Soviet Counterintelligence branch, he was authorized to call and meet Soviet agents, although he needed to get approval from his chain of command as well as the approval from a joint CIA-FBI task force.[40]

As part of his duties, Ames was authorized to meet and cultivate Sergey Chuvakhin, a diplomat in the Soviet Embassy. Ames and Chuvakhin had their first meeting set for April 1985; however, Chuvakhin never made the meeting. In fact, before the prearranged time to meet, Ames first stopped at a bar and calmed his nerves with a few drinks. After waiting for Chuvakhin, Ames decided to walk to the Soviet embassy and offer his services in a note to be delivered to the KGB resident.[41]

In this note, Ames became a double agent by offering the names of two Soviet double agents, as well as a CIA phone directory, that demonstrated that Ames was indeed a CIA officer who had access to information that would be greatly beneficial to the KGB and the Soviet Union.[42] In his position at the CIA, Ames:

oversaw CIA operations aimed directly at Moscow. His most important tasks were to think through CIA operations that utilized Soviet agents secretly working for the United States, to determine if those agents were really on our side, to help recruit new Soviet sources, and to counter efforts by the Soviets to recruit informers.[43]

His position in counterintelligence provided Ames with excellent access to information and intelligence that greatly benefited the KGB and the Soviet Union. In May 1985, Ames received $50,000 for his first installment of information. This significant amount of cash helped to alleviate the financial pressure on Ames.

By June 1985 Ames was meeting with Chuvakhin and passing him additional information on Soviet agents being used and cultivated by the CIA and the FBI. In return for this information, the KGB paid Ames well. For the duration of the Cold War, Ames continued to work as a double agent for the KGB in exchange for cash. By the time he was arrested in February 1994, he was the highest-paid agent in KGB history, having received roughly $3 million from the KGB, with a promise of an additional $2 million for future information.[44]

The damage done to CIA operations at the end of the Cold War and in the immediate post–Cold War period were significant as Ames was directly responsible for pinpointing agents such as Dimitri Polyakov, whom the KGB arrested and silenced. Due to his betrayal, the CIA lost its most valuable assets in Moscow, and the United States struggled to get good inside intelligence on the Soviet Union as the system collapsed and the Cold War came to an end. Unlike agents working for the KGB during the 1940s and 1950s, Ames was not driven by ideological convictions but rather by greed and other banal reasons.[45] Though the ideological convictions of the Cold War faded in the twilight of the era, the human side of the espionage game still remained as a central core of the operations.

THE CIA AFTER THE COLD WAR

The collapse of the Soviet Union and the demise of the Warsaw Pact had a profound influence on the espionage game between the CIA and the KGB. For roughly 50 years, the two intelligence agencies had tangled with one another in an attempt to ensure that their ideology would prevail. Now, at the close of 1991, the Soviet system had collapsed, and despite the immediate optimism, there was a period of trying to figure out the extent of the role of the CIA in the new world order, or more precisely, in the post–Soviet Union security environment.

In a curious connection to the CIA's support of the Mujahideen in Afghanistan, the rise of a transnational terrorism group called Al Qaeda (the base), started by Saudi Arabian businessman Osama bin Laden, shaped the emerging security environment. In the late 1990s, Al Qaeda slowly demanded the attention of the CIA, and by 2001, when the United States unleashed the global war on terrorism, Osama bin Laden and his transnational terrorist group emerged as a new focal point for the CIA in the early 21st century. Osama bin Laden had been part of the international Islamic effort to support and fight with the Mujahideen in Afghanistan in the 1980s.[46] Though it is a common misconception that the CIA's support for the Mujahideen in the 1980s produced Al Qaeda in the 1990s, this was simply not the case.

The rise of Al Qaeda stems from the coalition victory in Operation Desert Storm in which the United States and allies remained in the Middle East, even after Iraq's army had been forcibly removed from Kuwait. This "occupation" of traditional Muslim lands by Western powers led to an internal dispute between bin Laden and the Saudi royal family, because bin Laden believed that the Saudi royal family members were not operating as devout Muslims because they allowed the United States to stay in the region after Operation Desert Storm.[47] Due to what he saw as a ceding of traditional Islamic land to Western powers, bin Laden called for the establishment of a "true Islamic state" in Saudi Arabia.[48] In addition to his call for a new Islamic state in the Kingdom of Saudi Arabia, bin Laden called on the international contacts he had made in Afghanistan to start building an organization that would fight for a new and strictly traditional Islamic state, devoid of Western influence.[49] As a result of his calls for substantial political changes, the Saudi government stripped bin Laden of his Saudi Arabian citizenship and exiled him from the country. This only further fueled bin Laden's fight against what he saw as globalization by the West, which was ultimately led by the United States.[50]

His dismissal from Saudi Arabia coincided with the turbulent security environments in the Balkans, Chechnya, and Philippines of the mid-1990s, which bin Laden interpreted as Western encroachment into Islamic lands. This fueled his call to Muslims from around the globe to join his organization as a way to begin the fight against "unbelievers."[51] Based on what he saw in the early 1990s with Operation Desert Storm and later in Somalia, as well as military operations by Western forces in the Balkans, bin Laden built a transnational terrorism group that declared a jihad against the United States and struggled to liberate Muslim lands from the West.[52] Though he did not have a country, bin Laden bounced initially between Sudan and Pakistan as Al Qaeda built training camps and gathered fighters from throughout the Middle East and from around the world. With the stabilization of the political situation in Afghanistan due to the arrival of the Taliban, bin Laden had finally found a country where he could reside and build his international network of terrorists.

This long explanation demonstrates that Al Qaeda was not a product of the CIA's support for the Mujahideen in Afghanistan. Rather, the rise of Al Qaeda was the result of a complex mix of geopolitical circumstances that were rapidly shifting in the tumultuous geopolitical environment of the 1990s.[53] It was in this uncertain security environment that the CIA had to navigate.

During the 1990s the CIA had a difficult task because the basic need for strategic intelligence on the former Soviet Union did not immediately evaporate with the end of the Cold War. There were grave concerns about the potential of former Soviet republics potentially selling nuclear warheads as a means to obtain hard currency in the wildly fluctuating Russian economy. Furthermore, there were serious concerns on the part of the United States of the proliferation of transnational criminal organizations that appeared in the vacuum of power left after the collapse of the Soviet State. The CIA therefore had a rather difficult task of making sense of the former Soviet Union while also keeping track of significant changes in Somalia, the Balkans, and in Afghanistan. The agency that had spent 50 years focusing on stopping and rolling back communism had to adjust to a completely new security environment that had a host of enemies across a wide spectrum. While the intelligence service of the United States tried to adjust to the new reality of the post–Cold War security environment, it became increasingly clear through attacks in Somalia, Saudi Arabia, and Yemen that transnational terrorism—specifically Al Qaeda—was emerging as a primary threat to the West and the United States in particular.

The CIA's interest in Al Qaeda did not just blossom in the wake of the attacks on the United States on September 11, 2001. It started in the 1990s as bin Laden and his group moved between Sudan and Pakistan. With the Taliban's control of Afghanistan, the CIA needed information because the U.S. policy on Afghanistan disappeared with the Soviet Union's departure from Afghanistan and the eventual collapse of the Soviet Union at the end of 1991. However, by 1996, and with bin Laden's growing power within Al Qaeda, the CIA tracked and attempted to get more and more information about the structure and intent of the organization. However, one persistent problem troubled the CIA and presidents of the United States. This issue that concerned the CIA, was a scenario by which Al Qaeda could come to possess some of the stinger antiaircraft missiles that the CIA and shipped to the Mujahideen during their fight against the Soviet Union.[54]

The CIA's reentry into Afghanistan in 1996 with the objective of buying back the remaining stingers, roughly 600, provided foundational intelligence.[55] Working with Ahmed Shah Massoud, the CIA hoped not only that it could regain control of stingers but also that Massoud could provide information on bin Laden. By 1996 bin Laden had become a wanted international terrorist who was known to be harbored by the Taliban in Afghanistan. From caves in the Hindu Kush, he ran his growing terrorist organization that believed it was at war with the United States.[56]

Based on information and intelligence gained by its agents in Afghanistan, by 1997 the CIA had put together a plan to capture and remove bin Laden from Afghanistan.[57] The plan entailed paying money to members of what would later become the Northern Alliance to kidnap and detain bin Laden in a cave in Afghanistan, and this would allow the CIA to fly in and assume custody of bin Laden with the intent of taking him to the United States for trial.[58] Because Al Qaeda had been financing terrorist activities since the early 1990s, the United States believed that it had a case, which was secretly being put together by a New York grand jury.[59]

The reality was that bin Laden's Al Qaeda network was growing and expanding in power; however, due to the shifting geopolitical environment, it was very hard for the CIA and its counterterrorism team to convince the rest of the U.S. government that Al Qaeda and bin Laden were significant national security priorities that had to be focused on before it was a greater threat to the United States. However, despite all the planning, the raid to capture bin Laden was never briefed to President Bill Clinton, due to the risk of fallout from a failure in the operation.[60]

On the eve of the 21st century, the CIA was well aware of bin Laden and had plans to capture him; however, the political and international environment was such that the CIA had to suppress this well-developed operation. Writing in 2018, it is frustrating knowing that Al Qaeda attacked the United States on September 11, 2001, which makes the CIA's plans in 1996 and 1997 a great way to analyze a significant counterfactual outcome that could have had intense ramifications for the United States, its allies, and the global community in the post–Cold War security environment. The reality is that by the end of the 1990s, the CIA had identified Al Qaeda, bin Laden, and transnational terrorist organizations as the new significant national security threat to the United States.[61] Hence, the CIA had firmly embraced its new position as a chief operator in the counterterrorism game.

After Al Qaeda's stunning attacks on the World Trade Towers in New York and the Pentagon in Washington, D.C., in 2001, the CIA again blossomed to adapt to the new operational environment. Using the work it had culti-vated in the 1990s, the CIA became a strong intelligence and paramilitary organization that was vital in conducting the U.S.-led global war on ter-rorism. With the recognition that the attacks by Al Qaeda on the United States represented the first ideological war of the 21st century, the CIA, as it had done during the Cold War, expanded its capabilities and missions to ensure that the United States could effectively prevail in this new struggle. After spending the 1990s focusing on diffuse and diversified threats, the 21st century started with an identifiable enemy that allowed the agency to mobilize all its resources. Transnational terrorist groups such as Al Qaeda became the new focal point that allowed the CIA to once again reprise its role as a flexible and adaptive agency that worked to ensure that the United States remained secure and stable. However, the biggest noticeable differ-ence with the new fixation on Al Qaeda and the global war on terrorism was that the traditional foe was not the primary fixation. With the onset of the global war on terrorism, the espionage game between the United States and Russia had taken a very different turn, one that would only reappear years later as Russia sought to regain its lost prestige from the Cold War.

THE KGB AFTER THE COLD WAR

The KGB had a much more difficult time adjusting to the new era, because the Soviet Union collapsed. For the duration of the Cold War, the KGB had been a primary instrument to ensure the stability and perpetua-tion of the communist state. However, in 1991, the system had collapsed, and the KGB was left trying to find its way in this brave new world. At the time of the collapse, Kryuchkov was the chairman of the KGB, a position he had held since 1988.[62] As Gorbachev attempted to adjust the Soviet sys-tem in the closing days of 1991, Kryuchkov demonstrated the power and primary objective of the KGB by attempting to initiate a coup with the aim of removing Gorbachev from power in an attempt to save the crumbling Soviet system. Ultimately, the coup failed and led to the election of Boris Yeltsin.

The Yeltsin period in Russia history was a significant time for the former communist country. As detailed by Kalugin, there was a sense of openness and democratic ideas emanating within the country. However, these new ideas did not square with a vast intelligence community that was obsessed with maintaining the regime and preserving the status quo, even if it had to suppress its own citizens. Yeltsin's attempt to concede to the demands of the new era focused on changing the KGB. However, he did not have a grand strategic idea as to how to go about this vast undertaking.[63]

Despite posturing that his regime would fundamentally change the nature of the old system of Soviet intelligence, Yeltsin simply separated the internal structure of the KGB in an attempt to created smaller agencies with more focused objectives. But recognizing that the domestic political situation in Russia was still relatively unstable, he outlined three primary objectives that demanded the attention and focus of the intelligence services. The overarching theme of Yeltsin's adjustment focused on internal forces within Russia that posed the greatest threat to his regime.[64] First, Yeltsin wanted to ensure his position in power, so he used the newly structured FSB to support his position in "battles with political opponents."[65] The second mission Yeltsin envisioned for the FSB was the security of Russia's borders. This was not just about retaining the Border Guard sections of the old KGB; it also entailed the suppression of threats deemed detrimental the stability of the state.[66] Specifically, the Russian government was deeply concerned about "ethnic tension, terrorism, labor un-rest, drug trafficking, and organized crime."[67] The final mission for the FSB was to maintain a strong counterintelligence capability that meant focusing on "foreign spies within Russia."[68]

As compared to the vast capabilities of the old KGB, these tasks were pointed and directed internally. Furthermore, a parallel can be drawn between the way Lenin and the Bolsheviks built their intelligence system as a means to consolidate and advance the ideas of the October Revolution and the way Yeltsin worked to adjust the KGB to the political realities facing Russian at the close of the 20th century. In both cases the primary objective was the solidification of power, which meant that security forces had to focus on internal threats that directly challenged the regime.[69] The primary difference between the two eras was that this tendency to revert to tight internal control did not synchronize with the tenets of the new Russia.

To guide the new FSB, Yeltsin appointed Vladimir Putin, a former KGB officer who had begun his career at the close of the Cold War by working in Dresden, East Germany, as head of the FSB in 1998. Putin became a trusted agent for Yeltsin as he ensured that political detractors were effectively suppressed, and hence, the stability of the regime could be maintained.[70]

Under the Yeltsin era, the KGB system fractured into several new agencies that focused on departments or specialties formerly held within the old organizational structure of the intelligence service of the Soviet Union.[71] The primary agencies were the Ministry of Security (MB), the Federal Counterintelligence Service (FSK), the Federal Security Service (FSB), the Federal Agency for Government Communications and Information (FAPSI), and the Main Guard Directorate (GUO).

As a demonstration that Yeltsin merely split directorates and department out of the old structure, the MB assumed the operations of the old Second Chief Directorate, Third Chief Directorate, Fourth Directorate, and Protection of the Constitution (also known as the Fifth Directorate).[72] The FSK assumed the role of fighting crime and corruption, but it lacked the power to investigate crime, which was ceded to the FSB. Beyond crime and corruption, the FSK also focused on the actions of "non-Russian national-ists" and perceived acts of terrorism against the state but was again lim-ited in its investigatory powers.[73] The FSB had the ability to "investigate crimes that were national and international in scope."[74] Crimes that fell under this broad guidance were "terrorism, smuggling, treason, violations of secrecy laws, large-scale economic crimes, and corruption."[75] Beyond its law enforcement function, the FSB also had power to conduct intelligence operations both within and outside Russia that were deemed as "enhanc-ing the economic, scientific-technical, and defense potential of Russia."[76] Again, the parallels to the old KGB are not difficult to see.

FAPSI represented the combination of operations previously held by the Eighth Chief Directorate and the Sixteenth Directorate, which focused on "technical capabilities to monitor communications."[77] Beyond just a pas-sive mission, FAPSI, much like the FSB, also retained the authority and capabilities to run intelligence-gathering operations deemed necessary for the stability and preservation of the regime. The last new agency to emerge under Yeltsin was the Main Guard Directorate (GUO); it replaced the KGB's Fifteenth Directorate, which was charged with protecting gov-ernment buildings and the country's leaders.[78]

Despite the appearance of dismantling the old KGB, it can be seen by the previous discussion that the key Chief Directorates and Directorates, in addition to the departments and services of the KGB, were still entrenched within the new multiagency intelligence services of Russia. The most pow-erful of these "new organizations" was the FSB, which at the close of the 20th century came to be seen as the heir apparent to the KGB.

In 1999, Yeltsin appointed Vladimir Putin, head of the FSB, as prime min-ister. In the context of the evolution of intelligence services, this marked a move back toward a more unified and focused intelligence service within Russia. Under Putin's first term as president of Russia, he initially kept the structure of the Yeltsin era, but by the end of 2000, he began to make moves to eliminate redundancy between organizations and collapsed the Border Guard element of the MB into the FSB, and he also shifted the oper-ations of FAPSI back into the FSB.[79]

Through his tenure Putin worked to better organize and hone the intel-ligence services of Russia. By 2016, the efforts by Putin to restructure and better organize the intelligence services of Russia properly culminated with the development of the Ministry of State Security.[80] This new bureaucracy fused the Foreign Intelligence Service with the FSB, effectively reestablish-ing the old KGB under a new name and new bureaucratic structure.[81]

Therefore, in the roughly 20 years since the end of the Cold War, the KGB was quickly broken into separate departments, which at first func-tioned as independent agencies to ensure the stability of the new Russian regime. At the onset of the 21st century, under the leadership of Putin, the old Soviet tendencies of concentrating and building power within large organizations with many subordinates came back under the auspices of the Ministry of Security.[82] Old wine had indeed been placed in new bottles.

CONCLUSION

The end of the Cold War did not stifle the 50-year espionage game between the CIA and the KGB.[83] In the decade between the end of the Cold War and the collapse of the Soviet Union and the start of the global war on terrorism, the two main intelligence services faced daunting changes in the operational environment. However, before the United States and Russia dealt with the massive changes, they had to deal with residual issues that lingered as a result of their Cold War operations.

The case of Oleg Kalugin represents the immediate period between the end of old KGB and the start of a new era under Yeltsin. Kalugin, who had spent years living abroad and worked to generate intelligence and reliable agents within the United States, saw the reality of the corrupt Soviet system. His own case, in which he was suspected by Kryuchkov of being a possible double agent and, after years of dedicated service, left him in the cold, questioning the overall objectives of his career and the ultimate objective of the KGB as an institution. He did not discount the need for a strategic intelligence service such as the KGB; however, he questioned the steadfast and unwavering commitment by which the organization that, in the name of protecting the regime, suppressed, harassed, imprisoned, and even killed its own citizens.

Kalugin's decision to speak out about the ills of the KGB and the old system led him to a political career that again brought him into direct contact with his old comrades. It is worth noting that he even mentions that he and his wife were well aware that his outspoken criticism of the KGB and the old Soviet system could have dire—even fatal—consequences; yet, he persisted in his political commitment.[84] Kalugin's path unfolded as the Yeltsin era was emerging, and some adjustments to the KGB happened, at least structurally. However, the services' commitment to security was merely once again focused on the party in power and strove to suppress internal threats deemed hostile to Russia and the Yeltsin regime. So even though the KGB ceased to be an operating body, the powers and operations of the old KGB remained, but they were now mostly internally focused to ensure that Russia did not wither in the post–Cold War security environment.

The placement of Putin in charge of the new FSB signaled a slow, deliberate path back to the establishment of a KGB-like organization that slowly rebuilt its power. By the start of the 21st century, Putin worked his way to being elected president of Russia. As a former KGB officer in charge of the state, Putin slowly rebuilt the intelligence empire that was the KGB. This is not to say that he did not recognize the vast changes in the global security environment—he did, which is why he brought the external and internal intelligence services back into a single agency as a way to ensure that they were both focused on preserving Russian power within the international community as well as protecting it from a variety of domestic threats. With news of illegal networks of Russian spies in the United States and the hacking of U.S. elections, it is not a hard stretch to see the long-term patterns of the KGB and how it has regenerated in the 21st century.[85]

The CIA had a very different experience at the end of the Cold War, as there was never a major question as to the viability of a strategic intelligence service for the United States. In fact, after exposing the damage done by Aldrich Ames and arresting this double agent, the CIA quickly found itself in a vastly more complex and dynamic security environment that demanded a greater level of awareness. Beyond just tracking nuclear weapons and missile proliferation, which was a huge issue as the Soviet Union collapsed and the Russian Federation emerged, the CIA also had to be aware of rogue nations such as Iraq, Iran, and North Korea and their own quests for nuclear capabilities.

Against this demanding tempo, the CIA was also faced with a new international security environment that encompassed transnational terrorist organizations. Starting after Operation Desert Storm, Osama bin Laden built an international terrorist organization that strove to suppress and even eradicate Western influence in traditional Islamic lands. Bin Laden's group, Al Qaeda, emerged in the 1990s as a threat because it targeted the United States as the main source of Western influence in the Middle East. Al Qaeda and bin Laden were increasingly targeted by the CIA as they increased their attacks on U.S. military forces in Saudi Arabia and Yemen. However, in the tumultuous global security that came to characterize the 1990s, the level of threat to the stability and security of the United States seemed minor, despite the CIA's increased concern as the decade of the 1990s evolved.

On September 11, 2001, Al Qaeda attacked the United States by hijacking passenger jetliners and flying them into the World Trade Center and the Pentagon. These domestic attacks led the United States to build an international coalition to undertake the global war on terrorism. As part of this new military commitment, the CIA would play a vital role in the tracking, capture, interrogation, and eradication of Al Qaeda as well as other transitional terrorist groups that affiliated with Al Qaeda. The prosecution of the global war on terrorism demanded that the CIA once again actively engage in paramilitary operations as a means to protect the security of the United States. In the context of the end of the Cold War, the espionage game had certainly changed to meet the demands of the global security environment. However, as the 21st century emerged, the tension and mistrust between the United States and Russia reappeared with a stunning sense of familiarity.

Conclusion

Since 2016 the news has been filled with allegations of Russian interference in the November presidential elections of the United States. The general consensus from the intelligence services of the United States was that Russian operatives did indeed attempt to influence and hack into the U.S. system. In fact, in August 2018, the U.S. government indicted Russian military intelligence officers in absentia for these crimes.[1] Additionally, in England, the British government has indicted two men for the attempted assassination of a former Russian agent and his daughter. The two men, Alexander Petrov and Ruslan Boshirov, flew to the United Kingdom and allegedly dispensed the nerve agent Novichok, a Soviet-era concoction, on a doorknob to kill former Russian double agent Sergei Skripal.[2]

These sensational events, which could easily be part of any Cold War–era spy novel, are still part of the seemingly new Cold War between Russia and the West. The onset of this new era, which has slowly evolved in the last two decades, has once again placed the espionage game within the limelight of the general public. Within the context of the Cold War espionage game, these events further demonstrate one of the central themes of this work, which is that despite the evolution of technology in the use and analysis of intelligence, the human side of the operations are still very much the central actions conducted around the world. As stated in the introduction of this work, even after reviewing roughly 80 years of espionage games between the United States and the Soviet Union, and later the Russian federation, the essence of the game is "same as it ever was, same as it ever was!"[3]

To get a final appreciation for the maintenance within the continuity of espionage between the United States and the Soviet Union/Russia from the 1930s to the present, it is necessary to review the key themes from the chapters that compose this work.

STEALING INDUSTRIAL SECRETS AND INFILTRATING THE MANHATTAN PROJECT

In the period immediately after the Russian Civil War, V. I. Lenin realized that the newly established Soviet Union was significantly lacking in technological advancements in comparison to the West. The establishment of the ATC (Amtorg Trading Company), which was a front organization designed to allow the Soviet Union to steal industrial secrets from the west, and more specifically the United States, provided the Soviet Union with industrial and commercial secrets that greatly benefited the struggling economy of the Soviet Union.[4] This obsession with acquiring more and more technology and industrial secrets continued even as Stalin assumed command of the Soviet system and instituted the first in a series of five-year economic plans. As the rest of the world faced significant economic issues starting in 1928 with the Great Depression, the Soviet Union had what appeared to be a booming economy. No doubt that the industrial and commercial intelligence gathered in the late 1920s had assisted in this phenomenal boom.

With this boom in the Soviet Union's economy and the global downturn in the rest of the world, the communist system appeared from the outside as a real alternative to the boom and bust cycles of the capitalist systems. Communism therefore began to be debated as a possible alternative to other systems of governments. Sympathies for communist parties and the Soviet system helped to generate potential agents who believed they were working for the betterment of people around the globe. The intelligence services of the Soviet Union used these sympathies and viewed communist parties around the globe as hotbeds of future agents who would work for the Soviet Union under the guise of making the world a better place.[5]

Therefore, the ATC and the Communist Party of the United States (CPUSA) provided the Soviet Union with willing and committed agents who were driven by an ideological quest to make the world a better place. The ability to foster and build greater networks within the United States became easier for the Soviet Union after 1933, when Franklin Delano Roosevelt officially recognized the Soviet Union.[6] With this proclamation, the Soviet Union built its official diplomatic rezidenturas, which were more than just the traditional diplomats and embassy works. They also contained intelligence officers who worked to cultivate agents to spy for the Soviet Union.

The onset of World War II assisted the Soviet Union in the endeavor of spying, as its alliance with the United States and Great Britain provided a great cover for working toward the defeat of Hitler's Germany and the other Axis powers. When the United States began work on developing the atomic bomb and classified the program as the Manhattan Project, with an aim to provide the tightest security measures, little did the program's director, Leslie Groves, know that it was infiltrated by scientists with sympathies for the Soviet Union.

The spying done by Ted Hall, Klaus Fuchs, and David Greenglass are great examples of how the Soviet intelligence service played on the ideological tenets of communism to entice these men to spy for the Soviet Union. Furthermore, the information that the spies within the Manhattan Project provided to the Soviet Union allowed Stalin and his regime to build their own atomic bomb and test it in 1949, which was a complete shock to the United States.

Even though the Soviet Union's efforts to build and cultivate spies within the United States' work on the atomic bomb provided them with a treasure trove of information, the United States was aware of some of their efforts and released the Venona transcripts in the early Cold War era, which demonstrated that the United States also had capabilities to build counterintelligence information. However, as the alliance between the United States and the Soviet Union collapsed into the new Cold War, espionage received greater attention as the World War II allies become Cold War enemies.

For the duration of the Cold War, and even in its aftermath, both the United States and the Soviet Union worked to ensure that they had the necessary abilities to spy and keep track of each other. The espionage game had begun and continued to evolve beyond the means established in this first period. As the Cold War solidified, and both the United States and the Soviet Union sought more and more information on each other, the security services of each nation also evolved to ensure that not only was the necessary intelligence being collected, but that each nation could also capitalize on the political situation to assist in its goals in the Cold War. Europe, in the immediate years after World War II, became the first environment where the United States and Soviet Union worked to actively undermine each other.

ELECTIONS AND A NEED TO KNOW

As the Cold War evolved, Truman and his administration were focused on two main issues. The first was building a national security strategy that strove to contain the expansion of the Soviet Union, which was an issue as early as 1946. The primary focus beyond Central Europe was the overall domestic situation throughout Europe. The general idea within the administration was that displaced populations would be susceptible to communism.[7] The Truman administration was specifically focused on the turbulent situations in France and Italy, with a deep concern that the communist parties in both nations would make big gains.

As the concern over the fate of Western Europe was debated with the State Department and the executive branch, Truman was also trying to figure how to build a new intelligence community that would provide the United States with the tools to help shape the emerging security environment, or at least make sure that the United States was aware of the rapidly shifting political dynamics across Europe and the globe.[8] With the formation of the Central Intelligence Agency (CIA) within the National Security Act of 1947, Truman had a new intelligence agency that met the demands of the new Cold War.

The first operations that the new intelligence service conducted were operations in Italy and France that assisted in generating, dispensing, and reinforcing anticommunist propaganda for elections in France and Italy. It is interesting to note that since 2016, the United States has been debating and investigating Russian interference in U.S. elections, yet at the start of the Cold War, the United States covertly used its new intelligence service as a means to ensure that communists did not win elections in France or Italy.

Though officials in the Truman administration knew that the KGB was actively supporting the international communist movement, they believed that by using various overt and covert methods, they could combat the expansion of communism. The use of the newly created CIA was a significant expansion in the context of the espionage game, as the United States actively began to pursue not just the collection of intelligence but also the use of covert action as a means to shape the political and social environments in Europe toward a more Western stance. The Cold War game of espionage now had two major forces: the CIA and the KGB, both of whom worked to advance the goals and policies of their respective countries.[9]

The second major concern, also directly related to the espionage games, was that the United States had very limited means to assess the military strength of the Soviet Union. The largest concerns were new air defense systems, size and composition of the Red Army, and (after 1949) the atomic stockpile of the Soviet Union. Though the CIA had some covert capabilities to gather intelligence, the closed nature of the Soviet system stifled the ability of relying on HUMINT. Therefore, in this period, the espionage game took a technological leap. By developing specialized aircraft that could collect photographs, signals intelligence, and electronic intelligence, the United States expanded that collection of espionage to airborne operations. This adjustment to operational conduct of espionage started with the USAF, but as the CIA solidified and built on the Air Force's foundation, it became a mission conducted by joint teams of CIA and Air Force officers. Furthermore, the quest for more military and nuclear intelligence become of greater significance as the 1940s came to a close.

In just a few short years, the United States had built a new strategic intelligence organization designed to focus on the international community, not just for collecting information but also for running covert operations that supported the foreign policies goals of the United States and its allies. The KGB, for its part, tried to rebuild and grow its illegal network within the United States and Western Europe, which had been wrecked by the end of World War II as well as the release of the Venona intercepts in the United States.

Comparing the actions of the KGB and the CIA, they were both still heavily reliant on HUMINT, but the CIA began to seek other technological means to obtain the intelligence needed by the United States. The closed communist systems in the Soviet Union and Eastern Europe prevented great success with HUMINT, which ultimately drove the United States to seek airborne methods. The Soviet Union, on the other hand, had a much easier time infiltrating and developing agents within the United States and therefore continued to place greater reliance on traditional means of collecting intelligence. By the end of the 1940s, espionage between the CIA and the KGB had already expanded significantly, and by the start of the 1950s, the game evolved and expanded across the globe.

ILLEGALS, TUNNELS, AND SPY PLANES

As the Cold War expanded to cover the entire globe, the demands of the espionage game also increased. In addition to the expansion of the strategic context of the Cold War, the United States and the Soviet Union also confronted the proliferation of nuclear weapons within the military inventories of the militaries of the two primary adversaries. This expansion of the nuclear capabilities of the military forces of the Soviet Union and the United States also drove the nations in two different directions as they strove to ensure that they had the latest intelligence on each other.

In maintaining a commitment to use HUMINT, the Soviet Union used illegal KGB plants working deep undercover with Directorate S to build intelligence networks within the United States. This tactic was not new, but since the late 1940s, the Soviet Union had a renewed obsession with cultivating and expanding their network of KGB agents living as immigrants or citizens in the United States. The most famous agent of this era was William Fisher, AKA Rudolf Abel. Abel's objective was to build and run a network of agents to provide Soviet intelligence with information on U.S. military shipments, deployments, and other pertinent strategic issues; this was especially important to the Soviet Union as the United States led the United Nations' Coalition during the Korean War.

The KGB's reliance on legal spies within their *rezidenturas*, as well as illegal spies such as Abel, provided them with the possibility of building vast intelligence-gathering networks. However, even though the USSR was successful with placing Abel within the United States, he still had to convince U.S. citizens to become spies against their own country. While using communist ideals became a means to improve the world for humanity worked a generation earlier, with the onset of the Cold War and the subsequent

Red Scare in the United States, this avenue of recruitment withered away. Despite the KGB's eager attempts to recapture its pre–World War II success, the Soviet Union's intelligence service struggled to build a network that provided the USSR with all the information it needed.

This continued reliance on HUMINT did not mean that the KGB rejected the use of technology, but rather the openness of the American society provided the KGB with an easier venue to access and collect information. So HUMINT maintained itself as a primary means of collection for the KGB throughout the Cold War, even as other means of collections were developed by both sides.

The era of 1950–1960, which encompassed the Korean War and the space race, pushed the United States in a different direction vis-à-vis espionage. In addition to the use of HUMINT, the CIA also designed elaborate operations such as the Berlin Tunnel during Operation Gold that was an elaborate engineering and technology attempt to collect SIGNIT and ELINT on the Warsaw Pact and military of the Soviet Union. Again, the major problem that drove the United States to seek more advanced technological means for collecting intelligence was the difficulty of penetrating communist societies. Therefore, eavesdropping operations such as Silver and Gold were efforts by the British and the United States to leverage technology and tap into telephone communications in Central and Eastern Europe. The ultimate objective was to get a fuller understanding of the communist forces and their force structure behind the iron curtain. HUMINT did provide useful information and was used in coordination with technological means. Technology and advanced engineering such as the Berlin Tunnel, however, provided access to intelligence that was unobtainable by spies.

Moving beyond subterranean spying, the USAF and the CIA built the U-2 spy plane as a specifically developed aircraft that could fly over the Soviet Union and take photographs. In the tense days of the late 1950s, when the Soviet Union had already demonstrated its ability to build and launch missiles capable of carrying nuclear warheads, it became imperative that the United States have strong and accurate intelligence on the strategic capabilities of the Soviet Union. Once again, the secretive nature the closed Soviet system hampered the ability to use HUMINT as a reliable means to collect the needed strategic intelligence. The U-2 was the technological solution to the problem.

The CIA, on joint operations with the USAF, used the U-2 to collect much-needed intelligence on the alleged bomber and missile gap; however, the utility of the U-2 screeched to a halt on May 1, 1960, when the Soviet Union successfully shot down a U-2 piloted by Francis Gary Powers. To add further complications to this tense international event, the Soviet Union had captured Powers alive. Though Eisenhower had addressed the loss of a weather reconnaissance aircraft over the Soviet Union, he was forced to admit that the United States had been flying spy missions over the Soviet Union.

The incident of the U-2 acted as a catalyst. This drove the espionage game in yet another direction: outer space. Space became the next domain the Soviet Union and the United States sought to use to maintain awareness of each other. However, even as both sides worked to militarize space, the use HUMINT maintained itself along a steady track of intelligence gathering. For as much as both the United States and Soviet Union sought advanced technological means of intelligence collection, they could not abandon the use of officers and agents.

SATELLITES, PARAMILITARY OPERATIONS, AND OPPORTUNITIES

The evolution of the espionage game during the period 1961 to 1968 encompassed two major changes for the CIA. The first was an evolution of the use of aircraft, which had proven vulnerable with the Soviet Union's shootdown of Francis Gary Powers's U-2 on May 1, 1960. As a result, the CIA, working with the USAF and the new civilian space agency NASA, developed its abilities to use satellites for the collection of photographic and signals intelligence. The era between 1961 and 1968 saw the solidification of the use of satellites as a mainstay in intelligence work for both the United States and the Soviet Union.

The second major evolution for the CIA was the expansion of its covert operations into more paramilitary-style activities. This seemed like a natural evolution of the first covert mission authorized by President Truman in the late 1940s, especially as the Cold War heated up in places like the Middle East, Southeast Asia, and Latin America. However, by the end of the 1960s, the CIA began to wonder if it had stretched beyond its original charter. America's involvement in Vietnam, Cambodia, and Laos only served to further reinforce this systemic debate.

From the perspective of the KGB, the period between 1961 to 1968 represented two very different eras. From the start of the decade, the Soviet Union built upon the early successes with its space program, which had also been converted to provide satellites that could spy from space. Using the basic design of a few families of space vehicles, the Soviet Union and the KGB could at least also fly over the United States and its allies and collect photographic and signals intelligence. As the strategic nuclear balance of the Cold War arms race lurched forward, having up-to-date and photographic evidence of the strategic arsenal of the main adversary of the Soviet Union was critical to the stability of the tense years of the 1960s. Using space as a platform to collect intelligence therefore became a critical tool for both the United States and the KGB as they sought to understanding their respective positions in the strategic balance of the Cold War.

Furthermore, having the ability to "fly" over the enemy's territory and collect intelligence without the threat of being shot down also provided both the United States and the Soviet Union the ability to refine and build nuclear war plans that incorporated targets identified by space-based assets.

The use of space, especially by the Soviet Union, demonstrated that although that the KGB had been heavily focused on trying to rebuild its networks of agents in the United States, it was not against using advanced technological means to collect intelligence during the Cold War. In fact, as discussed within the chapter, the Soviet Union's ability to use space-based intelligence-gathering platforms was impressive—and in some ways more beneficial for intelligence gathering as they tended to have long life spans.

At the same time that the two main players in the espionage game had begun to use space as a new medium for intelligence collection, the CIA also began its evolution into paramilitary activities. Starting as an Eisenhower-era operation to train and support a small cadre of exiled Cuban rebels, the CIA wanted to cultivate and grow a rebellion within Cuba with the expressed objective of overthrowing Fidel Castro's regime. However, as the project evolved, it become more than the original operation, which came to include an amphibious landing by a much larger exiled Cuban force, with air support and other supporting fire from U.S. naval vessels. The fiasco that became the Bay of Pigs led to a slow and deliberate dis-cussion within the CIA as to the proper role for paramilitary activities conducted by the agency. With the various operations in Vietnam by the CIA, at the end of the decade, the CIA would finally be encouraged, if not forced, to move away from its development of paramilitary activities.[10]

As the decade of the 1960s came to a close, the KGB saw a major oppor-tunity to exploit the dwindling position of the United States in the third world. With the United States struggling in Vietnam, the KGB began to use the concept of imperial overstretch as a springboard from which to launch a new era of initiatives in Africa and Latin America with the belief that the United States and the West had finally begun to wither. Working within the context of the Brezhnev doctrine, the KGB believed that the global bal-ance of power had finally turned in favor of the Soviet Union and its allies.

The 1960s, therefore, was a pivotal period that ushered in the use of sat-ellites for intelligence collection, but it also saw a shift in the assessment of the Cold War global balance of power. At the end of the decade, the CIA had reached its apogee of operational success and appeared to be in decline, which would take roughly another decade to stabilize. From the KGB's perspective, its steadfast commitment to the cause was finally mak-ing international headway, and the "world was going their way."[11]

OPPORTUNITIES

At the close of the 1960s and in the early 1970s, the intelligence commu-nities of the United States and the Soviet Union faced two very different outlooks on the immediate future of the Cold War struggle. The KGB viewed this period as one of great opportunity that enabled them to move forward with advancing the objective of supporting burgeoning socialist/communist regimes around the world. After all, this was the central foundation of Brezhnev's doctrine. By the time the United States concluded a peace agreement in Vietnam, the KGB and the Soviet Union recognized that the image and influence of the United States had taken a serious international hit, which provided great possibilities the Soviet Union could capitalize on, especially in the third world.

To ensure that this period was not squandered, the KGB under the direction of Andropov empowered Kryuchkov and his First Chief Directorate (FCD) to work toward the development of larger networks of agents around the globe. Within the FCD, the focus moved from just rebuilding the illegal network within the United States with spies such as Rudolf Herrmann. While remaining fixated on illegals as a means to access intelligence within the United States, the FCD knew that it was difficult for these first-generation spies to penetrate deeply into the bureaucracies of the U.S. government. However, if the FCD could use the offspring of agents like Herrmann, who were born in the United States and were therefore U.S. citizens, then these second-generation potential spies would have no problem assimilating into positions within the U.S. government.

Peter Herrmann, the son of Rudolf Herrmann, is a great example of how the FCD expanded the Soviet's illegal network by directing Peter Herrmann to attend Georgetown University with an eye toward cultivating relationships with students and professors who had access to the U.S. government. Through Peter Herrmann and others like him, the KGB believed that it could finally insert KGB operatives within the deep recesses of its main adversary.

In addition to broadening its illegals operations, the KGB's renewed effort to capitalize on the post-Vietnam malaise of the United States can be seen in its actions toward the turbulent political situation in Chile, which had been a traditional focus of the United States and the CIA. As the CIA suffered through congressional scrutiny, the KGB overlooked Allende's questionable commitment to Marxism and simply made sure that he had intelligence that highlighted the CIA's attempt to undermine his regime.

The deliberate and calculating efforts by the KGB demonstrate the operational flexibility of the Soviet Union's intelligence service in the early 1970s and how it sought to use the tarnished image of the CIA and the United States as leverage to convince third-world governments that an alliance, however loose, with the Soviet Union was of greater benefit.

In contrast to the seemingly strengthening position of the KGB in the espionage game, as well as the Soviet Union in the strategic balance of the Cold War, the CIA was in a much different situation. Having to face intense external scrutiny for its past covert and paramilitary operations, the CIA was in a serious fight for its survival. Feeding off the social and political distrust of the U.S. government by a segment of the U.S. population after Vietnam and especially after Watergate, the CIA was caught in a position where it had to justify its actions and account for its past alleged abuses of power.[12]

Within this turbulent environment, the CIA's new director, William Colby, professionally led the intelligence service through this strenuous period. He provided details to congressional investigations into the CIA's past operations in which they spied on U.S. citizens, attempted to assassinate Fidel Castro, and planned and conducted operations to overthrow governments. Throughout the hearings in the Senate and the House of Representatives, the legislative branch found that the CIA may have engaged in improper actions, such as Operation CHAOS, but the CIA did not openly violate U.S. law or operate outside the parameters of its charter. The commissions asserted that Colby and the leadership in the CIA had gone far to correct the public perception that the CIA was a rogue intelligence service, running around the world toppling governments and assassinating leaders. To help soften the blow and yet still appease the public's suspicion of covert intelligence agencies, the blame focused on "presidents and senior government officials" who directed the CIA to conduct these operations.[13] This fixed the blame on the executive branch and assisted in curtailing the expansion of the imperial presidency. The end result of this era was that under the direction of Colby, the CIA had an opportunity to rebuild itself and demonstrate that it was a vital national security asset that provided critical intelligence to the president of the United States. An ethos of quiet professionalism was reinstalled within the CIA, which also coincided with a greater reliance on satellites and other advanced technological means to ensure that the United States kept track of the Soviet Union and its growing forces of nuclear weapons. It would take roughly a decade before the CIA regained its paramilitary fixation, which was driven by the Soviet Union's adventurism in Afghanistan.

FIRST STRIKES, HUMAN RIGHTS, AND STINGERS

The 12 years covered in this chapter represented a very dynamic and significant period, not just for the context of the Cold War but also in the consideration of the espionage game between the United States and the Soviet Union. The KGB's optimism of the early 1970s faded with the election of Ronald Reagan, which drove the KGB, and especially the FCD, to become obsessive about making sure that it had the latest intelligence on early indicators of any intention of Reagan to launch a nuclear strike on the Soviet Union. This obsession became a primary focus for the KGB as well as three of the last four leaders of the Soviet Union.[14]

Even while the KGB focused on adjusting the information collected and reported by the FCD to make sure it did not miss important indicators signaling the start of a third world war, the Soviet Union also realized, after 1983, that there was a major technological gap between the United States and its Western allies and the communist world.

Therefore, once the obsession over the first strike disappeared, the KGB refocused its efforts on collecting technological and scientific information that could assist the Soviet Union in improving and advancing its military, industrial, and computer technology. Much like its earlier days, when Stalin and his intelligence service developed ATC as a front to collect industrial, scientific, and agricultural intelligence from the United States, the KGB once again had to become a means by which the Soviet State strove to adjust to the rapidly changing political and strategic environment. For the duration of the Cold War and beyond, the KGB and its successor organizations became more and more fixated on the need to collection industrial, scientific, computer, and agricultural intelligence as a means to ensure that the Soviet/Russian State did not fall behind.

The CIA faced a much different evolution in the same period. Emerging from the early 1970s, President Carter had a deep suspicion of covert operations and the utility of the CIA. However, using the tenets of the Helsinki Accords, which highlighted the importance of nations providing basic human rights for their citizens, Carter saw an opportunity to once again use the CIA as a just and ethical tool for the advancement of moral and ethical objectives.

In relation to the tenets of the Helsinki Accords, Carter and his administration also saw a role for the CIA in the support of the blossoming Solidarity movement in Poland. By covertly supporting the labor union movement, which had strong democratic and human tenets, the Carter administration, specifically Brzezinski, believed that this operation was tailored for the CIA.

The importance of these two major recognitions by Carter's administration was that they provided an avenue by which the CIA could emerge from its post-Vietnam period and demonstrate that it could still plan, operate, and run covert operations that focused on perpetuating the tenets of democracy and freedom. This was significant for the CIA, because under the direction of Stansfield Turner, advanced technological means of collecting intelligence were preferred over HUMINT. Turner viewed HUMINT as a means to substantiate intelligence collected by satellites and other advanced means. However, by supporting human rights across the globe, but especially in Eastern Europe, Central Europe, and the Soviet Union, the CIA reinforced its ability to do more for the advancement of the Cold War objectives of the United States. Furthermore, the mission to support Solidarity covertly harkened back to the origins of the agency when President Truman authorized the intelligence service to assist the

French and Italians in their elections as a means to ensure communism did not come to control these two vital European allies. Hence, by the start of Reagan's first term as president of the United States, the CIA had moved well beyond its nadir of the 1970s.

Using programs started by Carter in Poland, as well as his support of supplying arms to the Mujahideen guerillas in Afghanistan, the CIA by 1981 was back to its objectives of not just supplying strategic intelligence but also running covert operations to roll back communism. This was the start of a much more activist role, one that the Carter administration had laid the foundation but Reagan and his DCI William Casey greatly expanded.

Casey and Reagan both saw the benefit of maintaining and continuing the covert operations in Poland and Afghanistan, but they believed that both provided greater opportunities to roll back the Soviet Union. In the case of Poland, Casey and Reagan worked with the Catholic Church and Pope John Paul II to get a better understanding of the circumstances on the ground and also gauge the Polish people's support for Solidarity. In conjunction with these operations to provide greater awareness, Casey and the CIA supported the expansion of covert operations to support the publication and distribution of materials. Again, this was a task in which the CIA had vast amounts of experience and also a task at which it excelled.

In Afghanistan, Casey and Reagan also saw the CIA's operations as a direct way to hedge against the Soviets' adventurism. Therefore, they authorized the sale of Stinger antiaircraft missile to the Mujahideen as a way to offset the Soviet Union's reliance on rotary-wing and fixed-wing airpower. Stingers were not the only adjustment the Reagan administration made; they also increased funding for communications equipment and training that allowed the Mujahideen to become a more effective fighting force. In 1989, Gorbachev pulled Soviet military forces out of Afghanistan, and by 1991, the Soviet Union collapsed.

In the last decade of the Cold War, the espionage game had become a menagerie of satellites, aircraft, ships, paramilitary operations, covert operations, and illegal spies. However, by examining its evolution, it is interesting to note that by the middle of the 1980s, both the CIA and the KGB had remained true to key operations that were outlined at the start of this study. Despite the march of technology and the new ways to collect intelligence, at the heart of the espionage game was still the need to collect intelligence and use covert operations as a way to advance the national security objectives of the major players in the Cold War. The foundation of these operations was the need to continue the use of HUMINT as the primary means to maintain a strong presence in the global strategic balance.

AFTER THE COLD WAR

With the collapse of the Soviet Union in December 1991, the espionage game that had been a staple of the Cold War suddenly changed. Even though the traditional tenets that had emerged remained in place, the essence and nature of the game between the KGB and the CIA fundamentally shifted. However, before these momentous shifts took place, both the CIA and KGB had lingering concerns that came to light in the new era.

For the KGB, the dissolution of the communist system brought with it an open and public distrust of the intelligence service, which not only spied on the enemies of the Soviet Union but also kept track of traitors who posed a threat to the regime from within. Oleg Kalugin, whose exploits as a legal spy working within the United States have been chronicled as part of this story, played a critical role in helping to dismantle the old KGB and attempted to replace it with a more traditional intelligence service that focused its efforts outside the country. This process that coincided with Kalugin's dismissal/retirement from the KGB also led to his running for elected office in the opening days of the new Russian Federation. However, as he recounts, the old Soviet intelligence service strove to maintain its grip on power and discredit all those who questioned the ideals of the old regime.

The coup pushed by the former head of the First Chief Directorate, Kryuchkov, who was now head of the KGB, sought to subvert the efforts of Gorbachev and maintain the tenets of the Brezhnev era. However, the old Soviet economy was broken, and the system itself was falling. Therefore, despite the best efforts of the KGB and its old guard, the forces of democracy seemed to prevail. Kalugin, despite being so strongly affiliated with the old regime, actually became an outspoken critic of the intelligence service and the old Soviet system. With the election of Boris Yeltsin, which resulted in massive reforms, Kalugin once again returned to the KGB as a reformer with an eye toward making the much-needed adjustments to the corrupt and oppressive intelligence service. The lackluster efforts to reshape the new intelligence service, which came to be generically called the Federal Security Service (FSB), resulted in a bureaucratic reshuffling and renaming for the various agencies that had been part of the old KGB. This diverse structure of roughly five agencies survived until the election of Vladimir Putin, a former KGB officer in the closing years of the Cold War and FSB head under Yeltsin's Russia. Under Putin, the FSB regained much of its powers and began to once again adapt to the changing international security environment.

While Kalugin and the former Soviet Union were going through massive changes as a result of the end of the Cold War, the CIA finally had answers to a roughly decade-long question as to why their agent networks within the Soviet Union had disappeared in the last years of the Cold War. Despite suspecting USMC embassy guards and others who had questionable backgrounds, the CIA was shocked to find that Aldrich Ames had been spying for the Soviet Union since 1985. In his position in the CIA's counterintelligence branch for Southeastern Europe, Ames had access to the names and networks of Soviet citizen who had been providing insider intelligence to the CIA. Ames passed this information to KGB handlers, not from some greater sense of duty but rather because he was unhappy with his professional position within the CIA and needed money to pay off an ever-increasing debt load.

The KGB greatly valued the information provided by Ames and paid him millions of dollars for his efforts. At the time of his arrest in 1994, he was the highest-paid spy in the history of the KGB and had provided the KGB with a significant amount of intelligence that effectively allowed it systematically to blind the CIA by removing its agents within the Soviet Union. By the time he was arrested, the CIA was already busy trying to find its way in the post–Cold War security environment.

The rise of Al Qaeda under the direction of Osama bin Laden provided the CIA with a focal point throughout the turbulent 1990s. As the first decade after the Cold War unfolded, transnational terrorism, and Al Qaeda specifically, emerged as a significant threat to the national security of the United States. With Al Qaeda's attacks on the United States in 2001, the CIA once again marshalled all its assets to include rebuilding its paramilitary capabilities in an effort to assist in the global war on terrorism. Even as the CIA came to play a significant and vital role in this long, demanding war, it also had to maintain its commitment to the strategic intelligence-gathering assets that came to define the Cold War.

Therefore, after 17 years of fighting transnational terrorist networks alongside the U.S. military, the CIA still had to keep the U.S. president abreast of potential security threats to the United States, such as the development of nuclear weapons and ballistic missiles being developed by Iran and North Korea. The diverse security climate of the 21st century has placed greater demands on the CIA, as it must fulfill many missions across a wide variety of threats and covert operations. Though the vast majority of these operations still remain highly classified, through open sources, it is evident that the game of espionage that evolved during the Cold War has expanded significantly in the post–Cold War security environment and now encompasses a much wider and more diverse set of operations that range from basic HUMINT to cyber operations. Simply, the CIA has made its adjustment to the new security environment and continues to excel at collecting espionage for the United States.

Russia also had to adjust to transnational terrorism, as well as homegrown terrorism in Chechnya and other former republics of the old Soviet Union. At first the FSB embraced the role and operated alongside Russian security and military forces as way to secure this new threat to the Russian federation as well as bring internal stability to the Russia state. Having to deal with the wars in Chechnya, the Beslan school siege, and the bombing of an apartment complex, the FSB again came to fulfill a vital role as an internal state security force focused on ensuring that the Russian State stayed strong. Although these operations seemed to focus on suppressing and eradicating a minority of terrorist organizations, the powers of the FSB expanded to ensure that internal dissent was also suppressed and eradicated, as with the Cold War, a vital function of Russian intelligence services was to protect the regime.

At the onset of the 21st century, more and more reports filtered out of Europe about former Russian spies or even Ukrainian government officials being mysteriously poisoned. This was a tactic used by the KGB during the Cold War as a way to silence those who knew too much information.[15] As the first decade of the 21st century unfolded, the FSB maintained its commitment to building vast internal intelligence networks within the United States. As late as 2018, the United States has identified at least ten Russian agents who have come to the United States under false names and pretenses with the assumed purpose of collecting intelligence for Russia.[16] In fact, as this book is being written, there is an active investigation into Russia's influence on the U.S. presidential election of 2016. Computer hacking and using agents to gain access to government officials are just two of the many issues being investigated. As chronicled by the chapters in this study, the KGB had these same obsessions, and its successor organization, the FSB, seems to be continuing in the traditional of the old KGB.

In 2018 the international security environment has significantly changed from the Cold War. However, based on the current tension between the United States and Russia, which has been evolving and morphing since the early 21st century, it is clear that the espionage game between the United States and the Soviet Union remains a vast, diverse effort as both nations strive to ensure the stability of their respective countries. In this quest for security, surely the game of espionage will continue to evolve.

Appendixes:
Organizational Charts

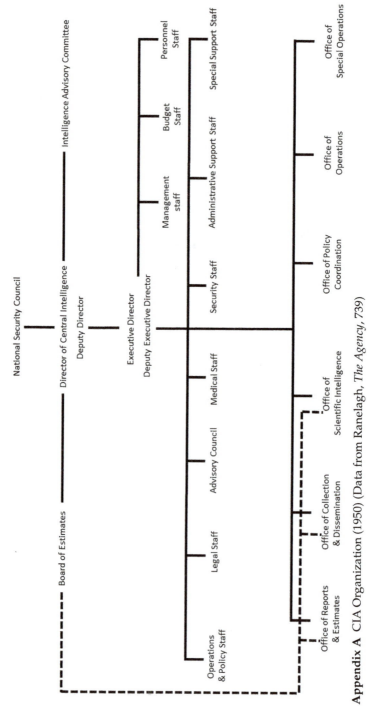

Appendix A CIA Organization (1950) (Data from Ranelagh, *The Agency*, 739)

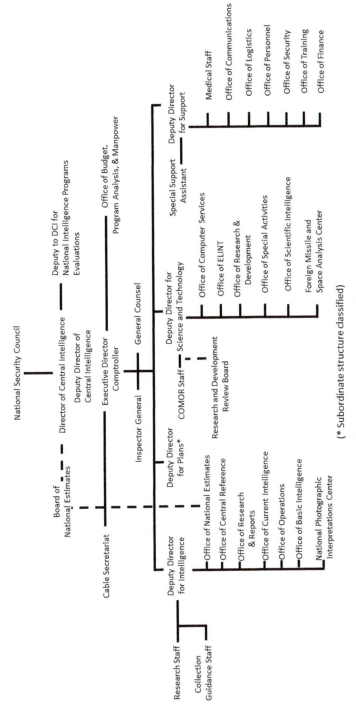

National Security Council

Board of National Estimates

Director of Central Intelligence

Deputy Director of Central Intelligence

Deputy to DCI for National Intelligence Programs Evaluations

Cable Secretariat

Executive Director Comptroller

Office of Budget, Program Analysis, & Manpower

Inspector General

General Counsel

Deputy Director for Plans*

COMOR Staff

Research and Development Review Board

Deputy Director for Science and Technology

Special Support Assistant

Deputy Director for Support

Deputy Director for Intelligence

Research Staff

Collection Guidance Staff

Office of National Estimates
Office of Central Reference
Office of Research & Reports
Office of Current Intelligence
Office of Operations
Office of Basic Intelligence
National Photographic Interpretations Center

Office of Computer Services
Office of ELINT
Office of Research & Development
Office of Special Activities
Office of Scientific Intelligence
Foreign Missile and Space Analysis Center

Medical Staff
Office of Communications
Office of Logistics
Office of Personnel
Office of Security
Office of Training
Office of Finance

(* Subordinate structure classified)

Appendix B CIA Organization (1964) (Data from Ranelagh, *The Agency*, 740)

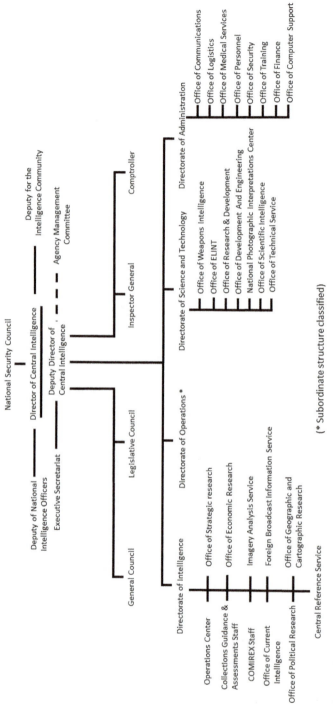

Appendix C CIA Organization (1975) (Data from Ranelagh, *The Agency*, 741)

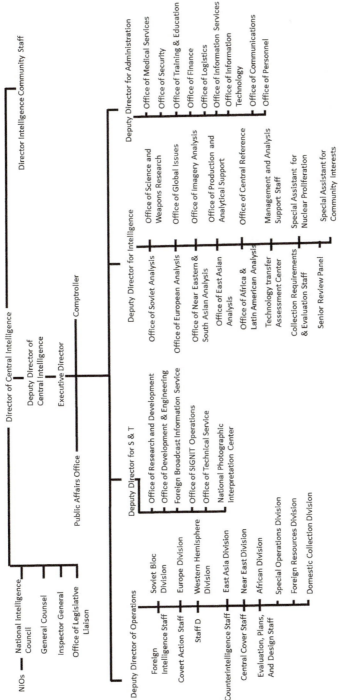

Appendix D CIA Organization (1985) (Data from Ranelagh, *The Agency*, 742)

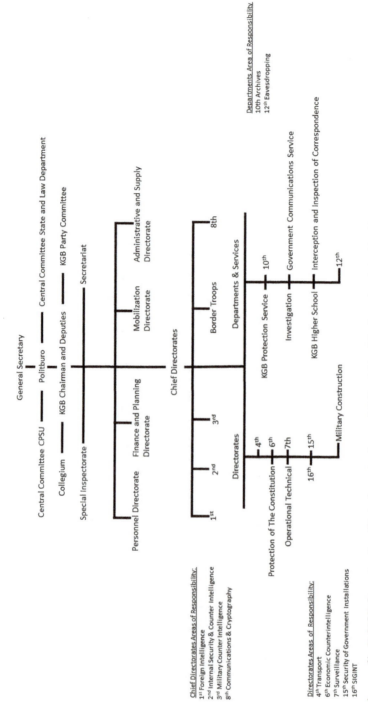

General Secretary

Central Committee CPSU — Politburo — Central Committee State and Law Department

Collegium — KGB Chairman and Deputies — KGB Party Committee

Special Inspectorate — Secretariat

Personnel Directorate

Finance and Planning Directorate

Mobilization Directorate

Administrative and Supply Directorate

Chief Directorates

1st 2nd 3rd 4th 6th 7th 8th

Directorates

Protection of The Constitution

Operational Technical

16th 15th

Military Construction

Border Troops

Departments & Services

KGB Protection Service

Investigation

10th

Government Communications Service

KGB Higher School

Interception and Inspection of Correspondence

12th

Chief Directorates Areas of Responsibility:
1st Foreign Intelligence
2nd Internal Security & Counter Intelligence
3rd Military Counter Intelligence
8th Communications & Cryptography

Directorates Areas of Responsibility:
4th Transport
6th Economic Counterintelligence
7th Surveillance
15th Security of Government Installations
16th SIGINT

Departments Area of Responsibility:
10th Archives
12th Eavesdropping

Appendix E KGB Organization (Data from Andrews & Mitrokhin, *The Sword and the Shield*, 1219)

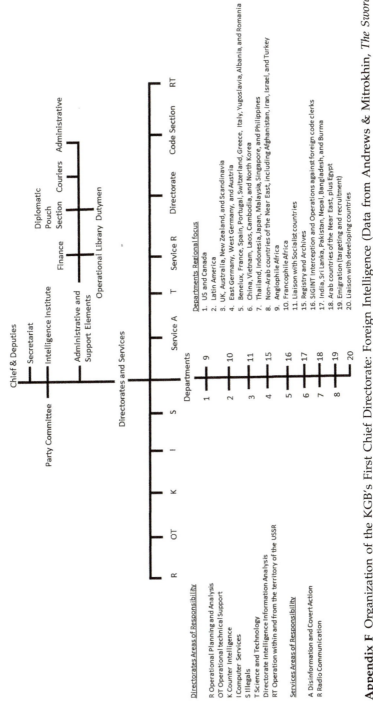

Chief & Deputies

Party Committee

Secretariat

Intelligence Institute

Administrative and Support Elements

Diplomatic Pouch

Finance Section Couriers Administrative

Operational Library Dutymen

Directorates and Services

R · OT · K · I · S · Service A · T · Service R · Directorate · Code Section · RT

Departments

1, 2, 3, 4, 5, 6, 7, 8 / 9, 10, 11, 15, 16, 17, 18, 19, 20

Departments Regional focus
1. US and Canada
2. Latin America
3. UK, Australia, New Zealand, and Scandinavia
4. East Germany, West Germany, and Austria
5. Benelux, France, Spain, Portugal, Switzerland, Greece, Italy, Yugoslavia, Albania, and Romania
6. China, Vietnam, Laos, Cambodia, and North Korea
7. Thailand, Indonesia, Japan, Malaysia, Singapore, and Philippines
8. Non-Arab countries of the Near East, including Afghanistan, Iran, Israel, and Turkey
9. Anglophile Africa
10. Francophile Africa
11. Liaison with Socialist countries
15. Registry and Archives
16. SIGINT Interception and Operations against foreign code clerks
17. India, Sri Lanka, Pakistan, Nepal, Bangladesh, and Burma
18. Arab countries of the Near East, plus Egypt
19. Emigration (targeting and recruitment)
20. Liaison with developing countries

Directorates Areas of Responsibility
R Operational Planning and Analysis
OT Operational technical Support
K Counter Intelligence
I Computer Services
S Illegals
T Science and Technology
Directorate Intelligence Information Analysis
RT Operation within and from the territory of the USSR

Services Areas of Responsibility
A Disinformation and Covert Action
R Radio Communication

Appendix F Organization of the KGB's First Chief Directorate: Foreign Intelligence (Data from Andrews & Mitrokhin, *The Sword and the Shield*, 1219)

Notes

INTRODUCTION

1. An "illegal" in the context of espionage during the Cold War was a was a spy for the Soviet Union who had assumed a false identity and entered the United States under an assumed name with the express purpose of spying for the KGB. Typically, Directorate S in the Soviet Embassy managed these spies, whose information was channeled through the First Chief Directorate.

2. Herbert Romerstein and Eric Breindel, *The Venona Secrets: Exposing Soviet Espionage and America's Traitors* (Washington, D.C.: Regency Publishing, 2000), 191–255.

3. William I. Hitchcock, *France Restored: Cold War Diplomacy and the Quest for Leadership in Europe, 1944–1954* (Chapel Hill: University of North Carolina Press, 1998), 41–72; Michael Creswell, *A Question of Balance: How France and the United States Created Cold War Europe* (Cambridge: Harvard University Press, 2006), 7–72; Robert A. Ventresca, *From Fascism to Democracy; Culture and Politics in the Italian Election of 1948* (Toronto: University of Toronto Press, 2004), 61–100; William J. Daugherty, *Executive Secrets: Covert Action and the Presidency* (Lexington: University Press of Kentucky, 2004), 113–118.

4. Igor Lukes, *On the Edge of the Cold War: American Diplomats and Spies in Postwar Prague* (New York: Oxford University Press, 2012), 85–111; Peter Kenez, *Hungary from Nazis to the Soviets: The Establishment of the Communist Regime in Hungary, 1944–1948* (New York: Cambridge University Press, 2006), 61–81.

5. Christopher Andrew and Vasili Mitrokhin, *The Sword and the Shield: The Mitrokhin Archive and the Secret History of the KGB* (New York: Basic Books, 1999), 197–200.

6. Romerstein and Breindel, *Venona Secrets*, 127.

7. Christopher Andrew and Vasili Mitrokhin, *The World Was Going Our Way: The KGB and the Battle for the Third World* (New York: Perseus Books, 2005), 1–27; Joseph J. Trento, *The Secret History of the CIA* (New York: MLF Books, 2001), xi–xvi.

8. Trento, *Secret History*, 69–75; Andrew and Mitrokhin, *Sword and the Shield*, 173–197.

9. Jeffery T. Richelson, *The Wizards of Langley: Inside the CIA's Directorate of Science and Technology* (Boulder: Westview Press, 2001), 39; William J. Burrows, *By Any Means Necessary: America's Secret Air War in the Cold War* (New York: Farrar, Straus, and Giroux, 2001), 267–272.

10. The Red Scare that evolved in the United States in the late 1940s and persisted into the 1950s was fueled by the release of Venona intelligence, which led to the arrest and break-up of the KGB's intelligence network within the United States. As a result of the loss of this valuable resource, the Soviet Union strove to rebuild its human network in the early Cold War.

11. Andrew and Mitrokhin, *World Was Going Our Way*, 1–27.

12. Trento, *Secret History*, 368.

13. Andrew and Mitrokhin, *Sword and the Shield*, 226–238.

14. Andrew and Mitrokhin, *Sword and the Shield*, 575–577.

15. Daugherty, *Executive Secrets*, 186.

16. Peter Schweizer, *Victory: The Reagan Administration's Secret Strategy That Hastened the Collapse of the Soviet Union* (New York: The Atlantic Monthly Press, 1994), 7.

17. Sean N. Kalic, "Reagan's SDI Announcement and the European Reaction: Diplomacy in the Last Decade of the Cold War," in *The Crisis of Détente in Europe: From Helsinki to Gorbachev, 1975–1985*, ed. Leopoldo Nuti (London: Routledge, 2009), 99–110.

18. Andrew and Mitrokhin, *Sword and the Shield*, 492.

19. Luke Harding, "Spies, Sleepers, and Hitmen: How the Soviet Union's KGB Never Went Away," in *The Guardian*, November 14, 2014, https://www.theguardian.com/world/2014/nov/19/spies-spooks-hitmen-kgb-never-went-away-russia-putin, accessed September 18, 2018.

20. The CIA did not just focus on the Soviet Union; since at least 1979, it had also begun to look at other radical Islamist threats to the United States.

21. "The KGB After the Breakup of the Soviet Union," http://factsanddetails.com/russia/Government_Military_Crime/sub9_5e/entry-5203.html, accessed September 18, 2018.

22. "The KGB After the Breakup of the Soviet Union," 1.

23. Talking Heads, "Once in a Lifetime," https://genius.com/Talking-heads-once-in-a-lifetime-lyrics, accessed September 18, 2018.

24. Ray S. Cline, *The CIA Under Reagan, Bush, and Casey* (Washington, D.C.: Acropolis Books, 1981), 107–109.

25. Trento, *Secret History*, 31.

26. Cline, *CIA Under Reagan, Bush, and Casey*, 113.

27. Ibid.

28. Ibid.

29. Ibid., 114.

30. According to Ray Cline in *The CIA Under Reagan, Bush, and Casey*, "the distribution of personnel in the CIG was roughly 600 officers deployed abroad and working covertly for OSO; with an additional 400 people working for OSO in Washington D.C. collecting and directing covert operations; which also had 600 more people working in supporting and administrative roles, which left the remaining 200 people for analysis and reporting" (p. 114).

31. In addition to the creation of the CIA, the National Security Act of 1947 also created the National Security Council (NSC), the Department of the Air Force, from which the United States Air Force became a separate military branch from the Army; also, the National Security Act as later amended in 1949 created the Secretary of Defense and the Chairman of the Joint Chiefs of Staff.

32. John Ranelagh, *The Agency: The Rise and Decline of the CIA* (New York: Touchstone Books, 1987), 739.

33. Ibid.

34. Ibid.

35. Ibid.

36. See Appendixes A, B, C, and D for the organizational charts of the CIA during the Cold War.

37. KGB is a general term used to identify Soviet Intelligence Services, as well as Soviet Security Services, as they evolved over the history of the Soviet State.

38. *The Russian Revolution and the Soviet State 1917–1921*, ed. Martin McCauley (London: MacMillan Press, 1975), 181–182, translated from *Pravda*, December 18, 1927.

39. Andrew and Mitrokhin, *Sword and the Shield*, 26.

40. Ibid.

41. For the duration of the Soviet Union, the tension between internal and external security and intelligence gathering was always persistent.

42. Specifically, the General Secretary, the Politburo, Central Committee of the Communist Party, and the Central Committee, State and Law Department; Andrew and Mitrokhin, *Sword and Shield*, 676.

43. Andrew and Mitrokhin, *Sword and Shield*, 676.

44. Ibid.

45. Ibid.

46. Ibid.

47. Andrew and Mitrokhin, *Sword and Shield*, 678.

48. Ibid.

49. Ibid. The breakdown is as follows: Department 1 U.S. and Canada; Department 2 Latin America; Department 3 UK, Australia, New Zealand, and Scandinavia; Department 4 East Germany, West Germany, and Austria; Department 5 Benelux Countries, France, Spain, Portugal, Switzerland, Greece, Italy, Yugoslavia, Albania, and Romania; Department 6 China, Vietnam, Laos, Cambodia, and North Korea; Department 7 Thailand, Indonesia, Japan, Malaysia, Singapore, and Philippines; Department 8 Non-Arab Countries Near East; Department 9 Anglophile Africa; Department 10 Francophile Africa; Department 11 Liaison with Socialist Countries; Department 17 India, Pakistan, Nepal, Bangladesh, and Burma; Department 18 Arab Countries of the Near East and Egypt; and Department 20 Liaison with Developing Countries.

CHAPTER 1

1. Michael D. Gordin, *Red Cloud at Dawn: Truman, Stalin, and the End of the Atomic Monopoly* (New York: Farrar, Straus, and Giroux, 2009), 63–89; David Holloway, *Stalin and The Bomb: The Soviet Union and Atomic Energy, 1939–1956* (New Haven, CT: Yale University Press, 1994), 105–108.

2. Katherine A. S. Sibley, *Red Spies in America: Stolen Secrets and the Dawn of the Cold War* (Lawrence: University Press of Kansas, 2004), 6.

3. Sibley, *Red Spies*, 8.

4. Ibid., 60.

5. Herbert Romerstein and Eric Breindel, *The Venona Secrets: Exposing Soviet Espionage and America's Traitors* (Washington, D.C.: Regency Publishing, 2000), 3–29.

6. William J. Daugherty, *Executive Secrets: Covert Action and the Presidency* (Lexington: University Press of Kentucky, 2004), 113.

7. Richard Pipes, *Russia Under the Bolshevik Regime* (New York: Vintage Books, 1995), 234.

8. Ronald Grigor Suny, *The Soviet Experiment: Russia, the USSR, and the Successor States* (New York: Oxford University Press, 1998), 134–159.

9. Since 1917 and the Bolshevik Revolution, there was a vigorous debate within the State Department over the issue of recognizing the Soviet Union. FDR ended the debate in 1933 when he officially recognized the USSR. One of the staunch advocates against recognition was Robert Lansing, who was also the uncle to John Foster Dulles and Allen Welsh Dulles.

10. Sibley, *Red Spies*, 8.

11. Ibid., 14.

12. Ibid.

13. Ibid.

14. Sibley, *Red Spies*, 17.

15. Ibid., 18.

16. Ibid., 19.

17. Ibid., 19.

18. Ibid., 20.

19. Of special note is that Lise Meitern, who had been a critical partner in the research with Hahn and Strassman, had fled Germany as a result of the rise to power of the National Socialist German Workers Party (NSDAP) in 1933 and their subsequent push for anti-Semitic laws in Germany under the direction of Adolf Hitler.

20. Sean N. Kalic, "The Manhattan Project," at The Robert J. Dole Institute for Politics, University of Kansas, Lawrence, Kansas, November 5, 2015, https://www.youtube.com/watch?v=MUv313lkU2s

21. Romerstein and Breindel, *Venona Secrets*, 268–272.

22. Ibid., 449.

23. Holloway, *Stalin and the Bomb*, 222.

24. Richard C. S. Trahair and Robert L. Miller, *Encyclopedia of Cold War Espionage, Spies, and Secret Operations* (New York: Enigma Books, 2012), 147; Michael D. Gordin, *Red Cloud at Dawn: Truman, Stalin, and the End of the Atomic Monopoly* (New York: Farrar, Strauss, and Giroux, 2009), 116.

25. Trahair and Miller, *Cold War Espionage*, 147.

26. Ibid.

27. Gordin, *Red Cloud*, 116; Trahair and Miller, *Cold War Espionage*, 147.

28. Trahair and Miller, *Cold War Espionage*, 147.

29. Gordin, *Red Cloud*, 116.

30. Ibid.; Trahair and Miller, *Cold War Espionage*, 147.

31. Ibid.

32. Gordin, *Red Cloud*, 117.

33. Romerstein and Breindel, *Venona Secrets*, 226.

34. Ibid., 226.

35. Trahair and Miller, *Cold War Espionage*, 157.

36. Ibid.

37. Ibid.

38. Ibid.

39. Romerstein and Breindel, *Venona Secrets*, 226.

40. Richard Rhodes, *The Making of the Atomic Bomb* (New York: Touchstone, 1986), 577–579, 588–598.

41. Romerstein and Breindel, *Venona Secrets*, 227. An example of how efficient the Soviet espionage program within the Manhattan Project was can be seen with Fuchs's passage of a report entitled "Fluctuations and the Efficiency of a Diffuse Plant" to Gold in June of 1944. Soviet intelligence had a copy of the report in Moscow only nine days after the report had been written at Los Alamos.

42. Robert H. Ferrell, *Harry S. Truman and the Bomb: A Documentary History*, (Worland, WY: High Plains, 1996), 33.

43. Rhodes, *Making of the Atomic Bomb*, 690.

44. Holloway, *Stalin and the Bomb*, 222.

45. Pavel Sudoplatov, Anatoli Sudoplatov, Jerrod L. Schecter, and Leona P. Schecter, *Special Tasks: The Memoirs of an Unwanted Witness—A Soviet Spymaster* (Boston: Little, Brown and Company, 1994), 208.

46. Sudoplatov et al., *Special Tasks*, 208–209.

47. Gordin, *Red Cloud*, 119; Trahair and Miller, *Cold War Espionage*, 178.

48. Trahair and Miller, *Cold War Espionage*, 178.

49. Ibid.

50. Suny, *Soviet Experiment*, 221–226.

51. Trahair and Miller, *Cold War Espionage*, 178–179.

52. Ibid.

53. Gordin, *Red Cloud*, 119.

54. Ibid., 119.

55. Romerstein and Breindel, *Venona Secrets*, 203.

56. Ibid.

57. Ibid.

58. Trahair and Miller, *Cold War Espionage*, 178.

59. Ibid.

60. Romerstein and Breindel, *Venona Secrets*, 204; Trahair and Miller, *Cold War Espionage*, 179.

61. Trahair and Miller, *Cold War Espionage*, 179.

62. John Earl Haynes and Harvey Klehr, *Venona: Decoding Soviet Espionage in America* (New Haven, CT: Yale University Press, 1999), 308; Trahair and Miller, *Cold War Espionage*, 171.

63. Haynes and Klehr, *Venona*, 308.

64. Trahair and Miller, *Cold War Espionage*, 171.

65. Haynes and Klehr, *Venona*, 308.

66. Ibid.

67. Ibid., 308–309.

68. Romerstein and Breindel, *Venona Secrets*, 233.

69. Ibid.; Haynes and Klehr, *Venona*, 309.

70. Haynes and Klehr, *Venona*, 309.

71. Ibid., 310.

72. Romerstein and Breindel, *Venona Secrets*, 235.

73. Trahair and Miller, *Cold War Espionage*, 172.

74. Ibid.

75. Romerstein and Breindel, *Venona Secrets*, 11.

76. Haynes and Klehr, *Venona*, 5.

77. Romerstein and Breindel, *Venona Secrets*, 4.

78. This is the method of infiltration used on the FX show *The Americans*, which is based on real events discovered through Venona.

79. Romerstein and Breindel, *Venona Secrets*, 10.

80. Ibid.

81. Trahair and Miller, *Cold War Espionage*, 511.

82. Haynes and Klehr, *Venona*, 9.

83. Romerstein and Breindel, *Venona Secrets*, 26–27.

84. Ibid.

85. Ibid.

86. Ibid.

87. Trahair and Miller, *Cold War Espionage*, 511.

CHAPTER 2

1. Melvin Leffler, *For the Soul of Mankind: The United States, The Soviet Union, and the Cold War* (New York: Hill and Wang, 2007), 37–48.

2. The Air Policy Commission had a robust debate over the perceived time it would take the USSR to develop an atomic bomb. Due to the lack of intelligence about the program, the members of the Commission believed that the date of 1953 was a safe guess. However, the USSR shocked the commission when it tested its first bomb in 1949.

3. Christopher Andrew and Vasili Mitrokhin, *The Sword and the Shield: The Mitrokhin Archive and the Secret History of the KGB* (New York: Basic Books, 1999), 212.

4. Andrew and Mitrokhin, *Sword and the Shield*, 50.

5. William J. Daugherty, *Executive Secrets: Covert Action and the Presidency* (Lexington: University Press of Kentucky, 2004), 114.

6. Daugherty, *Executive Secrets*, 114.

7. *Moscow Embassy Telegram # 511*, "The Long Telegram," February 22, 1946, in *Containment: Documents on American Policy and Strategy, 1945–1950*, ed. Thomas H. Etzold and John Lewis Gaddis (New York: Columbia University Press, 1978), 50–63.

8. George F. Kennan, "Sources of Soviet Conduct," in *Foreign Affairs* (July 1947), 556–582. The Policy Planning Staff, especially early in the Cold War, was an office within the State Department that worked on building national security policy and strategy within other executive-level agencies.

9. Michael Creswell, *A Question of Balance: How France and the United States Created Cold War Europe* (Cambridge, MA: Harvard University Press, 2006), 7.

10. William I. Hitchcock, *France Restored: Cold War Diplomacy and the Quest for Leadership in Europe, 1944–1954* (Chapel Hill: The University of North Carolina Press, 1998), 1.

11. Hitchcock, *France Restored*, 41.

12. Ibid.

13. Ibid.

14. Creswell, *Question of Balance*, 9.

15. Igor Lukes, *On the Edge of the Cold War: American Diplomats and Spies in Postwar Prague* (Oxford: Oxford University Press, 2012), 16–20; Creswell, *Question of Balance*, 9.

16. Creswell, *Question of Balance*, 8.

17. Ibid.

18. Ibid.

19. Creswell, *Question of France*, 11.

20. Hitchcock, *France Restored*, 83.

21. "Churchill Asks Red Barrier," *Kansas City Times*, March 16, 1946, vol. 109, no. 56, front page.

22. William J. Daugherty, *Executive Secrets: Covert Action and the Presidency* (Lexington: University Press of Kentucky, 2004), 113.

23. Daugherty, *Executive Secrets*, 114.

24. This was by no means unique to France. In fact, throughout Eastern and Central Europe, the Soviet Union used the communist parties of nations such as Hungary, Czechoslovakia, and Poland as the primary tools to shape the postwar political environment in their favor.

25. Andrew and Mitrokhin, *Sword and the Shield*, 206.

26. Ibid.

27. Ibid.

28. Ibid.

29. Ibid.

30. Ibid., 208.

31. Edward H. Judge and John W. Langdon, "The Truman Doctrine, 1947," in *The Cold War: A History through Documents* (Upper Saddle River, NJ: Prentice Hall, 1999), 24.

32. Ibid., 25.

33. Edward H. Judge and John W. Langdon, "The Marshall Plan, 1947," in *The Cold War: A History through Documents* (Upper Saddle River, NJ: Prentice Hall, 1999), 27.

34. Ibid.

35. Daugherty, *Executive Secrets*, 118.

36. Ibid.

37. Ibid.

38. Explain the key tenets of NSC 1/4.

39. Daugherty, *Executive Secrets*, 118-119.

40. Ibid., 119.

41. Ibid., 114-115.

42. Lukes, *On the Edge*, 163.

43. Antonio Varsouri, "Italy and Western Defence, 1948–55: The Elusive Alliance," in *Securing the Peace in Europe, 1945–62: Thoughts for the Post-Cold War Era*, ed. Beatrice Heuser and Robert O'Neill (New York: St. Martin's Press, 1992), 196.

44. Zachary Karabell, *The United States and the Third World and the Cold War 1946–1962: Architects of Intervention* (Baton Rouge: Louisiana State University Press, 1999), 38.

45. Ibid., 39.

46. Ibid.

47. NSC 1/1, 725; Karabell, *Architects of Intervention*, 39–40.

48. Pavel Sudoplatov, Anatoli Sudoplatov, Jerrold L. Schecter, and Leona P. Schecter, *Special Tasks: The Memoirs of an Unwanted Witness—A Soviet Spymaster* (Boston: Little, Brown, and Company, 1994), 296.

49. Daugherty, *Executive Secrets*, 114.

50. John Ranelagh, *The Agency: The Rise and Decline of the CIA* (New York: Touchstone, 1987), 176.

51. Ranelagh, *Agency*, 177.

52. Daugherty, *Executive Secrets*, 114.

53. Ibid., 116.

54. Ibid., 117.

55. Ibid.

56. Ibid., 119.

57. Ibid.

58. Ibid., 122.

59. Ibid.

60. Ibid., 126.

61. Michael S. Goodman, *Spying on the Nuclear Bear: Anglo-American Intelligence and the Soviet Bomb* (Stanford, CA: Stanford University Press, 2007), 9.

62. D. V. Gallery to John A. McCone, October 22, 1947, Harry S. Truman Presidential Library [hereafter HSTPL] Record Group 220, Box 41, File: MH3-4 Guided Missiles, 2.

63. Air Policy Commission to Colonel Boatner and Captain Pihl, Memorandum No. 39, undated, HSTPL, Record Group 220, Box 41, File: MH3-4 Guided Missiles, 2.

64. E. C. Sweeney, *Naval Air Research and Development: Notes of Meeting with Bureau of Aeronautics*, September 25, 1947. HSTPL, Record Group 220, Box 40, File: Weihmiller, H. E., MG1-14 Classified Material, 1.

65. L. Parker Temple III, *Shades of Gray: National Security and the Evolution of Space Reconnaissance* (Reston, VA: American Institute of Aeronautics and Astronautics, 2005), 23–43.

66. Air Policy Commission Report (draft), undated, HSTPL, Record Group 220, Box 41, File: ML1-10 Proposed Classified Report, 10.

67. Ibid.

68. Ibid.

69. Ibid., 10–11.

70. *Notes on Appearance of Donald M. Nelson, before the Executive Session*, October 23, 1947, HSTPL, Record Group 220, Box 40, File: Weihmiller, H.E., MG1-14 Classified Material, 2.

71. Paul H. Nitze was the main force behind the development of NSC-68, which became the basic U.S. national strategy for the majority of the Cold War. In NCS-68, Nitze specifically identified the Soviet Union as the primary enemy of the United States and recommended the United States needed to re-arm to confront and contain the expansionistic tendencies of the Soviet Union.

72. Paul H. Nitze, *From Hiroshima to Glasnost: At the Center of Decision: A Memoir* (New York: Grove/Atlantic, 1989), 96.

73. John Thomas Farquhar, *A Need to Know: The Role of Air Force Reconnaissance in War Planning, 1945–1953* (Maxwell Air Force Base, Montgomery, AL: Air University Press, 2004), 25.

74. Ibid., 28.

75. Ibid., 31.

76. Ibid., 35.

77. Ibid.

78. Ibid.

79. Ibid.

80. Ibid., 36.

81. Ibid., 40.

82. Ibid.

83. Ibid., 41.

84. Ibid., 55–56. Note that coverage for areas that highlight the wartime dates of 1941–1945 came from U.S. access to German military personnel that had fought and often may had been captured by the Soviet Union. This access to former German intelligence provided the only intelligence available at the time.

85. David Holloway, "Entering the Nuclear Arms Race: The Soviet Decision to Build the Atomic Bomb, 1939–1945," *Social Studies of Science* 11 (1981): 186-87.

86. David Holloway, *Stalin and the Bomb: The Soviet Union and Atomic Energy 1939–1956* (New Haven, CT: Yale University Press, 1994), 265.

87. Goodman, *Spying on the Nuclear Bear*, 46.

88. Ibid., 46.

89. Ibid.

90. Ibid., 47.

CHAPTER 3

1. William J. Daugherty, *Executive Secrets: Covert Action and the Presidency* (Lexington: University Press of Kentucky, 2004), 131–132.

2. Christopher Andrew and Vasili Mitrokhin, *The Sword and the Shield: The Mitrokhin Archive and the Secret History of the KGB* (New York: Basic Books, 1999), 238–246.

3. United States Department of State, "Estimate Prepared by Board of National Estimates," *Foreign Relations of the United States* (FRUS): *National Security Affairs, 1952–1954, Volume II Part 1*, November 21, 1952 (Washington, D.C.: Government Printing Office), 364.

4. Ibid., 365.

5. Ibid., 371.

6. Ibid.

7. Andrew and Mitrokhin, *Sword and the Shield*, 221.

8. Ibid., 221–223.

9. NSC 162/2, October 30, 1953, 1.

10. Ibid. The remainder of the focus is on the Soviet Union's continued reliance on "conspiracy and subversion."

11. NSC 162/2, 2.

12. It is important to note that by "threat," the NCS does not mean that they expect a Soviet bloc attack on the West, but rather that the Soviet Union and its

communist satellites will continue to challenge the West in an effort to weaken
the political and economic structure of the Western nations with an objective
of fomenting communist revolutions as the conditions solidify, as outlined by
Karl Marx.

13. NSC 162/2, 6.

14. Ibid.

15. Ibid.

16. NSC 162/2, 24–25.

17. NSC 162/2, 25.

18. Daugherty, *Executive Secrets*, 131–132.

19. Ibid., 133.

20. Ibid., 134.

21. Ibid., 135.

22. Andrew and Mitrokhin, *Sword and the Shield*, 220.

23. Rudolf Abel is a great example of how the Soviet Union used illegals to
penetrate the United States and assume citizenship with the intent of building
intelligence-gathering networks for the KGB.

24. In addition to illegals, the Soviet Union also used legal embassy or other
agency workers who were in the United States as on official government documents, but in reality, their day jobs were covers for their spying operations. Oleg
Kalugin is an example who will be discussed in later chapters.

25. Andrew and Mitrokhin, *Sword and the Shield*, 221.

26. Ibid.

27. Ibid., 221.

28. Pavel Sudoplatov, Anatoli Sudoplatov, Jerrod L. Schecter, and Leona P.
Schecter, *Special Tasks: The Memoirs of an Unwanted Witness—A Soviet Spymaster*
(Boston: Little, Brown and Company, 1994), 241; Andrew and Mitrokhin, *Sword
and the Shield*, 222.

29. Andrew and Mitrokhin, *Sword and the Shield*, 222.

30. Richard C. S. Trahair and Robert L. Miller, *Encyclopedia of Cold War Espionage, Spies, and Secret Operations* (New York: Enigma Books, 2012), 136.

31. Ibid.

32. Ibid.

33. Sudoplatov et al., *Special Tasks*, 241.

34. Ibid., 242.

35. Ibid. The Soviet Union had a long history of using illegal radio transmitters
to rely intelligence from both legal and illegal sources around the globe. Reference
Chapter 1 when the FCC found illegal radio transmitters operated by Soviets during routine scans for German illegal transmitters.

36. The Soviet Union had a history of using people who were deceased in the
1920s or even during the Second World War as a way to allow illegals to assume
identities to use as covers to enter the United States or Canada.

37. Sudoplatov et al., *Special Tasks*, 242.

38. Ibid.

39. Sudoplatov et al., *Special Tasks*, 245.

40. Trahair and Miller, *Cold War Espionage*, 137.

41. Ibid.

42. Sudoplatov et al., *Special Tasks*, 245.

43. Trahair and Miller, *Cold War Espionage*, 137.

44. Ibid.

45. Ibid.

46. Ibid.

47. When he was returned to the Soviet Union, Fisher was not faulted for disobeying orders but rather viewed as a casualty of the ineptness of other spies.

48. David Murphy, Sergei A. Kondrashev, and George Baily, *Battleground Berlin: The CIA vs. KGB in the Cold War* (New Haven, CT: Yale University Press, 1997), 229–230.

49. Trahair and Miller, *Cold War Espionage*, 387; Murphy et al., *Battleground Berlin*, 208–209.

50. Trahair and Miller, *Cold War Espionage*, 387.

51. Ibid.

52. Ibid., 388.

53. Ibid.

54. Ibid.

55. Murphy et al., *Battleground Berlin*, 208.

56. Joseph J. Trento, *The Secret History of the CIA* (New York: MJF Books, 2001), 136–140.

57. Murphy et al., *Battleground Berlin*, 209; Trento, *Secret History*, 141.

58. Murphy et al., *Battleground Berlin*, 209.

59. Ibid.

60. Ibid., 210.

61. Ibid., 211.

62. Ibid.

63. Trento, *Secret History*, 142.

64. Ibid.

65. Ibid.

66. Ibid.

67. Ibid.

68. Ibid.

69. Ibid., 143.

70. Ibid., 145.

71. Murphy et al., *Battleground Berlin*, 232.

72. Ibid., 235–237.

73. Trahair and Miller, *Cold War Espionage*, 45–46.

74. Michael R. Bechloss, *MAYDAY: Eisenhower, Khrushchev, and U-2 Affair* (New York: Harper Row, 1986), 74.

75. Norman Polmar, *Spyplane: The U-2 History Declassified* (Osceola, WI: MBI, 2001), 20–21.

76. Ibid., 22.

77. Ibid., 23.

78. Ibid.

79. Ibid.

80. Ibid.

81. Ibid.

82. Ibid., 26.

83. Ibid., 27.

84. Ibid., 29.

85. Ibid., 30.

86. Ibid., 42.

87. Ibid., 42–44.

88. Ibid. 45–46.

89. Ibid., 47.

90. Ibid., 50–51.

91. Some of the specific issues that had to be solved dealt with landing, brakes, and pressure suits.

92. Polmar, *Spyplane*, 70.

93. Ibid., 72.

94. Ibid., 87.

95. Eisenhower's Open Skies proposal was an attempt by the United States to provide an international framework that allowed nations to fly over other nations in an attempt to collect open intelligence. The rationale was that this open access to strategic intelligence would deescalate the tensions associated with not knowing about strategic military hardware.

96. Although the United States had little access to the international numbers of bomber production, Truman and, later, Eisenhower were deeply concerned that the Soviet Union had been secretly building bombers and hence had tipped the scales of the strategic nuclear balance in its favor.

97. Francis Gary Powers, *Operation Overflight: A Memoir of the U-2 Incident* (Washington, D.C.: Brassey's, 2004), 50–58.

98. Powers, *Overflight*, 54.

99. Due to Lee Harvey Oswald's work with the U-2 program as a result of his military experience, some connections have been asserted that he may have provided the Soviet Union with intelligence about the U-2, as he was a radar operator who worked with the U-2 units in Japan.

100. Powers, *Overflight*, 238.

CHAPTER 4

1. William J. Daugherty, *Executive Secrets: Covert Action and the Presidency* (Lexington: University Press of Kentucky, 2004), 151–152.

2. Ibid., 152.

3. Ibid.

4. Ibid.

5. Ibid., 153.

6. Joseph J. Trento, *The Secret History of the CIA* (New York: MJF Books, 2001), 192.

7. Daugherty, *Executive Secrets*, 146; Trento, *Secret History*, 192.

8. Trento, *Secret History*, 192.

9. Zachary Karabell, *The United States and the Third World, and the Cold War, 1946–1962* (Baton Rouge: Louisiana State University Press, 1999), 92–93.

10. Daugherty, *Executive Secrets*, 146.

11. Ibid.

12. Ibid.

13. Trento, *Secret History*, 192.

14. Richard C. S. Trahair and Robert L. Miller, *Encyclopedia of Cold War Espionage, Spies, and Secret Operations* (New York: Enigma Books, 2012), 379.

15. Trento, *Secret History*, 193.

16. Ibid.

17. Daugherty, *Executive Secrets*, 146–147.

18. Trento, *Secret History*, 193.

19. John Ranelagh, *The Agency: The Rise and Decline of the CIA* (New York: Touchstone Books, 1987), 358.

20. Ranelagh, *Agency*, 359.

21. Ibid., 360.

22. Ibid., 367.

23. Ibid., 368.

24. Ibid.

25. Ibid.

26. Ibid.

27. Ibid., 371.

28. Ibid.

29. Christopher Andrew and Vasili Mitrokhin, *The World Was Going Our Way: The KGB and the Battle for the Third World* (New York: Basic Books, 2005), 28–29.

30. Andrew and Mitrokhin, *World Was Going Our Way*, 29.

31. Oleg Kalugin, *Spymaster: My 32 Years in Intelligence and Espionage Against the West* (London: Smith Gryphon, 1994), 50.

32. Ibid., 1–2.

33. Ibid., 36.

34. Kalugin, *Spymaster*, 50.

35. Ibid.

36. Ibid., 51.

37. Ibid.

38. Ibid.

39. Ibid.

40. Ibid., 51–52.

41. Ibid., 52.

42. Ibid.

43. Ibid.

44. Trento, *Secret History*, 197–202.

45. Sean N. Kalic, *US Presidents and the Militarization of Space, 1946–1967* (Austin: Texas A&M University Press, 2012), 7–59.

46. Kevin C. Ruffner, ed., *Corona: America's Satellite Program* (Washington, D.C.: Center for the Study of Intelligence, 1995), xiii.

47. Ruffner, *Corona*, xiii.

48. Dwayne A. Day, John M. Logsdon, and Brian Latell, eds., "Introduction," in *Eye in the Sky: The Story of the Corona Spy Satellite* (Washington, D.C.: Smithsonian Institution, 1998), 5.

49. Kalic, *US Presidents*, 36.

50. Ibid., 37.

51. Day et al., "Introduction," 6.

52. Ibid., 7.

53. Kenneth E. Greer, "Corona," in *Corona: America's First Satellite Program* (Washington, D.C.: Center for the Study of Intelligence, 1995), 37.

54. Day et al., "Introduction," 7.

55. Peter A. Gorgin, "ZENIT: The Soviet Response to Corona," in *Eye in the Sky: The Story of the Corona Spy Satellite*, ed. Dwayne A. Day, John M. Logsdon, and Brian Latell (Washington, D.C.: Smithsonian Institution Press, 1998), 157.

56. Gorgin, "Soviet Response," 157.

57. Ibid., 158.

58. Ibid.

59. Ibid.

60. Gorgin, "Soviet Response," 158; Kalic, *US Presidents*, 137.

61. Gorgin, "Soviet Response," 158.

62. Ibid., 159.

63. Ibid.

64. Ibid., 160.

65. Ibid.

66. Ibid.

67. Ibid., 162.

68. Ibid., 165–166.

69. Ibid., 161–163.

70. Ibid., 162.

71. Ibid. Note that the territorial integrity of the United States is approximately 9,834 square kilometers.

72. Gorgin, "Soviet Response," 163.

73. Ibid., 164.

74. Ibid.

75. Ibid., 165. During the time between August 1960 and October 1963, the Soviet Union launched thirteen satellites with varying margins of success before they declared the program ready for operational capability.

76. Gorgin, "Soviet Response," 166.

77. Ibid., 167.

78. Ibid., 168–169.

79. Ibid., 170.

80. Andrew and Mitrokhin, *World Was Going Our Way*, 265.

81. Ibid.

82. A more detailed discussion of how the KGB used the U.S. war in Vietnam as a springboard to build greater support in the Third World will be covered in greater detail in Chapters 5 and 6.

83. The use of covert OSS forces in Indochina at the end of World War II is well documented and extensively written about; therefore, it will not be covered in much detail beyond a simple mention, because the focus of this section is to highlight how the CIA went from focusing on the importance of Vietnam within the context of the international strategic balance to making it a battleground on which the CIA actively fought for the preservation of South Vietnam.

84. Ranelagh, *Agency*, 417–418.

85. Ibid., 418.

86. Ibid., 420.

87. Ibid., 422.

88. Ibid., 425.

89. Ibid., 424–425.

CHAPTER 5

1. John Ranelagh, *The Agency: The Rise and Decline of the CIA* (New York: Touchstone Books, 1987), 585.

2. Ibid., 471.

3. James H. Willbanks, *The Tet Offensive, A Concise History* (New York: Columbia University Press, 2007), 5–6.

4. Ranelagh, *The Agency*, 472; Philip Agee, *Inside the Company: CIA Diary* (Harmondsworth: Penguin, 1975), 563–567.

5. Richard C. S. Trahair and Robert L. Miller, *Encyclopedia of Cold War Espionage, Spies, and Secret Operations* (New York: Enigma Books, 2012), 4; Ranelagh, *Agency*, 472.

6. Trahair and Miller, *Cold War Espionage*, 4.

7. Ranelagh, *Agency*, 480.

8. John Prados, *The Soviet Estimate: U.S. Intelligence Analysis and Russian Military Strength* (New York: The Dial Press, 1982), 196.

9. Ibid., 197.

10. Ibid., 217.

11. Ibid., 217.

12. William J. Daugherty, *Executive Secrets: Covert Action and the Presidency* (Lexington: University Press of Kentucky, 2004), 171; John Prados, *President's Secret Wars: CIA and Pentagon Covert Operations Since World War II* (New York: Morrow and Company, 1986), 315; Christopher Andrew and Vasili Mitrokhin, *The World Was Going Our Way: The KGB and the Battle for the Third World* (New York: Perseus books, 2005), 69.

13. Andrew and Mitrokhin, *World Was Going Our Way*, 69–70.

14. Ibid., 71.

15. Ibid.

16. Ranelagh, *Agency*, 513.

17. Ibid., 514.

18. Daugherty, *Executive Secrets*, 171.

19. Andrew and Mitrokhin, *World Was Going Our Way*, 73.

20. Ranelagh, *Agency*, 515.

21. Ibid.

22. Prados, *President's Secret* Wars, 316; Ranelagh, *Agency*, 515.

23. Prados, *President's Secret Wars*, 316; Ranelagh, *Agency*, 515.

24. Ranelagh, *Agency*, 515.

25. Andrew and Mitrokhin, *World Was Going Our Way*, 72–73.

26. Prados, *President's Secret Wars*, 317.

27. Ranelagh, *Agency*, 515.

28. Ibid., 516.

29. Ibid.

30. Ibid.

31. Prados, *President's Secret Wars*, 318.

32. Ranelagh, *Agency*, 517.

33. Ibid.

34. Ibid.

35. Ibid.

36. Ibid.

37. Ibid., 518.

38. Ibid., 519.

39. Andrew and Mitrokhin, *World Was Going Our Way*, 73.

40. Ibid.

41. Ibid.

42. Ibid., 78.

43. Ibid., 79.

44. Ibid., 80.

45. Ibid., 80–81.

46. Ibid., 83.

47. Ibid., 83–84.

48. Ranelagh, *Agency*, 534; Trahair and Miller, *Cold War Espionage*, 352.

49. Trahair and Miller, *Cold War Espionage*, 352–353.

50. Ranelagh, *Agency*, 534.

51. Ibid.

52. Ibid.

53. Ibid.

54. Trahair and Miller, *Cold War Espionage*, 353.

55. Ranelagh, *Agency*, 534–535.

56. Trahair and Miller, *Cold War Espionage*, 353.

57. Ranelagh, *Agency*, 535.

58. Ibid.

59. Christopher Andrew and Oleg Gordievsky, eds., *Comrade Kryuchkov's Instructions: Top Secret Files on KGB Foreign Operations, 1975–1985* (Stanford, CA: Stanford University Press, 1993), 2.

60. Melvyn P. Leffer, *For the Soul of Mankind: The United States, The Soviet Union, and the Cold War* (New York: Hill and Wang, 2007), 239–240.

61. Michael J. Sulick, *American Spies: Espionage against the United States from the Cold War to the Present* (Washington, D.C.; Georgetown University Press, 2013), 47-49.

62. Andrew and Gordievsky, *Comrade Kryuchkov*, 50.

63. Ibid., 25.

64. Ibid., 25–28.

65. Oleg Kalugin, *Spymaster: My 32 Years in Intelligence and Espionage Against the West* (London: Smith Gryphon, 1994), 126.

66. Ibid., 128–129.

67. Ibid., 129.

68. Ibid.

69. Ibid., 129–130.

70. Christopher Andrew and Vasili Mitrokhin, *The Sword and the Shield: The Mitrokhin Archive and the Secret History of the KGB* (New York: Basic Books, 1999), 459–460.

71. Ibid., 458.

72. Ibid., 448.
73. Ibid., 449.
74. Ibid.
75. Ibid.
76. Ibid.
77. Ibid., 460.
78. Ibid.
79. Ibid.
80. Ibid., 461.
81. Ibid.
82. Ibid.
83. Ibid.
84. Ranelagh, *Agency*, 587.
85. Ibid., 589.
86. Ibid., 591.
87. Ibid., 596.
88. Ibid., 597–598.

CHAPTER 6

1. William J. Daugherty, *Executive Secrets: Covert Action and the Presidency* (Lexington: University Press of Kentucky, 2004), 183.
2. Ibid., 184.
3. Melvyn P. Leffler, *For the Soul of Mankind: The United States, The Soviet Union, and the Cold War* (New York: Hill and Wang, 2007), 234.
4. Ibid.
5. Ibid.
6. Ibid., 235.
7. Ibid., 249.
8. Ibid.
9. Ibid.
10. Ibid.
11. John Ranelagh, *The Agency: The Rise and Decline of the CIA* (New York: Touchstone Books, 1987), 634.
12. Ibid., 633.
13. Ibid., 635.
14. Stansfield Turner, *Secrecy and Democracy: The CIA in Transition* (Boston: Houghton Mifflin, 1984), 27–28; Ranelagh, *Agency*, 635.
15. Ranelagh, *Agency*, 635–636.
16. Ibid., 636–637.
17. Ibid., 636.
18. Ibid., 637.
19. Ibid.
20. Ibid.
21. William E. Burrows, *Deep Black: Space Espionage and National Security* (New York: Random House, 1986), 226–227.
22. Ibid., 226.

23. Ibid. *Burrows in Deep Black* highlights that although the specified life span of the satellite was over two years, there have been instances where KH-11s have been in space for as long as 1,175 days.

24. Burrows, *Deep Black*, 248.

25. Ibid., 249.

26. Daugherty, *Executive Secrets*, 186.

27. Ibid., 187.

28. Ibid.

29. Ibid.

30. Ibid.

31. Christopher Andrew and Vasili Mitrokhin, *The World Was Going Our Way: The KGB and the Battle for the Third World* (New York: Basic Books, 2005), 19.

32. Ibid.

33. Christopher Andrew and Vasili Mitrokhin, *The Sword and the Shield: The Mitrokhin Archive and the Secret History of the KGB* (New York: Basic Books, 1999), 487.

34. Ibid., 488–498.

35. Ibid., 488.

36. Ibid., 490.

37. Ibid.

38. Ibid., 490–491.

39. Burrows, *Deep Black*, 267.

40. Ibid., 269.

41. Ibid., 267.

42. Andrew and Mitrokhin, *Sword and the Shield*, 492.

43. Ibid., 492.

44. Ibid.

45. Ibid.

46. Ibid., 493.

47. Ibid.

48. Christopher Andrew and Oleg Gordievsky, eds., *Comrade Kryuchkov's Instructions: Top Secret Files on KGB Foreign Operations, 1975–1985* (Stanford, CA: Stanford University Press, 1993), 74. It is interesting to note that within in this memorandum, the main adversary was identified as the USA, NATO, and the People's Republic of China. This inclusion of China is an interesting addition that does not seem to impact the operational focus, which still remained on the United States and its NATO allies.

49. Andrew and Gordievsky, *Comrade Kryuchkov's Instructions*, 75. Though the PRC is referenced in the previous quotation, it appears as Kryuchkov further justified and explained this new shift for the KGB; the real and primary focus was indeed the United States and NATO.

50. Andrew and Gordievsky, *Comrade Kryuchkov's Instructions*, 75–76.

51. Andrew and Mitrokhin, *Sword and the Shield*, 492.

52. Sean N. Kalic, "Reagan's SDI Announcement and the European Reaction: Diplomacy in the Last Decade of the Cold War," in *The Crisis of Détente in Europe: From Helsinki to Gorbachev, 1975–1985*, ed. Leopoldo Nuti (London: Routledge, 2009), 102.

53. Andrew and Mitrokhin, *Sword and the Shield*, 493.

54. Andrew and Mitrokhin, *Sword and the Shield*, 494.

55. Rodric Braithwaite, *Afgansty: The Russian in Afghanistan, 1979–1989* (New York: Oxford University Press, 2011), 331.

56. Ibid.

57. Ibid.

58. Ibid.

59. Archie Brown, *The Gorbachev Factor* (New York: Oxford University Press, 1997), 155–156.

60. Ibid., 158.

61. Mikhail S. Gorbachev, *Perestroika: New Thinking for Our Country and the World* (New York: Harper Collins, 1987), 24.

62. Brown, *Gorbachev Factor*, 211.

63. Andrew and Mitrokhin, *Sword and the Shield*, 496.

64. Michael J. Sulick, *American Spies: Espionage against the United States from the Cold War to the Present* (Washington, D.C.: Georgetown University Press, 2013), 103.

65. Andrew and Mitrokhin, *Sword and the Shield*, 498.

66. Ibid., 501.

67. Ibid., 500.

68. Ibid., 500–501.

69. Ibid., 503.

70. Ibid.

71. Andrew and Mitrokhin, *Sword and the Shield*, 505.

72. Ibid., 503.

73. Ibid., 507.

74. Peter Schweizer, *Victory: The Reagan Administration's Secret Strategy That Hastened the Collapse of the Soviet Union* (New York: The Atlantic Monthly Press, 1994), 7.

75. Schweizer, *Victory*, 32; Daugherty, *Executive Secrets*, 188.

76. Daugherty, *Executive Secrets*, 188.

77. Schweizer, *Victory*, 34.

78. Ibid., 34–35.

79. Ibid., 38–39.

80. Ibid.

81. Ibid., 60–61.

82. Schweizer, *Victory*, 69.

83. Ibid.

84. Ibid., 75.

85. Christopher Simpson, *National Security Directives of the Reagan and Bush Administrations: The Declassified History of U.S. Political and Military Policy, 1981–1990* (Boulder, CO: Westview Press, 1995), 64; Schweizer, *Victory*, 77.

86. Daugherty, *Executive Secrets*, 188–189.

87. Ibid.

88. Ibid., 189.

89. Ibid.

90. Schweizer, *Victory*, 116.

91. Schweizer, *Victory*, 116.

92. The White House, "U.S. Policy, Program, and Strategy in Afghanistan," National Security Decision Directive (NSDD) 166 [hereafter NSDD 166], March 27, 1985, Ronald Reagan Presidential Library, website accessed on August 1, 2018, https://www.reaganlibrary.gov/digital-library/nsdds, 1.

93. NSDD 166, 1–2.
94. Schweizer, *Victory*, 116.
95. Schweizer, *Victory*, 151. Lester Grau, ed. and trans., *The Bewar Went Over the Mountain: Soviet Combat Tactics in Afghanistan* (Washington, D.C.: National Defense University Press, 1996), xvii-xx.
96. Schweizer, *Victory*, 151.
97. Andrew and Mitrokhin, *The World Was Going Our Way*, 12–24.

CHAPTER 7

1. Christopher Andrew and Vasili Mitrokhin, *The Sword and the Shield: The Mitrokhin Archive and the Secret History of the KGB* (New York: Basic Books, 1999), 507.
2. Ibid,. 508.
3. Ibid., 509.
4. Ibid.
5. Ibid., 510.
6. Oleg Kalugin, *Spymaster: My 32 Years in Intelligence and Espionage Against the West* (London: Smith Gryphon, 1994), 288.
7. Ibid., 290.
8. Ibid., 291.
9. Ibid., 291–293.
10. Kalugin, *Spymaster*, 328. Despite his vast experience in intelligence matters, Kryuchkov had a deep distrust of Kalugin. Suspecting that that Kalugin was possibly a CIA double agent at the end of his career in the Soviet Union the KGB, shuffled around and gave Kalugin assignments that kept him from the hierarchy of power, as he was deemed a threat to the entrenched system of the KGB, and hence the longevity of the Soviet Union. This was a shocking blow to Kalugin, who had been seen as a very strong candidate to head the KGB after Kryuchkov.
11. Kalugin, *Spymaster*, 332.
12. Ibid.
13. Ibid., 334.
14. Ibid., 335.
15. Ibid.
16. Kalugin, *Spymaster*, 336–344. In a very interesting and innovative attempt to subvert Kalugin's campaign, the KGB hired a local pilot to fly low and slow over head to drown out his speech. This is just one of several stories that Kalugin recounts in his memoirs.
17. Kalugin, *Spymaster*, 344.
18. Kalugin's recommendations for a "new" KGB were to reduce its manpower and diffuse the power across its internal branches. However, as Vadim Batakin, the new head of the KGB, attempted to implement the recommendations offered by Kalugin, the rapid demise of the Soviet Union essentially stopped the efforts as the KGB had balkanized and began to consolidate its power as the Soviet Union fell apart.
19. Richard C. S. Trahair and Robert L. Miller, *Encyclopedia of Cold War Espionage, Spies, and Secret Operations* (New York: Enigma Books, 2012), 427.
20. Ibid., 426–427.
21. Ibid., 426.

22. Ibid.

23. Ibid., 588.

24. Michael J. Sulick, *American Spies: Espionage against the United States from the Cold War to the Present* (Washington, D.C.; Georgetown University Press, 2013), 116–117; Trahair and Miller, *Cold War Espionage*, 220.

25. Sulick, *American Spies*, 116–117.

26. Trahair and Miller, *Cold War Espionage*, 221; Sulick, *American Spies*, 118–120.

27. Sulick, *American Spies*, 125.

28. Ibid., 128.

29. Ibid.

30. Lonetree never saw Violetta after his transfer to the U.S. Embassy in Vienna. Trahair and Miller, *Cold War Espionage*, 294–295.

31. Trahair and Miller, *Cold War Espionage*, 295.

32. Tim Weiner, David Johnston, and Neil Lewis, *Betrayal: The Story of Aldrich Ames, An American Spy* (New York: Random House, 1995), 170–171.

33. Trahair and Miller, *Cold War Espionage*, 13.

34. Weiner et al., *Betrayal*, 14–16; Trahair and Miller, *Cold War Espionage*, 13.

35. Trahair and Miller, *Cold War Espionage*, 13. During the Cold War, the Soviet Union had a large embassy in Mexico City, and it became a hotbed of espionage activity for both the United States and the Soviet Union.

36. Sulick, *American Spies*, 191.

37. Trahair and Miller, *Cold War Espionage*, 13.

38. Ibid.

39. Sulick, *American Spies*, 191.

40. Ibid.

41. Ibid., 192.

42. Ibid.

43. Weiner et al., *Betrayal*, 17.

44. Trahair and Miller, *Cold War Espionage*, 13.

45. Ibid., 14.

46. Brian Michael Jenkins, *Countering Al Qaeda: An Appreciation of the Situation and Suggestions for Strategy* (MR-1620-RC, Santa Monica: RAND Corporation, 2002), 3.

47. Rohan Gunaratna, "Blowback," *Jane's Intelligence Review*, August 2001, 43.

48. Ibid.

49. Sean N. Kalic, *Combating A Modern Hydra: Al Qaeda and the Global War on Terrorism* (Occasional Paper #8, Fort Leavenworth: Combat Studies Institute 2006), 23. It is interesting to note that this government publication was found on bin Laden's personal computer when it was recovered during the now-famous raid on bin Laden's compound in Pakistan by U.S. Navy Seals.

50. Jenkins, *Countering Al Qaeda*, 3; Kalic, *Combating a Modern Hydra*, 23.

51. Rohan Gunaratna, *Inside Al Qaeda: Global Network of Terror* (New York: Berkley Book, 2002), 56.

52. "Declaration of Jihad Against the Americans Occupying The Land of the Two Holy Sanctuaries," in *Al Qaeda in Its Own Words*, ed. Gilles Kepel and Jean Pierre Milelli, trans. Pascale Chazaleh (Cambridge: Belknap Press, 2008), 47–50.

53. The Secretary of Defense's (William J. Perry) *Annual Report to the President and Congress* for 1996 listed the following as the primary threats to the United

States: "Attempts by regional powers hostile to U.S. Interests to gain hegemony in their regions through aggression or intimidation; Internal conflicts among ethnic, national, religious, or tribal groups that threaten innocent lives, force mass migrations, and undermine stability and international order; threats by potential adversaries to acquire or use nuclear, chemical, or biological weapons and their means of delivery; threats to democracy and reform in the former Soviet Union, Central and Eastern Europe, and elsewhere; Subversion and lawlessness that undermine friendly governments; Terrorism; Threats to U.S. prosperity and economic growth; Global environmental degradation; Illegal drug trade; and international crime." William J. Perry, *Annual Report to the President and Congress* (Washington, D.C.: Government Printing Office, March 1996), 1–2.

54. Steve Coll, *Ghost Wars; The Secret History of the CIA, Afghanistan, and Bin Laden from the Soviet Invasion to September 11, 2001* (New York: Penguin Press, 2004), 10–11.

55. Coll, *Ghost Wars*, 11.

56. "Declaration of Jihad Against the Americans Occupying the Land of the Two Holy Sanctuaries," 47–50.

57. Ibid., 375–377.

58. Ibid., 376–377.

59. Ibid., 376.

60. Ibid., 396.

61. William S. Cohen, Secretary of Defense, *Annual Report to the President and Congress* (Washington, D.C.: Government Printing Office, 2000), 20–21.

62. Trahair and Miller, *Cold War Espionage*, 273. It is important to note that Kryuchkov had been head of the First Chief Directorate since 1971, where he focused his efforts on build networks in foreign countries. See Appendix F.

63. Andrei Soldatov, "Putin Had Finally Reincarnated the KGB," *Foreign Policy*, September 21, 2016, 2, https://foreignpolicy.com/2016/09/21/putin-has-finally-reincarnated-the-kgb-mgb-fsb-russia/, accessed September 18, 2018.

64. Interestingly, enough this was the same rationale use by the Bolsheviks to develop the Cheka and begin the process of suppress counterrevolutionaries.

65. "The KGB after the Breakup of the Soviet Union," 2, http://factsanddetails .com/russia/Government_Military_Crime/sub9_5e/entry-5203.html, accessed September 18, 2018.

66. Ibid.

67. Ibid.

68. Ibid.

69. The Bolsheviks quickly established the Cheka, which was an organization designed to arrest, torture, and imprison enemies of the regime. Led by Felix Dzerzhinsky, the Cheka became a comprehensive power used by the Bolsheviks to maintain order and discipline to the tenets of the Revolution. Though originally established as a means to check the efforts of Whites and other counter-revolutionaries, the need to control and suppress contradictory ideas and other interpretation beyond those advocated by the Bolsheviks, only further solidified the extraordinary police powers of this repressive tool of the regime. Despite the passage of roughly 80 years, the new Russian intelligence/security service focused on similar objectives.

70. "The KGB after the Breakup of the Soviet Union," 2.

71. See Appendix E for the general structure of the KGB.

72. "The KGB After the Breakup of the Soviet Union," 2; see Appendix E.

73. "The KGB After the Breakup of the Soviet Union," 5.

74. "The KGB After the Breakup of the Soviet Union," 5.

75. Ibid.

76. Ibid., 6.

77. See Appendix E, "The KGB after the Breakup of the Soviet Union," 6.

78. "The KGB after the Breakup of the Soviet Union," 6–7; see also Appendix E.

79. Soldatov, "Putin Had Finally Reincarnated the KGB," 4.

80. Ibid., 1.

81. Ibid.

82. An example of this structure can be seen by looking at Appendix E and Appendix F. It is important to note that Appendix F is just the diagram for the First Chief Directorate. Each Chief Directorate and Directorate would have a similar diffuse and deep organizational structure.

83. It is recognized that the KGB was disbanded as an institution after 1991 and replaced by various other agencies discussed in this chapter. The use of the term "KGB" here is intended to reinforce the parallels between the Ministry of State Security and the old Soviet-era KGB.

84. Kalugin, *Spymaster*, 334–336.

85. Jerry Markon, "FBI Arrests 10 Accused of Working as Russian Spies," *Washington Post*, June 29, 2010, http://www.washingtonpost.com/wp-dyn/content /article/2010/06/28/AR2010062805227.html, accessed September 18, 2018; Mark Mazzetti and Katie Benner, "12 Russian Agents Indicted in Mueller Investigation," *New York Times*, July 13, 2018, https://www.nytimes.com/2018/07/13/us /politics/mueller-indictments-russian-intelligence.html, accessed September 18, 2018; Luke Harding, "Spies, Sleepers, and Hitmen: How the Soviet Union's KGB Never Went Away," *Guardian*, November 14, 2014, https://www.theguardian.com /world/2014/nov/19/spies-spooks-hitmen-kgb-never-went-away-russia-putin, accessed September 18, 2018.

CONCLUSION

1. Mark Mazzetti and Katie Benner, "12 Russian Agents Indicted in Mueller Investigation," *New York Times*, July 13, 2018, https://www.nytimes.com/2018/07 /13/us/politics/mueller-indictments-russian-intelligence.html, accessed September 18, 2018.

2. Laura Smith-Spark and Milena Veselinovic, "Russians Charged over UK Novichok Nerve Agent Attack," CNN, September 5, 2018, https://www.cnn .com/2018/09/05/uk/uk-russians-novichok-intl/index.html, 1, accessed September 18, 2018.

3. Talking Heads, "Once in a Lifetime," https://genius.com/Talking-heads -once-in-a-lifetime-lyrics, accessed September 18, 2018.

4. Katherine A. S. Sibley, *Red Spies in America: Stolen Secrets and the Dawn of the Cold War* (Lawrence: University Press of Kansas, 2004), 6–8.

5. The ideological force that drove many of the spies in the period between 1920 and 1950 looked at the manufactured and heavily censored outside image of the Soviet System as the reality and possibility of communist systems. However, onlookers were totally unaware that the Soviet Union's intelligence services

worked to ensure that the positive benefits of the regime were greatly exaggerated, propagated throughout the international community. The reality was that the Soviet system, since its inception in 1917, had strong tendencies to suppress, imprison, and harass citizens who did not adhere to the tenets of the regime.

6. Due to the ideological tension between the tenets of Marxism/Leninism, the State Department was strongly against FDR's decision to recognize the Soviet Union.

7. John Lewis Gaddis, *Strategies of Containment: A Critical Appraisal of the Postwar American National Security Policy* (New York: Oxford University Press, 1982), 16–24; William I. Hitchcock, *France Restored: Cold War Diplomacy and the Quest for Leadership in Europe, 1944–1954* (Chapel Hill: University of North Carolina University Press, 1998), 11; Michael Creswell, *A Question of Balance: How France and the United States Created Cold War Europe* (Cambridge, MA: Harvard University Press, 2006), 8–21.

8. William J. Daugherty, *Executive Secrets: Covert Action and the Presidency* (Lexington: University Press of Kentucky, 2004), 114–124.

9. The British, French, Germans, and other Central and Eastern European nations also had intelligence services; however, the focus of the study is on the intelligence services of the United States and the Soviet Union.

10. The post-Vietnam period may have assisted in halting the CIA's propensity to use and develop paramilitary operations, but by the time of the Reagan administration, these ideas were once again welcomed by William Casey as DCI.

11. Christopher Andrew and Vasili Mitrokhin, *The World Was Going Our Way: The KGB and the Battle for the Third World* (New York: Basic Books, 2005), 11.

12. John Ranelagh, *The Agency: The Rise and Decline of the CIA* (New York: Touchstone Books, 1987), 587.

13. Ibid., 596.

14. Brezhnev, Andropov, and Chernenko were fixated on the potential for a nuclear first strike from the United States. This obsession started with Andropov as head of the KGB and was maintained as he became General Secretary of the Party. Only when Gorbachev assumed power did this paranoia dissolve.

15. It is interesting to note that Oleg Kalugin, in his memoirs, recounts how aware he and his wife were of the very possibility that he could be poisoned when he was running for office.

16. Jerry Markon, "FBI Arrests 10 Accused of Working as Russian Spies," *Washington Post*, June 29, 2010, http://www.washingtonpost.com/wp-dyn/content /article/2010/06/28/AR2010062805227.html, accessed September 18, 2018.

Bibliography

BOOKS

Andrew, Christopher, and Oleg Gordievsky, eds. *Comrade Kryuchkov's Instructions: Top Secret Files on KGB Foreign Operations, 1975–1985.* Stanford: Stanford University Press, 1993.

Andrew, Christopher, and Vasili Mitrokhin. *The World Was Going Our Way: The KGB and the Battle for the Third World.* New York: Basic Books, 2005.

Baer, Robert. *See No Evil: The True Story of a Ground Soldier in the CIA's War on Terrorism.* New York: Three Rivers, 2002.

Bagley, Tennet H. *Spymaster: Startling Cold War Revelations of a Soviet KGB Chief.* New York: Skyhorse, 2013.

Bamford, James. *Body of Secrets: Anatomy of the Ultra-Secret National Security Agency from the Cold War through the Dawn of a New Century.* New York: Doubleday, 2001.

Baumann, Robert F. *Russian-Soviet Unconventional Wars in the Caucasus, Central Asia, and Afghanistan.* Leavenworth Paper No. 20. Fort Leavenworth: Combat Studies Institute, 1993.

Beschloss, Michael R. *MAYDAY: Eisenhower Khrushchev and the U-2 Affair.* New York: Harper and Row, 1986.

Burrows, William E. *Deep Black: Space Espionage and National Security.* New York: Random House, 1986.

Burrows, William E. *By Any Means Necessary: America's Secret Air War in the Cold War.* New York: Farrar, Straus and Giroux, 2001.

Cadbury, Deborah. *Space Race: The Epic Battle between America and the Soviet Union for Dominion of Space.* New York: Harper/Perennial, 2006.

Cline, Ray S. *The CIA under Reagan, Bush, and Casey: The Evolution of the Agency from Roosevelt to Reagan.* Washington, DC: Acropolis, 1981.

Coll, Steve. *Ghost Wars: The Secret History of the CIA, Afghanistan, and Bin Laden, from the Soviet Invasion to September 10, 2001.* New York: Penguin, 2004.

Cowell, Alan S. *The Terminal Spy: A True Story of Espionage, Betrayal, and Murder.* New York: Double Day, 2008.

Daugherty, William J. *Executive Secrets: Covert Action and the Presidency.* Lexington: The University Press of Kentucky, 2004.

Day, Dwayne A., John M. Logsdon, and Brian Latell, eds. *Eye in the Sky: The Story of the Corona Spy Satellite.* Washington, DC: Smithsonian Institution Press, 1998.

Gordin, Michael D. *Red Cloud at Dawn: Truman, Stalin, and the End of the Atomic Monopoly.* New York: Farrar, Straus, and Giroux, 2009.

Grose, Peter. *Allen Dulles, Spymaster: The Life and Times of the First Civilian Director of the CIA.* London: André Deutsch, 2006.

Haynes, John Earl, and Harvey Klehr. *VENONA: Decoding Soviet Espionage in America.* New Haven, CT: Yale University Press, 1999.

Heuser, Beatrice and Robert O'Neill, eds. *Securing Peace in Europe, 1945–62: Thoughts for the Post-Cold War Era.* New York: St. Martin's Press, 1992.

Holloway, David. *Stalin and the Bomb: The Soviet Union and Atomic Energy, 1939–1956.* New Haven, CT: Yale University Press, 1994.

Jacobsen, Annie. *Operation Paperclip: The Secret Intelligence Program That Brought Nazi Scientists to America.* New York: Little, Brown, and Company, 2014.

Kalic, Sean N. *US Presidents and the Militarization of Space, 1946–1967.* Austin, TX: Texas A&M University Press, 2012.

Kalugin, Oleg. *Spymaster: My 32 Years in Intelligence and Espionage against the West.* London: Smith Gryphon, 1994.

Karabell, Zachary. *Architects of Invention: The United States, the Third World, and the Cold War, 1946–1962.* Baton Rouge: Louisiana State University Press, 1999.

Kessler, Ronald. *Moscow Station: How the KGB Penetrated the American Embassy.* New York: Charles Scribner's Sons, 1989.

Khalidi, Rashid. *Sowing Crisis: The Cold War and American Dominance in the Middle East.* Boston: Beacon, 2009.

Kirkpatrick, Lyman B., and Howland H. Sargeant. *Soviet Political Warfare Techniques: Espionage and Propaganda in the 1970s.* New York: National Strategy Information Center, 1972.

Leffler, Melvyn P. *For the Soul of Mankind: The United States, the Soviet Union, and the Cold War.* New York: Hill and Wang, 2007.

Lingen, Kerstin von. *Kesselring's Last Battle: War Crimes Trials and Cold War Politics, 1945–1960.* Translated by Alexandra Klemm. Lawrence: University Press of Kansas, 2009.

Litvinenko, Alexander, and Yuri Felshtinsky. *Blowing Up Russia: The Secret Plot to Bring Back KGB Terror.* New York: Encounter, 2007.

Miles, Jonathan. *The Nine Lives of Otto Katz: The Remarkable Story of a Communist Super Spy.* London: Bantam, 2010.

Murphy, David E., Sergei A. Kondrashev, and George Bailey. *Battleground Berlin: CIA VS. KGB in the Cold War.* New Haven, CT: Yale University Press, 1997.

Nuti, Leopoldo, ed. *The Crisis of Détente in Europe: From Helsinki to Gorbachev, 1975–1985.* London: Routledge, 2009.

Oberdorfer, Don. *From the Cold War to a New Era: The United States and the Soviet Union, 1983–1991*. Baltimore, MD: The Johns Hopkins University Press, 1998.

Osgood, Kenneth. *Total Cold War: Eisenhower's Secret Propaganda Battle at Home and Abroad*. Lawrence: University Press of Kansas, 2006.

Polmar, Norman. *Spyplanes: The U-2 History Declassified*. Osceola, WI: MBI, 2001.

Powers, Gary Francis, and Curt Gentry. *Operation Overflight: A Memoir of the U-2 Incident*. Washington, DC: Brassey's, 2004.

Prados, John. *The Soviet Estimate: U.S. Intelligence Analysis and Russian Military Strength*. New York: The Dial Press, 1982.

Prados, John. *President's Secret Wars: The CIA and Pentagon Covert Operations since World War II*. New York: William Morrow and Company, 1986.

Ranelagh, John. *The Agency: The Rise and Decline of the CIA*. New York: Touchstone, 1987.

Reynolds, David, ed. *The Origins of the Cold War in Europe: International Perspectives*. New Haven, CT: Yale University Press, 1994.

Richelson, Jeffery T. *The Wizards of Langley: Inside the CIA's Directorate of Science and Technology*. Boulder, CO: Westview, 2001.

Romerstein, Herbert, and Eric Breindel. *The Venona Secrets: Exposing Soviet Espionage and America's Traitors*. Washington, DC: Regency, 2000.

Ruffner, Kevin C., ed. *Corona: America's First Satellite Program*. Washington, DC: Center for the Study of Intelligence, Central Intelligence Agency, 1995.

Schecter, Jerrold, and Leona Schecter. *Sacred Secrets: How Soviet Intelligence Operations Changed American History*. Washington, DC: Brassey's, 2003.

Schwarz, Guri. *After Mussolini: Jewish Life and Jewish Memories in Post-Fascist Italy*. Translated by Giovanni Noor Mazhar. London: Vallentine Mitchell, 2012.

Schweizer, Peter. *Victory: The Reagan Administration's Secret Strategy That Hastened the Collapse of the Soviet Union*. New York: The Atlantic Monthly Press, 1994.

Sibley, Katherin A. S. *Red Spies in America: Stolen Secrets and the Dawn of the Cold War*. Lawrence: University Press of Kansas, 2004.

Simpson, Christopher. *National Security Directives of the Reagan and Bush Administrations: The Declassified History of U.S. Political and Military Policy, 1981–1991*. Boulder: Westview Press, 1995.

Spires, David N. *Beyond Horizons: A Half Century of Air Force Space Leadership*. Maxwell Air Force Base, Montgomery, AL: Air University Press, 1998.

Sudoplatov, Pavel, Anatoli Sudoplatov, Jerrod L. Schecter, and Leona P. Schecter. *Special Tasks: The Memoirs of an Unwanted Witness, a Soviet Spymaster*. Boston: Little, Brown, and Company, 1994.

Sulick, Michael J. *American Spies: Espionage against the United States from the Cold War to the Present*. Washington, DC: Georgetown University Press, 2013.

Taubman, Philip. *Secret Empire: Eisenhower, the CIA, and the Hidden Story of America's Space Espionage*. New York: Simon and Schuster, 2003.

Trahair, Richard C. S., and Robert L. Miller. *Encyclopedia of Cold War Espionage, Spies, and Secret Operations*. New York: Enigma Books, 2012.

Trento, Joseph J. *The Secret History of the CIA*. New York: MJF Books, 2001.

Ventresca, Robert A. *From Fascism to Democracy: Culture and Politics in the Italian Election of 1948*. Toronto: University of Toronto Press, 2004.

Waller, J. Michael. *Secret Empire: The KGB in Russia Today*. Boulder, CO: Westview Press, 1994.

Weiner, Tim, David Johnston, and Neil A. Lewis. *Betrayal: The Story of Aldrich Ames, an American Spy*. New York: Random House, 1995.

West, Nigel. *Mortal Crimes: The Greatest Theft in History: Soviet Penetration of the Manhattan Project*. New York: Enigma, 2004.

ARTICLES

Alder, Ken. "America's Two Gadgets: Of Bombs and Polygraphs." *Isis* 98, no. 1 (March 2007): 124–137.

Ball, Desmond. "Controlling Theatre Nuclear War." *British Journal of Political Science* 19, no. 3 (July 1989): 303–327.

Barnes, Trevor. "The Secret Cold War: The C.I.A. and American Foreign Policy in Europe, 1946–1956. Part I." *The Historical Journal* 24, no. 2 (June 1981): 399–415.

Barnes, Trevor. "The Secret Cold War: The C.I.A. and American Foreign Policy in Europe 1946–1956. Part II." *The Historical Journal* 25, no. 3 (Sep. 1982): 649–670.

Brands, H. W., Jr. "A Cold War Foreign Legion? The Eisenhower Administration and the Volunteer Freedom Corps." *Military Affairs* 52, no. 1 (Jan. 1988): 7–11.

Cain, Frank. "Venona in Australia and Its Long-Term Ramifications." *Journal of Contemporary History* 35, no. 2 (April 2000): 231–248.

Cloud, John. "Imaging the World in a Barrel: CORONA and the Clandestine Convergence of the Earth Sciences." *Social Studies of Science* 31, no. 2, Science in the Cold War (April 2001): 231–251.

Crist, Stephen A. "Jazz as Democracy? Dave Brubeck and Cold War Politics." *The Journal of Musicology* 26, no. 2 (Spring 2009): 133–174.

"FBI Releases Papers on Russian Spy Ring That Involved Anna Chapman." *The Guardian*, October 31, 2011, https://www.theguardian.com/world/2011/oct/31/fbi-russian-spy-ring-anna-chapman

Garthoff, Raymond L. "Estimating Soviet Military Force Levels: Some Light from the Past." *International Security* 14, no. 4 (Spring 1990): 93–116.

Gentry, Philip. "Leonard Bernstein's The Age of Anxiety: A Great American Symphony during McCarthyism." *American Music* 29, no. 3 (Fall 2011): 308–331.

Granville, Johanna. "Reactions to the Events of 1956: New Findings from the Budapest and Warsaw Archives." *Journal of Contemporary History* 38, no. 2 (April 2003): 261–290.

Haas, Mark L. "The United States and the End of the Cold War: Reactions to Shifts in Soviet Power, Policies, or Domestic Politics?" *International Organization* 61, no. 1 (Winter 2007): 145–179.

Harding, Luke. "Spies, Sleepers and Hitmen: How the Soviet Union's KGB Never Went Away." *The Guardian*, November 19, 2014, https://www.theguardian.com/world/2014/nov/19/spies-spooks-hitmen-kgb-never-went-away-russia-putin

Holden, Robert H. "Securing Central America against Communism: The United States and the Modernization of Surveillance in the Cold War." *Journal of Interamerican Studies and World Affairs* 41, no. 1 (Spring 1999): 1–30.

Kaiser, David. "The Atomic Secret in Red Hands? American Suspicions of Theoretical Physicists During the Early Cold War." *Representations* 90, no. 1 (Spring 2005): 28–60.

Katz, Basil. "U.S. Russia to Swap Spies after 10 Plead Guilty," in *Reuters*, July 8, 2010, https://www.reuters.com/article/us-russia-usa-spy/u-s-and-russia-to-swap-spies-after-10-plead-guilty-idUSTRE66618Y20100708

"The KGB after the Breakup of the Soviet Union," 2, http://factsanddetails.com/russia/Government_Military_Crime/sub9_5e/entry-5203.html

Krammer, Arnold. "Russian Counterfeit Dollars: A Case of Early Soviet Espionage." *Slavic Review* 30, no. 4 (Dec. 1971): 762–773.

Krige, John. "Atoms for Peace, Scientific Internationalism, and Scientific Intelligence." *Osiris* 21, no. 1, Global Power Knowledge: Science and Technology in International Affairs (2006): 161–181.

Kuperman, Alan J. "The Stinger Missile and U.S. Intervention in Afghanistan." *Political Science Quarterly* 114, no. 2 (Summer 1999): 219–263.

Lambeth, Benjamin S. "Uncertainties for the Soviet War Planner." *International Security* 7, no. 3 (Winter 1982–1983): 139–166.

Leonard, Raymond W. "Studying the Kremlin's Secret Soldiers: A Historiographical Essay on the GRU, 1918–1945." *The Journal of Military History* 56, no. 3 (July 1992): 403–422.

Macrakis, Kristie. "Technophilic Hubris and Espionage Styles during the Cold War." *Isis* 101, no. 2 (June 2010): 378–385.

Markon, Jerry. "FBI Arrests 10 Accused of Working as Russian Spies," *Washington Post*, June 29, 2010, http://www.washingtonpost.com/wp-dyn/content/article/2010/06/28/AR2010062805227.html

Mazzetti, Mark, and Katie Benner. "12 Russian Agents Indicted in Mueller Investigation." *The New York Times*, July 13, 2018, https://www.nytimes.com/2018/07/13/us/politics/mueller-indictments-russian-intelligence.html

McAuliffe, Mary S. "Eisenhower, the President." *The Journal of American History* 68, no. 3 (Dec. 1981): 625–632.

Minkley, Gary, and Martin Legassick. "'Not Telling': Secrecy, Lies, and History." *History and Theory* 39, no. 4, Theme Issue 39 (Dec. 2000): 1–10.

Nathan, James A. "A FRAGILE DETENTE: The U-2 Incident Re-examined." *Military Affairs* 39, no. 3 (Oct. 1975): 97–104.

Prados, John. "Notes on the CIA's Secret War in Afghanistan." *The Journal of American History* 89, no. 2, History and September 11: A Special Issue (Sep. 2002): 466–471.

Rosenbaum, David M. "Nuclear Terror." *International Security* 1, no. 3 (Winter 1977): 140–161.

Rubinstein, Alvin Z. "The Soviet Union and Iran under Khomeini." *International Affairs* 57, no. 4 (Autumn 1981): 599–617.

Siddiqi, Asif A. "Germans in Russia: Cold War, Technology Transfer, and National Identity." *Osiris* 24, no. 1, Science and National Identity (2009): 120–143.

Simon, Sheldon W. "ASEAN's Strategic Situation in the 1980s." *Pacific Affairs* 60, no. 1 (Spring 1987): 73–93.

Smith-Spark, Laura, and Milena Veselinovic. "Russians Charged over UK Novichok Nerve Agent Attack." Retrieved September 5, 2018, from https://www.cnn.com/2018/09/05/uk/uk-russians-novichok-intl/index.html

Soldatov, Andrei. "Putin Had Finally Reincarnated the KGB." *Foreign Policy,* September 21, 2016, 2. https://foreignpolicy.com/2016/09/21/putin-has-finally-reincarnated-the-kgb-mgb-fsb-russia/

Stafford, David. "'Intrepid': Myth and Reality." *Journal of Contemporary History* 22, no. 2, Intelligence Services during the Second World War (April 1987): 303–317.

Strobel, Warren. "Fewer Russian Spies in U.S. But Getting Harder to Track." *Reuters,* March 28, 2018, https://www.reuters.com/article/us-usa-russia-spies/fewer-russian-spies-in-u-s-but-getting-harder-to-track-idUSKBN1H40JW

Talbott, Strobe. "Scrambling and Spying in SALT II." *International Security* 4, no. 2 (Fall 1979): 3–21.

University of California Press, Institute for Palestine Studies. "The Jonathan Pollard Case." *Journal of Palestine Studies* 15, no. 3 (Spring 1986): 173–180.

White, Stephen, and Ol'Ga Kryshtanovskay. "Public Attitudes toward the KGB: A Research Note." *Europe-Asia Studies* 45, no. 1 (1993): 169–175.

Index

About the Author

DR. SEAN N. KALIC is a professor of military history in the Department of Military History at the U.S. Army Command and General Staff College, where he has taught since 2004. He specializes in Cold War history and the history of terrorism. He has contributed to numerous major publications, including "Post–Cold War Conflicts," in *The Handbook of American Military and Diplomatic History, 1865 to the Present* (Routledge, 2013); "Eisenhower," in *Generals of the Army: Marshall, MacArthur, Eisenhower, Arnold, Bradley* (University of Kentucky Press, 2013); "Terrorism in the Twenty-First Century: A New Era of Warfare," in *An International History of Terrorism: Western and Non-Western Experiences* (Routledge, 2013); "Framing the Discourse: The Rhetoric on the War on Terrorism," in *Legacies of the Cold War* (Hamburg Institute for Social Research, 2013); *U.S. Presidents and the Militarization of Space, 1946–1967* (Texas A&M Press, 2012), which was recognized by CHOICE as a top academic work of 2012; and as editor for *Thinking about War: Past, Present, and Future* (Inter-Disciplinary Press, 2011).